Pop Culture
FREAKS

Pop Culture

FREAKS

Identity, Mass Media, and Society

Dustin Kidd

WESTVIEW
PRESS

A Member of the Perseus Books Group

Westview Press was founded in 1975 in Boulder, Colorado, by notable publisher and intellectual Fred Praeger. Westview Press continues to publish scholarly titles and high-quality undergraduate- and graduate-level textbooks in core social science disciplines. With books developed, written, and edited with the needs of serious nonfiction readers, professors, and students in mind, Westview Press honors its long history of publishing books that matter.

Find us on the World Wide Web at http://www.westviewpress.com.

Every effort has been made to secure required permissions for all text, images, maps, and other art reprinted in this volume.

Westview Press books are available at special discounts for bulk purchases in the United States by corporations, institutions, and other organizations. For more information, please contact the Special Markets Department at the Perseus Books Group, 2300 Chestnut Street, Suite 200, Philadelphia, PA 19103, or call (800) 810-4145, ext. 5000, or e-mail special.markets@perseusbooks.com.

Designed by Trish Wilkinson
Set in 10.5 point Minion Pro

Library of Congress Cataloging-in-Publication Data

Kidd, Dustin.
    Pop culture freaks : identity, mass media, and society / Dustin Kidd.
        pages   cm
    Includes bibliographical references and index.
    ISBN 978-0-8133-4912-1 (pbk.) — ISBN 978-0-8133-4913-8 (e-book)
1. Popular culture—21st century. 2. Identity (Psychology) and mass media 3. Advertising—Social aspects. 4. Mass media—History. I. Title.
HM621.K5293 2014
306.4'0905—dc23   2013037175

10 9 8 7 6 5 4 3 2 1

CONTENTS

Acknowledgments   *vii*

1. The Matrix Is Everywhere:
   An Introduction to the Sociology of Popular Culture   1

2. The Revolution Will Not Be Available on iTunes:
   Racial Perspectives   31

3. Movin' on Up: Class Perspectives   63

4. Men Are from Marlboro Country, Women Are
   from Wisteria Lane: Gender Perspectives   95

5. Not That There's Anything Wrong with That:
   Sexuality Perspectives   129

6. Handi-Capable: Disability Perspectives   165

7. Translating Harry Potter: Global Perspectives   191

8. Freaks in the Matrix: A Conclusion and an Invitation   217

Appendix 1: A Brief History of Printing and Publishing   229
Appendix 2: A Brief History of the Music Industry   233
Appendix 3: A Brief History of Film   235
Appendix 4: A Brief History of Television   239
Appendix 5: A Brief History of the Internet   245
References   249
Glossary   261
Index   265

ACKNOWLEDGMENTS

This book is dedicated to all of the students in my classes on popular culture since I started teaching in this area in 2001. Their thoughtfulness, creativity, and high expectations have made me the scholar and teacher that I am. I thank them all. Students from my fall 2010 popular culture course played an important role in the collection of the television data, along with graduate students in my spring 2011 seminar on culture. Students from my fall 2012 popular culture course played an important role in the collection of the film data. Dr. Corrine Castro served as a valuable research assistant in the early stages of this project while she was a graduate student at Temple University.

I first engaged the sociology of popular culture as a teaching assistant for Bethany Bryson. Bethany provided a road map through this exciting terrain that is evident throughout this book. I also thank my other intellectual role models, Sarah Corse, Sharon Hays, and Julia Ericksen.

Eric Crawford produced the wonderful illustrations in this book. The team at ChatterBlast Media guided me gently into the world of social media.

The team at Westview was great to work with. Leanne Silverman and Evan Carver played particularly big roles in moving this project forward.

And finally, thank-you to all of the creative professionals, devoted fans, and rigorous scholars who demand that we take popular culture seriously. You are the true pop culture freaks!

REVIEWERS

We would like to thank the following peer reviewers for their time and comments toward making this a better book:

Rhonda E. Dugan, California State University, Bakersfield
Celestino Fernández, University of Arizona
Joshua Gamson, University of San Francisco
Stephen P. Hagan, McKendree University
Danielle Hedegard, Boston College
Andrew R. Jones, California State University, Fresno
Anne Lincoln, Southern Methodist University
Ryan Moore, Florida Atlantic University
Lori Waite, Tennessee Wesleyan College
Lorna Lueker Zukas, National University

The Matrix Is Everywhere
AN INTRODUCTION TO THE
SOCIOLOGY OF POPULAR CULTURE

Image I.I. Amber Riley, who plays Mercedes Jones on the Fox television show *Glee* (SOURCE: EVERETT COLLECTION).

THE SOCIOLOGY OF *GLEE*

Hold up your right hand. Form a right angle with your thumb and index finger while folding the other three fingers down. Keeping that shape, place the back of your hand against your forehead and look in the mirror. Loser! That is what you have just called yourself. If you were a character on the Fox television show *Glee*, you would deserve a slushy. In case you never saw the show, *Glee* is a dramedy about a high school chorus formed by a group of (mostly) losers, assembled by a frustrated Spanish teacher named Will Schuester. Whenever these so-called losers start to achieve some modicum of success or even popularity, they are quickly cut down to size by a jock dumping a red slushy on them. *Glee* deliberately explores what it means to be a loser in contemporary American society, both for high school kids and for adults like Will Schuester.

Image 1.1 depicts Mercedes Jones, one of the founding members of New Directions, the glee club at William McKinley High School. Is Mercedes a loser? She's a beautiful woman with a tremendous voice. Sure, she has a larger body type than is glorified on television and in magazines, but no one really looks like those women anyway. She is a black woman in a majority white school, but McKinley High has plenty of black students, many of whom are not outcasts in the least. Maybe calling Mercedes a loser is unfair. But *loser* certainly describes how she feels—not about her character, but about her position within the hierarchy of the high school. "Loser" also becomes a rallying cry for Mercedes and the other glee club members, who embrace the term as a description of what makes them unique and special in a world that turns everyone into cookie-cutter cheerleaders and football stars.

Glee presents us with an array of archetypes for the loser. Mercedes Jones is the curvy black woman. Rachel Berry is the awkward, artsy Jewish girl. Artie Abrams is the wheelchair-bound nerd. Tina Cohen-Chang is the shy, stuttering Asian. Kurt Hummel is the obviously gay white kid with flamboyant fashion taste. Santana Lopez is the loud, angry Latina from Lima Heights Adjacent.

LOSERS, STRANGERS, AND FREAKS

Losers, freaks, misfits, cripples, and queers: the world of popular culture has a way of telling us that we do not fit in, then turning around and selling us a ticket to conformity, to the pop culture prom with a gorgeous date. But the ticket is always a counterfeit; we never get into the prom, at least not for long, and we have to buy yet another ticket. Unless we fight back, organizing our own alternative prom and turning around the weapons of mass culture.

We might compare the loser in *Glee* to the stranger in a 1908 essay by the early sociologist Georg Simmel. He begins "The Stranger" with a discussion of wanderers—traveling merchants in particular—who roam into a new community, bringing with them an awareness of everything that is beyond and outside of that community. Simmel is most intrigued by the wanderer who then lingers, settling into his surroundings, but always being identified as an outsider, someone who never attains full membership in the community because he is not organically a part of it. The persistent presence of this stranger provides for the larger community what Simmel calls a "union of closeness and remoteness involved in every human relationship . . . an element whose membership within the group involves being both outside it and confronting it" (2010, 302–303).

In the same way, the loser is a member of the high school social world who is nevertheless excluded from full participation in that milieu and whose refusal or inability to be just like everyone else creates a persistent confrontation with the world. The popular kids' status depends on having a large mass of other kids who seek to mimic them. The losers cannot or will not mimic the cool kids. They may have the wrong body, the wrong hair, the wrong skin tone, or simply the wrong tastes, the wrong desires, or the wrong values. Indeed, a survey of the nonlosers often reveals a little "loserness" in everyone, just as many of the popular kids at McKinley High eventually cycle into the glee club as they confront their own inability to fully embody the popular ideal. Consider the following scene from a season 1 episode of *Glee*. A popular boy named Finn, who has joined the glee club and befriended the losers there, has been pressured by his football teammates to cut a glee kid down to size. They want Finn to confirm that he is one of the ruling cool kids, not a loser, so he has been ordered to throw a slushy at confirmed loser Kurt. Kurt's glee club friends Mercedes and Rachel intervene.

Mercedes Jones: "You are not gonna slushy on my man Kurt."
Rachel Berry: "Why wouldn't he? He's made his choice. He doesn't care about us losers anymore."
Finn Hudson: "No, that's not true! It's just if I don't do it, the guys on the team are gonna kick the crap out of me!"
Kurt Hummel: "Well we can't have that, can we?"
[*Grabs the slushy from Finn.*]
Finn Hudson: "What are you doing?"
Kurt Hummel: "It's called taking one for the team."
[*Splashes himself in the face with the slushy, then pauses.*]
Kurt Hummel: "Now get out of here. And take some time to think whether or not any of your friends on the football team would have done that for you." (Brennan, Falchuk, and Murphy 2009c)

The slushy confirms both the "closeness and remoteness" between Kurt and Finn, and in turn between the losers and the jocks. Finn and Kurt know each other and even care about each other, but the social distance remains, even though these two students and the groups they represent live in the same town, attend the same school and the same classes in that school, and eat in the same cafeteria.

This book explores how the popular culture we produce and consume creates a sense of closeness and remoteness for all of us, living in a world in which we are pressured to conform, in ways that few of us can fully achieve. The very same traits that make us unique individuals also prevent us from realizing the popular ideals of our time, which we affirm and produce through the music we dance to, the television shows and films we turn to for entertainment, the books we read, and even the websites we access for diversion or information. This is a book about the intersections of identity—the associations that make us who we are and give us a sense of belonging to the tribe—and popular culture, the somewhat mechanical set of meanings and values that dominate our world, regardless of our tribal membership.

Why freaks? The word *freak* can be very off-putting; it is an insult. Interestingly, it is a slur that has never attached itself to any particular group. Kids who are gay have been called freaks for their sexuality. Christians have been called freaks for their faith. Artists have been called freaks for their self-expression. People with disabilities have been called freaks for the unique qualities of their bodies or minds. Smart people have been called freaks for their high IQs. Anyone is susceptible to being called a freak. The word is a mechanism for undermining the social power of the person at whom it is targeted. It implies that the recipient has been poorly socialized to be a member of the community. On the surface, *freak* is an accusation against the individual target, but it also implies that our mechanisms of socialization may be suspect. Who is responsible for these freaks? Parents? Neighborhoods? Schools? The media?

I embrace the word *freak* in this book, first because I believe that we operate within a commercial culture system that treats us all as freaks. The system's goal is to push us to spend and consume, and that means that we can never be satisfied. We are told that we can find peace and satisfaction when we achieve the right lifestyle, but nothing is ever good enough. There is always another gadget to buy, another imperfection in our bodies, another reason to feel like a freak. If we are not maligned for our race, class, gender, sexuality, or bodies, then we are maligned for our religion, age, ethnicity, political ideology, or cultural tastes.

How do we escape the freak cycle, in which popular culture tells us that we are not good enough, then sells us a path to supposed perfection, then says we failed to follow that path successfully and have to buy into the next path that it offers? As I look at audiences, the people who consume popular culture—which is to say, all of us—I notice that those who seem to find some peace and satisfaction are the ones who lean into the identity of the freak. When commercial culture says they are not good enough, they say "hell, yeah!" and laugh. They take the messages embedded in popular culture and twist them around to find new kinds of meaning that allow them to experience empowerment and pride.

I argue that we are all pop culture freaks in a commercial culture system that is inescapable and needs all of us to feel insufficient. But I also argue that embracing our freak status may provide us with the tools to find some agency within that system and have some control over how the culture industries influence our lives.

DEFINING POPULAR CULTURE

The term **popular culture** has a variety of meanings, and I will be very specific about which ones I am using in this book. The word *popular* is from the Latin *populus*, meaning "the people." Historically, both in Roman times and in other societies, "the people" referred not to all people, but rather to a very specific and very large mass of poor and working people. It excluded a tiny group of ruling elites, who were associated with a very different kind of culture—a privileged set of cultural goods like paintings, classical music, literature, and other forms of creative expression—that we now refer to as **high culture**. Everyone else had what we now call **folk culture**—local music, crafts, oral traditions, morality plays, and many other types of expression. If *popular* means the people, then popular culture could be associated with this folk culture, and many analyses of popular culture do focus on it. But folk culture is just one of the meanings associated with popular culture and is not the focus of this book. Folk culture is local, rooted in regional identity. The popular culture that I discuss in this book has been carefully scrubbed of that kind of localism to make it appealing across regions.

Although categories like high and folk culture are still relevant, both in the United States and around the world, they do not apply to a lot of the culture that is now produced and consumed. This is attributable in part to the growth of the middle class, as sociologist Herbert Gans explains in *Popular Culture and High Culture* (1999). *Middle class* is both an economic and a cultural category. As an economic category, it refers to a vast middle ground between wealthy elites and the poorest of the poor. In the United States, despite tremendous and growing economic inequality, nearly all Americans identify themselves as middle class. As a cultural category, middle class refers to a set of lifestyles that are characterized largely by **consumption**, the purchase of goods on the market. Members of the middle class have enough money to purchase almost everything they need, rather than making these goods at home. But they do not have so much money that they can commission a craftsperson to make these goods for them individually. For example, they do not typically sew their own dresses, nor do they hire dressmakers; instead, they purchase mass-produced clothing.

The growth of the middle class, both economically and culturally, has resulted in a shift in how we think of popular culture, from the working masses to the vast middle class. Middle-class cultural practices are so ubiquitous that middle-class consumption has become the norm for everyone. Even those who might sew their own dresses out of economic necessity or commission custom-made dresses because they are economically privileged probably also purchase most of their clothing at the fashion mall. This book focuses on the culture associated with this middle class, which has become so broad as to functionally include all Americans, even those who are desperately poor or fantastically rich.

This brings me to the word *culture*, which also has a variety of meanings, some of them rather contradictory. On the one hand we have the notion that something "cultured" is somehow refined because it has been cultivated. Some process has occurred to move it from a raw, uncultured state to an elevated, cultured state. In this sense, *culture* may refer to sacred elements of society such as religious artifacts or high culture art. But in sociological analysis, culture is much broader than just high culture and much bigger than just the sacred. It is also everyday, or as the scholar Raymond Williams puts it, "culture is ordinary" (2002, 91). So what is this *thing* that is both sacred and everyday? It is shared meaning.

Shared meaning is the meat and bones of culture. Meaning ranges from our highest beliefs about god and the sacred to our everyday tastes about food and fashion. It is the political ideologies we fight over and the everyday assumptions we take for granted. These meanings are structured into our languages and the various other ways that we communicate. Some meanings are relatively fixed and hard to change; others are constantly being debated and negotiated. Culture is produced within families, neighborhoods, schools, and churches— and it is also produced by the entertainment industry. The mass media floods our homes and lives with stories about the human experience, and each story includes a set of claims about what the world means. Two critical theorists of the twentieth century—Theodor Adorno and Max Horkheimer—referred to the mass media as the **culture industry**, because it is capitalism's mechanism for producing art as a market commodity, and in turn capitalism's primary mechanism for the production and distribution of meaning.

The culture in question in this book is that of the culture industry: commercially produced meanings embedded in expressive works that include text, audio, and video. I said that we are looking at the culture of the vast middle class. To be more specific, we are looking at the **commercial culture** that is produced in a society driven by middle-class identification, even for those who are very rich and those who are very poor.

Unlike culture that is produced and enjoyed within a community, commercial culture separates the **production** and **reception** processes in very clear ways. *Reception* refers to the ways that audiences receive a cultural good, such as a television show, and make use of it. It refers to both *consumption*—how we access and select a cultural good—and *interpretation*—how we determine what the cultural good means and how we act on those meanings. When a cultural object is made within a community, production and reception are part of the same social moment. The local singer, performing in a coffee shop or bar, stands immediately in front of her audience. The sociologist examining that moment is able to study both production and reception and unlikely to invest in a distinction between the two. In commercial culture, a very clear division of labor separates producers from audiences and separates the process of production temporally and geographically from that of reception. Television shows are made in Hollywood and distributed across the United States; films are shot in Hollywood or "on location" and shown in theaters across the country. Fashion magazines are edited in New York and devoured by readers all over. Music is recorded in Los Angeles, New York, or Nashville and downloaded on computers, phones, and iPods everywhere. It might make sense to ask Ryan Murphy, creator of *Glee*, what television shows he watches when he gets home from the set, but we would not ask the average *Glee* fan what new TV show she is working on. Production is reserved for a lucky few.

Wendy Griswold (1994) provides a visual representation of the relationship between producer and audience in her concept of the **cultural diamond** (see following diagram). We see that creators and receivers—that is, producers and audiences—are placed at opposite ends of the diamond, as are the social world and the cultural object. *Social world* refers to the totality of the community in which the cultural object acts. It might be hip-hop culture, America, global culture, or any other social unit we could imagine. Of course creators, objects,

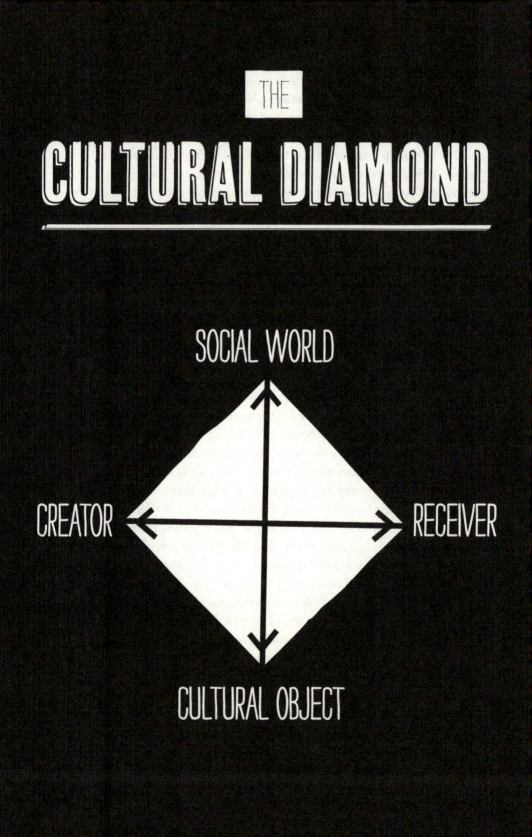

and receivers are embedded in this world, but for our analytical purposes we are teasing out cultural objects to better understand how they work. As we do so, we learn that these cultural objects are connected to the larger social world through both production *and* reception, so we need to study both to understand the objects.

Consider the example of *Glee*. The show is a cultural object created by a team of producers, writers, directors, actors, and many others. It depicts a social world that centers on a high school in the small city of Lima, Ohio. But it is meant to represent the social world of high schools in general, not just that of William McKinley High School. To get from the real high schools of the social world to the fictional representation, the content of the show is filtered through the perspectives and interests of the people who make it. Those creators are acting in part on the perceived desires of their audience. The interests of the creators and the desires of the audience probably disrupt the show's capacity to offer an accurate reflection of the social world of American high schools. **Reflection theory**, a sociological approach to literature and other forms of cultural objects, examines the ways that culture reflects the social world. Although the theory has its critics,* it nevertheless offers a powerful way of understanding the content of culture. Ryan Murphy did not invent the high school that we see in his television show out of thin air. He built it with elements from the social world: his memories of high school, other shows and films that feature high schools, stories about high school that he has seen in the news. There are probably some aspects that he creatively invented, and certainly the accumulation of those elements into this particular fictional school can be credited to Murphy and his creative team, but for the most part William McKinley High School is a reflection of the creator's experiences and interests *and* of the intended audience's desire. The influence of the audience is probably limited to focus group tests and market research in the early stages of a show, but it grows over time as ratings and other mechanisms allow audiences to weigh in.

As audiences watch the show, they may internalize the meanings they make from it. That is an important claim that we need to examine. I am not saying that audiences internalize the meanings that Murphy and the other creators infuse into the show. Rather, I am saying that the meaning is made by the audience itself. The audience has limited tools for this meaning-making work, but the work is theirs. Audience members are limited by the available

---

* Griswold (1981) offers one of the best examinations of reflection theory.

interpretations of the content and by the personal experiences they bring to the viewing, including those with similar content. But these interpretations and experiences generate what one sociologist calls a **tool kit**. Ann Swidler suggests that "cultures provide a 'tool kit' of resources from which people can construct diverse strategies of action" (1986, 281). If Swidler's notion is correct, then we draw on past cultural experiences to construct meaning and make choices in new situations. Even though I graduated from high school many years ago, I may draw on my exposure to the episodes of *Glee* to decide how to act when I feel the world is treating me like a loser. If I were a current high school student, this exposure might be especially useful—or especially harmful. But I might learn from what Finn says to his friend Puck in the pilot episode:

> Don't you get it, man? We're all losers—everyone in this school. Hell, everyone in this town. Out of all the kids who graduate, maybe half will go to college, and two will leave the state to do it. I'm not afraid of being called a loser 'cause I can accept that that's what I am. But I am afraid of turning my back on something that actually made me happy for the first time in my sorry life. (Brennan, Falchuk, and Murphy 2009a)

Maybe, just maybe, remembering a moment like that would help me choose my own happiness over the fear of being called a loser.

In sum, this book asks questions about the ways the culture industry generates a wide array of social meanings through the production, content, and reception of commercial culture objects that, taken as a whole, are consumed by the mass of society. Attention is given to all four points of the cultural diamond: creators, cultural objects, audiences (receivers), and the social world.

RESEARCH QUESTIONS AND ARGUMENTS

Now that I have clarified what *popular culture* means in this book, let me articulate the research questions that I am asking about popular culture. *What is the relationship between popular culture and identity?* This seems like a relatively straightforward question—setting aside for the moment the definition of identity, which I address later. However, from a social science perspective, it is not clear what direction of influence I am querying. Asking how popular culture shapes identity is very different from asking how identity shapes popular culture. To do the former, I would need to examine the stages in the formation of various identities—racial identities, gender identities, class identities, and so forth—to see where popular culture plays a role. That is *not* what I do in this book; although it is a very important question—aspects of which appear from time to time throughout the book—it is not the focus.

I ask the opposite question: *How does identity influence popular culture?* To answer this question, we need to make our way around the cultural diamond—from the social world, to production, to cultural objects, to audiences, and back again to the social world—to see where and how identity shows up at each point. I focus on five dimensions of identity: race, class, gender, sexuality, and disability. The first three dimensions—race, class, and gender—have been heavily studied by sociologists for years, including in the context of popular culture. The last two—sexuality and disability—are now being studied by sociologists to an increasing degree, but have received less attention in the context of popular culture. These five dimensions are not by any means the only aspects of identity. We could also ask about religion, region, age, political ideology, and many other factors that both make us who we are and give us a connection to others like us. The kinds of identity that I am examining are all collective rather than individual. They are associations we make that connect us with others. The choice of these five dimensions may seem somewhat arbitrary in comparison to the longer list of collective identities that we could formulate, but what links them together is the particular prominence they have in contemporary US *and* global politics. I have devoted a chapter to examining commercial culture systems in a few select locations around the world.

Although I have not limited the formats of popular culture discussed in this book—there are many, and technology continually allows for new formats to emerge—some have been so prominent and so heavily studied that I discuss them at length. These include television, music, film, magazines, books, and the Internet (including variations on telephones, iPads, and other devices).

To formulate my question one more time: *How do race, class, gender, sexuality, and disability influence the production, content, audience, and social world for television, music, film, magazines, books, and the Internet, both in the United States and abroad?* Now I have a large research question that is also very specific. It spells out the variables (types of media, types of identity), gives some indication of how I operationalize them, and clarifies the locations where the question is addressed. The work of answering this question is limitless. For some aspects of the question there are excellent studies that I can draw from and synthesize.

For others there is enough relevant work that I can begin to speculate what the answers might be. And yet for some aspects of the question the best I can do is suggest what finding the answer might look like. Even as I, and other researchers, work on answering this enormous question about the relationship between popular culture and identity, the terrain is moving. New technologies create new media formats with new possibilities. Changing political and economic climates shift the meanings that we attach to various aspects of identity. So even the questions that we have answered before need to be answered again. The notion that everything we could possibly say has already been said is the farthest thing from the truth. We have only just scratched the surface!

Although the work of examining the relationship between identity and popular culture is vast, the process of synthesizing the work to date into this book does allow me to make some preliminary arguments.

Argument 1: Popular culture serves the dual and contradictory role of integrating us into the social world while also insisting that we have failed to fully integrate. We are invited into the mass media matrix, but after accepting that invitation we are constantly made to feel that we do not deserve to be at the party. Popular culture normalizes our identities even as it also brands us as freaks and strangers.

Consider the characters on *Glee*. Their glee club, New Directions, gives them a place where they can be themselves and connect with others. It does not automatically make them popular, but it certainly makes them less alone. It pulls them collectively into the social world of the high school, where before they had just been marginalized individuals. As New Directions finds some success, and as more popular kids begin to join it, all of the characters become more integrated into William McKinley High School. But that integration is never fully complete, and we learn from *Glee* that everyone is on the verge of descent into loserdom.

Fans of the show may get the message that being a loser is fine, and that even losers will get their moments to shine. That is a great message. But in my lowest moments, when I am making a decision to stand up for myself, I never have the luxury of a backup orchestra ready to play the latest pop song that reminds me of my inner power. No matter how many power ballads I break into as I walk down the halls at work, the music never kicks in. That is the impossibility of popular culture. It presents us with cultural goals—physical perfection, relationship bliss, fantastical sex—but the means to achieve those goals never actually get us there.

TABLE I.I. Robert Merton's Five Types of Cultural Adaptation		
	Cultural Goals	Institutionalized Means
Conformity	+	+
Innovation	+	−
Ritualism	−	+
Retreatism	−	−
Rebellion	±	±

+ indicates access and/or acceptance; − indicates rejection; ± indicates rejection and the substitution of new goals or means
(SOURCE: MERTON 1938.)

Sociologist Robert Merton (1938) suggests that full social participation requires both embracing the cultural goals of a society and access to the means to achieve those goals. (See Table 1.1 for Merton's five types of cultural adaptation.) He uses the term *ritualist* to refer to those who embrace the means—in this case consumption—but never achieve the goals. So we could say that contemporary popular culture transforms us all into ritualists. We keep consuming popular culture and buying the products that it sells, even though we never attain the perfection that it promises.

I am suggesting that the goals celebrated by commercial culture are actually unobtainable through the means presented by that culture. Merton's notion of conformity simply is not possible. For example, if you want to achieve the body the media keep telling you to have, you cannot eat the food that the media tell you to eat. A few people manage to achieve the cultural goals, but only by rejecting the official means. These are the models and actors who attain gorgeous bodies, but only by rejecting all the food that is advertised in the commercials that punctuate their work. They are the successful business elites who attain influential careers, but only by rejecting the lifestyle of leisure and consumption that is celebrated by the businesses they lead. In Merton's model, these people are innovators because they achieve the goals of society, but only by rejecting the institutionalized means.

The ubiquity of commercial culture means that retreatism is also not possible. We may turn off our televisions (though few do), but we are still faced with commercial culture on billboards, in stores, in the magazines that litter the doctor's waiting room, and in a thousand other aspects of our day-to-day lives. However, although it may be impossible to retreat, creative audiences are showing us that it is possible to rebel by taking the cultural goals and the institutional means and transforming them into something new. This creative work by audiences is discussed at various points throughout this book.

Argument 2: Production, content, and reception are deeply connected and are deeply embedded in the larger social world, so any attempt to understand popular culture without paying attention to all four points of the cultural diamond is inevitably flawed.

Consider the production, content, and reception of *Glee*. Using the Internet Movie Database (IMDb), I identified the gender breakdown for the first-billed cast, just for the pilot episode. It is a near-even mix: of the fifteen first-billed cast members, eight were men and seven were women. In the larger social world, the gender scales tip just slightly in the other direction, with about 51 percent of the US population being women.* On television in general, studies have shown that women are significantly underrepresented, constituting just 41 percent of all prime time characters in the 2010–2011 TV season, a *decline* of 2 percentage points from three years prior (Lauzen 2012). So *Glee* is offering a higher proportion of female characters than most other shows. But who is responsible for making these images of women? As it turns out, the female characters in *Glee* come from a predominantly male creative staff. Of the ten people who served as creators, writers, directors, or producers for the pilot episode, only one was a woman—which means the lives of the women we see on *Glee* are largely authored by men. Could this skew the ways that women are represented? Answering that question requires more evidence than we have at the moment, but it is a very important one to ask.

How might male executives misrepresent the lives of women? Certainly some persistent stereotypes come through in the show. The women of *Glee* are obsessed with relationships, are consumed with doubts about their bodies and about sex, and show little interest in their academic endeavors—although they appear to keep doing fine in school. The one character who seems most confident is eventually revealed as a closeted lesbian—an interesting plot twist that nevertheless undermines her confident sexuality. Women and men who watch *Glee* are unlikely to internalize these stereotypes wholesale, because they do watch TV critically. But if they are bombarded with the same messages about women in nearly every show they watch, then hear that same message in the

---

* http://quickfacts.census.gov/qfd/states/00000.html.

music they listen to, repeated across a host of cultural formats, it becomes difficult for them to imagine that cultural images are anything other than a perfect
reflection of social reality. I suggest that when the dominant cultural messages
are that women are obsessed with relationships and men are obsessed with sex,
it is even harder for either gender to be fully engaged with the political and
economic issues of our time, including the politics of gender itself.

Argument 3: The primary way that identity influences popular culture is by
creating deep disparities, which are found especially in the labor force demographics for production, the quantitative and qualitative representations
found in the content, and the interpretive experiences of the audience.

Identity is more than a marker of difference; it is also a mechanism of stratification. For any dimension of identity, there are some people who are socially
privileged and others who face marginalization, discrimination, and oppression.
We may all feel individually privileged to be the people we are, regardless of our
gender or sexuality or any other aspect of our lives, but when we move from the
individual to the social level, those identities have very real consequences and
create deep disparities. At the production level, the key disparity is found in the
labor market and its recruitment processes. Women, racial minorities, working-class people, people with disabilities, gays and lesbians, transgender (trans)
men and women, and people who are not American (or not American enough)
often play little to no role in how their own stories are told through commercial
culture. They are either recruited less often than their privileged counterparts or
recruited unevenly—pushed more into some jobs or roles than others.

In terms of content, the issues are both quantitative and qualitative. Quantitatively, we have to look at who is overrepresented, who is proportionally represented, who is underrepresented, and who is missing entirely from our cultural
outlets. We can compare the demographics of content to the national and global
demographics, to the demographics of the audience, and to the demographics
of producers. Qualitatively, we have to examine stereotypes and other kinds of
images that produce distorted notions about certain groups, including both minority and majority groups. Some of these images are not widespread enough
to qualify as stereotypes, but they still function as what sociologist Patricia Hill
Collins (1990) refers to as **controlling images**. These images are designed to
remind us of social hierarchies and to put us in our place within them. Media
culture is also full of counterimages, which offer a disruption from stereotypes
and other controlling images. However, even as new counterimages are continually produced, the stereotypes persist, and they produce very different stories

for different identity groups. Consider the following review of the third season of *Glee*, posted by Alyssa Rosenberg on the website ThinkProgress. The name should clearly indicate that Rosenberg is critiquing the show from a liberal perspective, which is interesting because some of the most vocal criticisms of *Glee* have come from social conservatives. Rosenberg says:

> It's become impossible to escape the conclusion that Glee is an immoral show, but not for the reason cultural conservatives believe. It's become a show that's not just sloppy but exploitative and manipulative of serious societal issues and human experiences. And it's time to walk away, even for hate-watching purposes. . . . It's one thing for bringing the underexamined lives of gay teenagers, of abused women, of people of color into the mainstream of popular culture. But spotlighting them only to use their pain to accrue credit to yourself isn't admirable. (Rosenberg 2012)

Rosenberg laments the way that the show brings up serious issues facing one group or another, but only treats them across a one- or two-episode arc and contrasts them with much less important issues—for example, intertwining a story about domestic abuse with the tale of two students' auditions at a drama academy.

Finally, for audiences, identity creates disparate patterns of interpretation. In other words, audiences bring different experiences with them when they consume culture, and they access culture in uneven ways. Some groups watch television more than others, and economics plays a role in determining how we all access television.

Having laid out my questions and arguments, I now address two key issues: the mass media matrix and the matrix of identity.

THE MASS MEDIA MATRIX

Popular culture is ubiquitous. I have students, friends, and colleagues who approach me all the time with questions about current trends in popular culture. They often preface their questions by telling me that they are not popular culture consumers. They presume that I am a pop culture know-it-all and insist that they are pop culture imbeciles. There are two problems with this. First, popular culture involves such a dizzying array of cultural objects that no one person—not even a scholarly expert—can keep up with more than a fraction of it. Second, the array of cultural objects is so insidious in our lives that no one really escapes it. When one friend told me she had no interest in popular culture, I asked her what kind of music she liked. Her answer was alt country. That genre of music does not come from the Tennessee hills or the back roads of Texas; it was created by the popular music industry and places my friend in a very clear category of cultural consumer. She likes the storytelling of country music, but not the religious values. She thinks of farms as the place where organic food is made. She probably drives a Volvo or a Subaru, definitely not a pickup or an SUV. We do not have to watch prime time TV, or go see the latest blockbuster, or download the number one pop song, to be engaged with popular culture. The film at the bottom of the box office is still a form of popular culture, as is the book that never cracks the best-seller list or the canceled show that a handful of people happen to discover and fall in love with when it comes out on DVD. They all come from the same industry.

The most important point to note about the culture industry is that it is controlled by a very small handful of corporations. In 1988 media scholars Edward S. Herman and Noam Chomsky complained that a mere twenty-four companies controlled the US media output (Herman and Chomsky 1988). In 1999 Robert McChesney updated that number to six: Time Warner, Disney, Viacom, Seagram, News Corporation, and Sony—although he noted also the significant holdings of AT&T and General Electric. The actual list of the major media giants shifts a little every year, because some holdings are sold or simply spun off as their own entities. Sometimes when this happens, the company names make it difficult for the novice researcher to keep track. For example, in 2008 Time Warner Cable split from Time Warner, making them separate financial entities. Or consider the case of Sony Music Entertainment, a division of the Sony Corporation. Moving backward in time, Sony Music Entertainment has also been known as Sony BMG (during a partnership with Bertelsmann), Columbia Records, and the American Record Corporation. Many Americans think of Columbia Records as an important part of American music history, but may not realize that it still exists as a corporate entity under the name Sony Music Entertainment, owned by the Japanese Sony Corporation.

How we identify the major media corporations depends in part on how we define the media. If we focus on types of media formats produced, then we would likely start with television, radio, film, music, print media, and digital outlets. If we also consider distribution mechanisms, then cable and telecommunications (such as mobile phones) are added to the list.

As an experiment, we will use the five major broadcast networks as an entry point to this analysis: NBC, ABC, CBS, Fox, and the CW. This analysis is

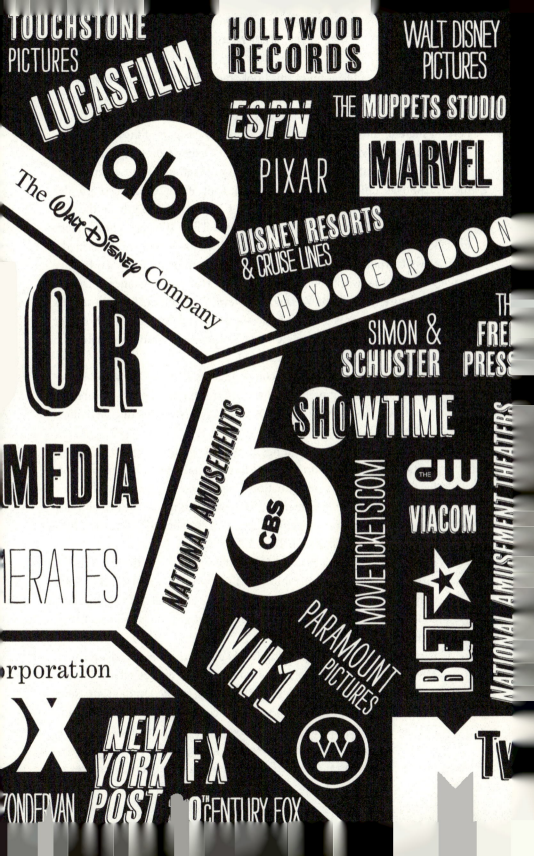

accurate as of the publication of this book, but subject to change as holdings shift. NBC is part of the larger company NBC Universal, which was jointly owned by Comcast and General Electric until Comcast purchased GE's 49 percent share of the company in March 2013. ABC is part of the Disney-ABC Television Group, which is owned by the Walt Disney Company. CBS is part of the CBS Corporation, which is a subsidiary of National Amusements. Formerly, CBS was a division of Viacom, but it split off in 2005. Viacom is also a subsidiary of National Amusements. The CW is owned jointly by the CBS Corporation and Warner Bros. (a subsidiary of Time Warner). The C stands for CBS, and the W stands for Warner. Finally, Fox is owned by the media giant News Corporation as part of its Fox Entertainment Group. So the five major broadcast networks point us to the powerful role of Comcast, Disney, National Amusements, Time Warner, and News Corporation. "5 Major Media Conglomerates" presents a visual indicator of the relative size and holdings of some of the major media conglomerates. These corporations constitute a *media oligopoly*, a term explained in Table 1.2.

An analysis of the major media conglomerates reveals four key observations that will help us comprehend how powerful these corporations are and how insignificant the role of competition is for understanding their activities.

1. Each conglomerate has holdings at multiple points in the chain of production and distribution. In television, a conglomerate may have holdings in production studios, national networks, and local broadcasters. In film, the same conglomerate may have holdings in studios, film distributors, and national theater chains. This is referred to as *vertical integration*, a term explained in Table 1.2.

2. Each major conglomerate has broad holdings within the main media formats. Comcast's ownership of NBC Universal gives it control not only of NBC, but also of Bravo, the Weather Channel, Syfy, Telemundo, and USA. This is referred to as *horizontal integration*, a term explained in Table 1.2.

3. Each conglomerate has broad holdings across the main media formats. News Corporation has holdings in publishing (HarperCollins, Zondervan), newspapers (*New York Post*, *Wall Street Journal*), radio (Fox News Radio), sports teams (the Brisbane Broncos in Australia, the Colorado Rockies in the United States), film (Twentieth Century Fox), and television (Fox, FX, Fuel). This of course allows for significant cross-promotion. In *Glee*'s first season, the teen characters made frequent references to

TABLE I.2. Keywords for Understanding Media Consolidation

Oligopoly: An industry that is controlled by a small handful of corporations that are functionally no longer competing with each other. The media industry is an oligopoly, because a small group of companies controls the industry, and they are deeply interconnected and share the same interests (McChesney 1999).

Vertical Integration: A cost-saving method for businesses that involves controlling every aspect of the creation and distribution process. For example, a corporation that owns a music studio may also seek to own a song publishing business, a music distribution business, etc. Moreover, corporations that own businesses across different media formats can cross-promote cheaply and easily, such as when *Glee* promoted MySpace during its first season (Peterson and Berger 1975).

Horizontal Integration: A cost-saving method for a business that involves controlling ever higher proportions of the market production within a field. A corporation that owns a music studio may purchase other music studios in order to control a significant segment of music production (McChesney 1999).

Interlock: The situation when a board member of a major media organization is also a board member of another corporation, making the media organization more favorable to the interlocking corporation. One team of researchers found that the boards of ten major media outlets are composed of 118 individuals who are on the boards of 288 different corporations, which indicates significant interlock. They also found that many of these media board members are also board members for major colleges and universities, and that many have served in political office, creating interlocks among the leadership of the media, the political leadership of the country, the educational leadership of the country, and the international corporate community (Thornton, Walters, and Rouse 2006).

Federal Communications Commission (FCC): An independent federal agency created by the Communications Act of 1934, charged with regulating the use of wire and radio communications, which are concerned public goods belonging to the citizens. The Internet was added to the FCC's charge by the Telecommunications Act of 1996, which also created new allowances for cross ownership. The FCC's ownership rules are reviewed and potentially revised every two years, which means that further deregulation is always a possibility. The FCC is funded entirely by licensing fees and fines.

their MySpace pages, even though MySpace was swiftly losing users to its rival, Facebook. Why would *Glee* promote MySpace? Because News Corporation owned MySpace at the time, before selling it in 2011 to Justin Timberlake and Specific Media Group. MySpace, now Myspace, has been transformed into a "social entertainment" service, focusing especially on music.

4. The various conglomerates are interlocked by joint holdings and joint ventures. Hulu, the popular online service provider, primarily of television but also of film, is a joint venture of Fox, NBC, and ABC. The popular television show *Scrubs*, which aired from 2001 to 2010, was produced by ABC Studios, but aired until 2008 on NBC. When NBC canceled the show, ABC picked it up and aired it for two more seasons. These are just two among scores of joint ventures that significantly interlock the financial interests of these media conglomerates, while also undermining the power of consumers. Table 1.2 explains the concept of interlocks and the various forms that an interlock can take.

The term *culture industry* is most associated with the mid-twentieth-century scholars Theodor Adorno and Max Horkheimer in their 1944 book, *The Dialectic of Enlightenment*. Adorno and Horkheimer viewed the culture industry as the inevitable conclusion of capitalism, which they believed was a cultural process of turning everything into a commodity. Early discussions of capitalism focused on factory production of the goods and resources necessary for survival and rarely touched on the commodification of art. But Adorno and Horkheimer observed that capitalism was extending its grasp into every aspect of human life, including the arts. Their critique of the culture industry was that it churned out mass-produced and dumbed-down works of culture that would only numb or deceive the masses:

> The culture industry perpetually cheats its consumers of what it perpetually promises. The promissory note which, with its plots and staging, it draws on pleasure is endlessly prolonged; the promise, which is actually all the spectacle consists of, is illusory: all it actually confirms is that the real point will never be reached; that the diner must be satisfied with the menu. (Horkheimer and Adorno 2002, 44)

The diner must be satisfied with the menu because, in the authors' view, the culture industry sells nothing other than itself—no life lesson, no enlightenment, no new possibility for the human experience. The institutionalized means never allow us to achieve the cultural goals. The stranger never gains full citizenship.

I refer to the culture industry as a matrix because of the incredible ways that media conglomerates are interlocked across production chains, media formats, and the globe. Their size, and the fact that they have no vested interest in competing with one another, leaves consumers with little influence over the industry. They are a large and powerful force that feels invisible in many ways. A studio may put its stamp on a particular product, usually in the opening or closing credits, but it remains difficult for consumers to see how interconnected all of these products are.

THE MATRIX OF IDENTITY

The mass media is just one of two major matrices that I examine in this book. The other is the matrix of identity, or what Patricia Hill Collins calls "the matrix of domination" (Collins 1990, 18). Identity is ubiquitous. It is a central political issue in an era of identity politics—gay marriage, "postracial" America, confusion over how to court women voters—and it is a growing research interest for scholars in both the humanities and social sciences. Sometimes my students complain about the constant focus on identity, not just in my classroom but also in many of their other classes. They tell me that they do not feel discriminated against and do not discriminate against others, and they wonder why we have to talk about discrimination and oppression all the time. Although I am certain we do not discuss discrimination and oppression *all the time*, I have no trouble defending the centrality of identity and inequality in the college curriculum. Identity is a matrix of *social* mechanisms and is not reducible to individual interpersonal interactions, although it certainly has an impact on those. Scholars are not the inventors or authors of identity; at best, we can hope to describe its parameters and central organizing principles. Identity captures a core aspect of the human experience: the sorting of humans into groups that give us a sense of belonging and connection and also clarify who is excluded (and when and why).

Identity is a structural principle. It creates the boundaries of social groups and defines the norms of the people within these groups. Identity is an economic principle. It creates the basic divisions of labor, determining who will work in which occupations and how they will prepare for those fields. Identity is a cultural principle. It creates the central value systems that shape what we believe and what our lives mean.

In our time, the dimensions of identity that receive the most attention are race, class, and gender. Key social movements, including the civil rights movement, the labor union movement, and the women's liberation movement, have placed these dimensions of identity at the forefront of structural change by extending full social participation to previously excluded groups. To a lesser degree, these movements have also created economic changes, opening up new possibilities in the labor market for women and racial minorities and improving the lives of the working and middle classes. Culture, by comparison, has proven much more durable. The social meanings of racial, class, and gender labels are difficult to change. These identities may be performed—as suggested by the sociological concept of "doing gender" (West and Zimmerman 1987)—but that should never be misinterpreted as a suggestion that we can perform them any way we want at any time. Performances become scripted and institutionalized, making it very difficult to significantly alter them.

The key sociological concept that is used when we bring race, class, and gender together is *intersectionality*, a concept coined by the legal scholar Kimberle Crenshaw (1989) in her early work on critical race theory. Patricia Hill Collins expands on this concept in *Black Feminist Thought* (1990). It refers to the overlapping effects of race, class, gender, and other dimensions of identity to shape the human experience by situating the individual within a complex system of stratification. Although intersectionality creates degrees of privilege and oppression for most people, it also creates important categories for collective organizing and social challenge. In both Crenshaw's and Collins's work, intersectionality is defined primarily in terms of race, class, and gender, but the concept is defined in such a broad way that other dimensions of identity are easily included as well. Indeed, they must be included to fully understand how intersectionality works. These additional dimensions include sexuality, disability, religion, and nationality. The core idea of intersectionality is that we cannot understand the full story of stratification if we look only at one dimension at a time. Take gender as an example. If someone were to ask me to name key stereotypes associated with masculinity, I might use words like toughness, leader, strong, and "can't cry." But if the question became more specific, and I was asked for stereotypes associated with black masculinity, or Hispanic masculinity, or gay masculinity, then the words would change pretty significantly. That raises the question of whether my original list of stereotypes refers only to white or straight masculinity. When we don't explicitly identify an intersection, our assumptions are often directed at those groups who *benefit* from the dimension of identity in question. When thinking about gender, whether masculinity or femininity, we too often focus on whites, people who are straight, people who are not disabled, and those in the middle class.

An important corollary to intersectionality, then, is **privilege**, a concept most associated with Peggy McIntosh's consideration of white privilege and male privilege. McIntosh discusses the blithely privileged statements that her male students made in classes in which she explored gender issues (McIntosh 2009). As she realized that these statements were not deliberately malicious, but rather reflections of deeply seated, taken-for-granted assumptions, she began to question her own assumptions, which resulted from her privilege as a white person. She refers to these assumptions as an "invisible knapsack," a set of tools and resources that privileged people carry around without ever realizing that many people do not have the same resources. Bringing intersectionality and privilege together allows us to see that most people experience some level of privilege *and* some level of oppression. For example, a white, gay, middle-class male might feel oppressed in a homophobic culture, without recognizing that he is also privileged by his gender and class. A straight black woman may feel oppressed by the combination of sexism and racism, without recognizing the ways that she is privileged by her sexual orientation and her status as nondisabled. Because of the important but often-overlooked role of privilege as a mechanism of inequality, I prefer the phrase "matrix of privilege and oppression" over "matrix of domination." *Domination* is a much stronger term than privilege, to be sure, but it is too easy to focus on who is being dominated. The concept of privilege forces our attention to the question of who benefits from this system of inequality.

In a memorable scene from *Glee*, the cheerleading coach, Sue Sylvester, invokes identity markers to call out a set of students from New Directions: "Santana, wheels, gay kid . . . Asian, other Asian, Shaft" (Brennan, Falchuk, and Murphy 2009b). She is referring, in order, to the Latina named Santana (one of her Cheerios), the disabled student Artie Abrams, the as-yet-not-out gay kid Kurt Hummel, an Asian student named Tina Cohen-Chang, another Asian student named Mike Chang (no relation to Tina), and a black student named Matt Rutherford. In that moment, Sue Sylvester is doing to these students something that popular culture does to many minorities: reducing them to one dimension of their identities. Only Santana, as one of Sue's favorites, is let off the hook and given the full subjectivity that is implied when we are identified by our names, not just by a single aspect of who we are. The effect of these one-dimensional labels is to render each recipient a stranger in the very sense that Simmel discussed: both a part of the community and apart from it.

As mentioned previously, in this book I examine five dimensions of identity: race, class, gender, sexuality, and disability status. I also address questions of national identity in a chapter on global comparisons. Although I tease these dimensions apart for analytical purposes, I always include as much intersectional analysis as possible. For instance, when discussing sexuality I try to include comparisons between gays and lesbians to allow for gender analysis and to include racial comparisons as well. The fact that I discuss these dimensions separately should in no way obscure the fact that they are intricately linked. But it is very difficult to be fully intersectional at every moment of analysis. The matrix of the culture industry and the matrix of identity are two powerful social forces that work together to significantly shape modern life.

A FIELD GUIDE FOR ANALYSIS

This book is designed as a field guide for any student or scholar who is interested in studying the influence that identity has on commercial culture. It summarizes the ways that this influence has been explored, along with the major relevant findings. It brings a wide variety of sociological theories and methods to bear on this issue. I try to focus primarily on sociological research, especially from the sociology of culture, but I also draw heavily from both communications studies and cultural studies. Communications studies offers an excellent perspective on the organization and influence of the media industries. Cultural studies provides a method for close textual analysis of cultural objects. The sociology of culture has emphasized the meaning-making strategies that audience members use in transforming cultural objects into a set of meanings and values that guide their daily actions and preferences. In addition, I draw from both classical and contemporary theories and theorists. Table 1.3 summarizes the theoretical approaches used in this book.

In addition to a range of theories, I also introduce several methodological approaches. In each of Chapters 2–6, I discuss three methodological approaches: production studies, content studies, and audience studies. These methods include both quantitative and qualitative approaches and demonstrate a range of ways that social research questions can be answered. Table 1.4 summarizes the methods discussed in this book.

TABLE I.3. Theoretical Approaches Used, by Chapter

Chapter and Topic	Classical Perspectives	Contemporary Perspectives
Chapter 1, Introduction	Georg Simmel's "The Stranger."	Theodor Adorno and Max Horkheimer's analysis of the culture industry, along with recent similar work by Robert McChesney. Patricia Hill Collins's discussion of intersectionality from *Black Feminist Thought*.
Chapter 2, Racial Perspectives	W. E. B. Du Bois's insights into race from several of his key works.	Howard Winant and Michael Omi's analysis of race and racial formation in *Racial Formation in the United States*.
Chapter 3, Class Perspectives	Karl Marx's perspectives on class and capitalism from several of his key works.	Pierre Bourdieu's analysis of cultural capital from several of his key works.
Chapter 4, Gender Perspectives	Beatrice Potter Webb's introduction to *The Awakening of Women*.	Judith Lorber's social construction approach to gender in *Paradoxes of Gender*.
Chapter 5, Sexuality Perspectives	Emile Durkheim's functionalism, as presented in *The Rules of Sociological Method*, as well as his concepts of anomie, regulation, and authority from *Suicide*.	Michel Foucault's discussion of the relationship between sexuality and power from *The History of Sexuality, Volume 1*.
Chapter 6, Disability Perspectives	Max Weber's discussion of meaning and culture in *Economy and Society*.	Peter Conrad's analysis of medicalization.
Chapter 7, Global Perspectives	George Herbert Mead's conception of symbolic interactionism.	George Ritzer's conception of McDonaldization.
Chapter 8, Conclusion	This chapter treats the films *The Matrix* and *Freaks* as alternative sources of social theory about popular culture.	

TABLE I.4. Methodological Approaches Discussed

Chapter and Topic	Approach
Chapter 2, Racial Perspectives	*Cultural Efficacy*: A method introduced by Michael Schudson for examining the social potency of a cultural object: how and why a piece of culture works. *Labor Force Analysis*: Using demographic data to examine the labor force participation of various groups within culture industries. *Audience Ethnography*: Using participant observation to study the ways consumers engage with cultural objects and experiences.
Chapter 3, Class Perspectives	*Qualitative Content Analysis*: Recording key observations about how social issues are represented and discussed within cultural objects. *Production Ethnography*: Using participant observation to study the process of cultural production. *Audience Surveys*: Using closed questions to gather broad data about audience consumption patterns and preferences.
Chapter 4, Gender Perspectives	*Descriptive Analysis*: An open-ended approach to understanding the kinds and types of representations that occur in popular culture. *Interviewing Creators*: Using directed questions to interrogate the process of production through the lens of cultural producers. *Cultural Controversies as Ethnomethodology*: The study of culture wars and other conflicts that reveal deep-seated assumptions about meaning.
Chapter 5, Sexuality Perspectives	*Quantitative Content Analysis*: Using coding sheets to examine and compare large amounts of popular culture content. *Production Surveys*: The use of closed questions to generate quantitative information about what producers make and how they think about the production process. *Audience Interviews*: Using directed questions to examine the processes of consumption and interpretation.

continues

TABLE I.4. *continued*	
Chapter and Topic	Approach
Chapter 6, Disability Perspectives	*Thick Description*: Studying cultural texts in depth and in context to deeply understand the kinds of meanings they convey and the ways that these meanings are enacted.
	Organizational Reports: Reviewing key organizational documents to understand how associations within the culture industries, such as labor unions and guilds, assess and act on their varied interests.
	Autoethnography: A method through which researchers examine themselves and their position within the groups they are examining.

WRAP-UP

To sum up, this book is a field guide to the many ways that social researchers can answer the following question: How do race, class, gender, sexuality, and disability influence the production, content, audience, and social world for television, music, film, print media, and digital culture? Although most of the book focuses on the contemporary United States, Chapter 7 turns to global comparisons. I argue that the relationship between identity and popular culture creates a kind of contradiction that tells us that cultural goals can be achieved without providing the means to realistically achieve them—because in fact the goals are truly unattainable. I further argue that in our analysis we must continually look at the connections among production, content, and audience and at how these key points are embedded in a social milieu. Finally, I argue that identity creates deep disparities that do far more than carve out niche markets—they drive us apart from one another and exacerbate cultural, economic, and structural hierarchies.

Sociology provides us with a powerful set of theoretical and methodological tools for answering our questions and exploring the arguments that I make. Several theoretical perspectives are explored throughout this book, but many more are not covered. This is also true of the methods reviewed here. Some sociologists choose a particular theoretical frame and a particular method and commit to them throughout their careers. I advocate an alternative approach in which all theories and all methods are available tools in our tool kit for sociological analysis. This allows us to choose the best tools for the job depending on the question we are asking and the realities of the data that we produce.

RESOURCES

Resources for Understanding the Culture Industry

- Video: Douglas Rushkof's *The Merchants of Cool.* A Frontline Special from PBS, available in streaming format on the Frontline website: http://www.pbs.org/wgbh/pages/frontline/shows/cool.
- Video: Robert McChesney's *Rich Media, Poor Democracy*, from the Media Education Foundation. Available in many libraries. Some clips can be found on YouTube.
- Website: Internet Movie Database. An online database of information on both movies and television programs, including credits for both on- and offscreen roles: https://imdb.com.
- Website: By the Numbers. Tracks tickets sales and other information for film: http://www.the-numbers.com.
- Website: TV By the Numbers. Tracks ratings information and other television statistics: http://tvbythenumbers.zap2it.com.
- Website: Billboard. Tracks sales information for popular music: http://www.billboard.com.

Resources for Examining Identity

- Website: Project Implicit. A set of online tests that help to reveal a variety of biases we may hold: https://implicit.harvard.edu/implicit.
- Website: Census Quick Facts. A broad overview of demographic information on the US population: http://quickfacts.census.gov/qfd/states/00000.html.

2

The Revolution Will Not Be Available on iTunes

RACIAL PERSPECTIVES

Image 2.1. Musician Janelle Monae sings fun songs that also make powerful statements about race, identity, and inequality (SOURCE: EVERETT COLLECTION).

YOUR FREEDOM'S IN A BIND

In contemporary commercial popular culture, race is both ubiquitous and invisible. On the one hand, it is everywhere. Racial labels are sprinkled throughout popular culture like markers on a map. Sometimes they are used to invoke a kind of racial attraction, such as when Missy Misdemeanor Elliot raps, "Boys,

boys, all types of boys; Black, White, Puerto Rican, Chinese boys" (Elliot 2002). Sometimes racial labels are used to invoke messages of equality, such as when Lady Gaga sings, "You're Black, White, beige, Chola descent, you're Lebanese, you're orient . . . Rejoice and love yourself today 'cause baby, you were born this way" (Lady Gaga 2009). Racial labels are used frequently and quite casually. This attitude about racial categories marks a dramatic departure from the popular culture of the 1990s, in which discussions of race were generally characterized by discomfort, especially with regard to labels. Confusion over whether to use black or African American, white or Caucasian, Indian or Native American, along with many other ambiguities (including the lines between race and religion, between race and ethnicity, and between race and nationality) resulted in a broad discomfort with race in popular culture. This uncertainty is captured quite well in the documentary *Hip-Hop: Beyond Beats and Rhymes*, when the film's host, Byron Hurt, interviews a young white kid from Ohio who is visiting BET's Spring Bling in Daytona Beach, Florida:

Byron Hurt: "How long you been listening to hip-hop, man?"

White kid: "Seven or eight years, since it started to come out in '91 and '92, ever since then."

Byron Hurt: "What is it that draws you to hip-hop?"

White kid: "Just the pure emotion in the beats. I love the beats. I love every lyric that they spit. Everything about it is my style. You guys, colored people, could say that it's their music, but I can get down to it just as much as they can."

Byron Hurt: "Did you just say colored people?"

White kid: "I don't know, what term do you want me to use? I'm not a racist at all. That's why I feel like I can come down here and just roll in and I can have no problem. No one is going to try to do anything. I'm just trying to have a good time down here." (Hurt 2006)

This "white kid" demonstrates the kind of general discomfort that popular culture had with race in the 1990s, but which seems to have passed. Now, instead of causing anxiety, these labels are a source of humor, or drama, or tension, which is really just to say that they have been incorporated into the broader repertoire of storytelling with which popular culture is engaged.

But the white kid above also demonstrates the ways that race has become invisible in popular culture. Although the categories of race remain salient, the concept of race as a powerful and politically charged social institution is missing. Thus, the kid in Byron Hurt's interview sees no substantial difference between his consumption of hip-hop music and the consumption of that music by black people, a group that he is clearly aware of and yet not sure how to name. Although racial controversy is rampant in American society, there has been little of it evident in recent music, television, film, books, and digital culture. In the 1980s and 1990s rap and hip-hop were major sources of controversy, resulting in multiple hearings in the US Congress.* Today these genres are just additional channels on the radio and extra sections in the (online) record store.

Why should I expect the situation to be any different? At one time racial culture was talked about in revolutionary terms. The question today is, where's the revolution? In 1970 the poet Gil Scott-Heron composed what would become his most famous work, "The Revolution Will Not Be Televised." Scott-Heron, who passed away in 2011, was a spoken-word artist whose work is considered by many a forerunner to rap music. He recorded his poetry and set it to music, rather than committing it to the page. "The Revolution Will Not Be Televised"—which is easy to find on YouTube and other sources—is a powerful political song that speaks specifically about a racial revolution: "Green Acres, The Beverly Hillbillies, and Hooterville Junction will no longer be so damned relevant, and women will not care if Dick finally gets down with Jane on *Search for Tomorrow* because Black people will be in the street looking for a brighter day. The revolution will not be televised" (Scott-Heron 1970). Scott-Heron offers a very clear answer to a question about the relationship between popular culture and race: popular culture is not going to liberate black people from racial oppression. It is a distraction from *real* racial politics. The last line of the track is telling: "The revolution will be live." Here, "live" references the notion of live TV, in contrast to recorded television, but actually invokes something even more immediate. The live revolution, as described by Scott-Heron, is in person, and it is not mediated by commercial culture.

Fast-forward from 1970 to 2008, to another performer who draws together music and the spoken word: Janelle Monae (see Image 2.1). Monae is not known for selling large numbers of records, but she has a strong cult following. Her fan base was solidified by the release of her music video for the song "Many Moons," which is available on YouTube. In the video, Monae adopts an alter ego known as Cindi Mayweather, a character she says is based in part on

---

* See, for example, Binder (1993).

Neo from the film series *The Matrix*. The video, however, is a tribute to Fritz Lang's 1927 film *Metropolis*, which was also an inspiration for *The Matrix*. *Metropolis* tells the story of a dystopian future in which the world is divided into a race of workers, who live below the ground, and a race of privileged elites, who live in a golden city in the sky. An inventor named Rotwang invents a robot that is indistinguishable from humans, and that robot becomes a revolutionary leader who frees the underground workers. In the video for "Many Moons," Cindi Mayweather is a similar robot, and she has been mass produced so that she is available for purchase by those in the golden city. The setting for the video is a product release event at which one of the robots is performing for the audience while other versions are demonstrating the diverse capacities of this artificial life form. The people in the audience do not seem to notice the revolutionary character of the song they are hearing. Consider the lyrics, paying attention to the ways that Monae has interwoven the story of *Metropolis* with a story about racial politics. She opens the song with the line "We're dancing free but we're stuck here underground" (Monae 2007), which implies tension between a free soul and a feeling of being trapped by external circumstances. She then says that "all we ever wanted to say, was chased, erased, and then thrown away." She has not identified who "we" are, but clearly is referring to a group of people who have been oppressed and mistreated. According to the song, this group is proclaiming: "We long for freedom (for freedom). You're free but in your mind, your freedom's in a bind." In a lengthy spoken word section called the "cybernetic chantdown," Monae includes many racial images in a long list of concerns about society, including "Civil rights, civil war . . . Black girl, bad hair, broad nose, cold stare . . . Creative black, love song, stupid words, erased song . . . White House, Jim Crow." Notice how "erased song" sounds almost like "a race song."

What story does this song, and its accompanying video, tell about the relationship between race and popular music? First, the topic of race has not been dropped from musical content, but rather has gone "underground," even in a time of "dancing free." The word *underground* invokes both the underground workers' city in *Metropolis* and the underground railroad that once ferried escaped slaves to freedom. Second, the freedom that is experienced in contemporary culture is limited and problematic, for as she sings, "your freedom's in a bind." Third, a revolution is coming: "Revolutionize your lives and find a way out." According to the lyrics, that way out may involve flying, perhaps to Shangri-la. She sings that she can "use my wings when storms come around" and then chants "Shan, shan shan shan-gri la" at the end of the song. The idea of flying away on personal wings returns us to the notion that the oppressed workers in *Metropolis* are trapped underground while the elites live in the sky. It also invokes the legend of the flying Africans. According to folklore found throughout the Americas, some black Africans kidnapped into slavery escaped by sprouting wings and flying away. Flying off to Shangri-la would mean escaping to paradise. The questions then are: What does popular culture tell us about the world that needs escaping, and what does it tell us about how to escape? Moreover, what role does race play in the formation of these messages?

POPULAR CULTURE AND RACIAL THEORY

We can examine these questions through the lens of sociological theories of race. The work of W. E. B. Du Bois is an excellent starting point. Du Bois was a sociologist who lived from 1868 to 1963, from just after the Civil War to the midst of the civil rights movement. His 1899 book *The Philadelphia Negro* (Du Bois 1995) was one of the earliest major works of empirical sociology produced in America. But Du Bois is probably best known for his 1903 book of essays and commentary, *The Souls of Black Folk* (Du Bois 1903), in which he presented his concept of double consciousness, a theory of the unique experience of being black and American in a country where, and at a time when, it seemed one simply could not be both:

> It is a peculiar sensation, this double-consciousness, this sense of always looking at one's self through the eyes of others, of measuring one's soul by the tape of a world that looks on in amused contempt and pity. One ever feels his two-ness—an American, a Negro; two souls, two thoughts, two unreconciled strivings; two warring ideals in one dark body, whose dogged strength alone keeps it from being torn asunder. The history of the American Negro is the history of this strife—this longing to attain self-conscious manhood, to merge his double self into a better and truer self. (Du Bois 1903, 3–4)

I think the key to understanding Du Bois's concept of double consciousness is in the word *unreconciled*. This is not just a matter of having an identity shaped by two forces, race *and* nationality. All identities are shaped by a multitude of forces. What Du Bois is describing is the social position in which blackness was culturally represented as perpetually *less than* and subverted to the American identity. In a nation where, and a time when, American meant white, what national claims were available to the black American?

This discussion of double consciousness is reminiscent of Simmel's discussion of the stranger. The black American is a stranger within his own society, who can never fully escape being a stranger. Du Bois wrote *The Souls of Black Folk* before the full development of the American culture industry, but examining the concept of double consciousness today, we can identify popular culture as one of its sources. It is through popular culture that we now imagine ourselves through the eyes of others, or rather through the lens of the camera. For racial minorities, **representations** become incredibly important as they confront myths and stereotypes and seek authentic and compelling stories about their communities. The quantitative side of representation focuses on how many minority depictions are found in popular culture, whereas the qualitative side focuses on the nature of those depictions: positive or negative, real or distorted, one-dimensional or fully developed.

Du Bois took cultural representations very seriously. He once wrote: "I do not care a damn for any art that is not used for propaganda. But I do care when propaganda is confined to one side while the other is stripped and silent" (Du Bois 1926, 296). He saw art and other forms of cultural expression as being of central concern to the racial politics of his time. He spoke out against harmful stereotypes in white representations of black culture, but he also objected to demands by black audiences that black characters always be portrayed only in the best light possible, preferring that all dimensions of black life come through in cultural representations.

The contemporary sociologists of race Michael Omi and Howard Winant, who together wrote an important analysis called *Racial Formation in the United States*, might refer to popular culture representations of race as forms of racial formation:

> We define *racial formation* as the sociohistorical process by which racial categories are created, inhabited, transformed, and destroyed. Our attempt to elaborate a theory of racial formation will proceed in two steps. First, we argue that racial formation is a process of historically situated *projects* in which human bodies and social structures are represented and organized. Next we link racial formation to the evolution of hegemony, the way in which society is organized and ruled. (Omi and Winant 1994, 55–56)

By this definition, each of the songs discussed at the beginning of this chapter is a kind of racial formation project that is situated at a specific moment in history, provides a representation of both racialized bodies and broad forms of social structure, and speaks to the way that society is organized and ruled. For example, "The Revolution Will Not Be Televised" tells a powerful story about the role that television plays in the maintenance of racial **hegemony**. "Many Moons" produces a prophetic vision of the future in which individuals are freed from racial domination and led into paradise.

The centrality of race in the contemporary era means that any television show, film, song, novel, or website is a kind of racial formation project. Even a work that is silent on the topic of race must still depict racialized people (even when they are all white), and silence around the topic is still a powerful message about race.

RACE IN THE SOCIAL WORLD

"Racial Breakdown of the United States," using census data from 2010, tells a story about the politics of racial categories. The categories that the census includes and leaves out reveal the role that American political history has played in shaping how the Census Bureau treats race. For example, "Hispanic" is treated as a separate category from race altogether and is asked about in a separate question. Many Hispanics identify their race as white, then also identify as Hispanic, whereas others identify their race as "Other." This is why we often see the category "White, non-Hispanic," because the people who identified as both can be subtracted out. In the data presented throughout this book, I present "White, non-Hispanic" data as simply "White" and allow Hispanic to be a separate category. Also interesting, the census does not ask about Middle Eastern identity and defines those people as racially white.

The reality is that there is no fixed list of racial categories. The perception that race is a biologically discernible distinction has been effectively destroyed by scientists, who have made it very clear that race is a social category, not a scientific one. For the purposes of this chapter, I use census numbers as a reference point for comparing the demographics of popular culture to the demographics of the social world of the contemporary United States.

Moving beyond demographics, we know that whites are the group most privileged by the racial hegemony of the United States. Although Asian Americans do report higher incomes than whites, as well as high rates of educational success and occupational prestige, they also experience higher rates of poverty than whites and face a tremendous amount of discrimination. Across the board, racial minorities in the United States confront stereotypes and disparaging assumptions in their everyday interactions. At the same time, white

RACIAL BREAKDOWN
OF THE UNITED STATES

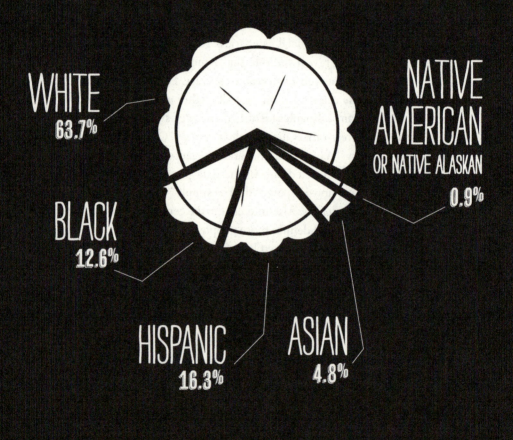

WHITE
63.7%

NATIVE
AMERICAN
OR NATIVE ALASKAN
0.9%

BLACK
12.6%

HISPANIC
16.3%

ASIAN
4.8%

privilege is often overlooked and undertheorized, allowing it to go unmentioned in many discussions of race.

RACIAL DEMOGRAPHICS IN POPULAR CULTURE

In popular culture, whose stories are told the most, whose are told the least, and whose stories are missing? When we compare the demographics of representation to the demographics of the social world, who is represented accurately, who is overrepresented, who is underrepresented, and who is invisible?

In film, white characters have dominated screens since the beginning of the industry, but nonwhite characters have always been very important as well, especially considering film's fascination with race and racial hierarchy, which dates back to 1915's *The Birth of a Nation* (Griffith). This film caused significant controversy when it was released, because it celebrates the role of the Ku Klux Klan in the Reconstruction era and also portrays black characters as violent, sexual, and insidious. It was a divisive film that is important for both American film history and American race relations.

The best analysis of racial representation in film today is found in Stacy Smith and Marc Choueiti's study of the one hundred top-grossing films of 2008 (Smith and Choueiti 2009). They find that whites constitute 71.2 percent of speaking and/or named characters. So whites are heavily overrepresented. Blacks are also overrepresented, but not by much, constituting 13.2 percent of roles, compared to 12.6 percent of the US population. Asians are overrepresented as well. Making up 4.8 percent of the US population, Asians have 7.1 percent of speaking or named roles in the one hundred top-grossing films of 2008.

So if Asians, blacks, and whites are all overrepresented, who is getting pushed out? The answer is Hispanics, the second largest and fastest growing racial group in the United States. Hispanics make up 16.3 percent of the population, yet they only have 4.9 percent of roles in films. That is a massive underrepresentation. "Racial Representation in Film" shows the breakdown. Smith and Choueiti do not count Native American characters.

Turning to television, one scholar who has devoted particular attention to the relationship between race and television is sociologist Darnell Hunt. He conducted a content analysis of prime time television in the 2002 new fall season, counting characters by their racial identity (Hunt 2003). He found that whites accounted for 74.3 percent of roles, which makes them overrepresented in comparison to their proportion of the American population at the time, 69.1 percent.

RACIAL
REPRESENTATION
IN FILM

ASIAN
7.1%

HISPANIC
4.9%

BLACK 13.2%

WHITE
71.2%

Perhaps surprisingly, blacks were also overrepresented. At the time they accounted for 12.1 percent of the population, but made up 15.9 percent of prime time roles. The overrepresentation of whites and blacks was made possible yet again by the underrepresentation of Hispanics. Hispanics comprised 12.5 percent of the population, but only 3.2 percent of prime time roles. Asians made up 2.7 percent of roles, which approaches their portion of the population at the time of 3.6 percent. Native Americans were completely absent from prime time television that year.

To update this information, I conducted my own analysis of the 2010–2011 television season. I coded characters by their race, gender, sexuality, and disability status, following protocols established in similar research, such as Hunt's methods for coding race in the report just described. "Race Representation in Prime Time TV" shows the results. In the area of race, I found patterns that are only slightly different. White overrepresentation not only persists, it has increased. I found that whites accounted for 81.8 percent of prime time roles in 2010–2011. Representation of whites in prime time has increased during a period when the white proportion of the population has decreased, to 63.7 percent. The increase in white representation is largely explained by the decline of black representation, which is down to just 9.6 percent. Over a period of eight years, blacks went from being overrepresented to being underrepresented. The reasons for this decline may be varied, but certainly the merger of UPN, a network that was known to feature black characters, with the WB, into a new network, the CW, explains much of the change. The CW targets white teenagers and has none of the black-themed shows that once appeared on UPN. But one network alone cannot explain such a dramatic decline. During the years between the two studies, the black proportion of the population increased slightly, from 12.3 to 12.6 percent.

Underrepresentation of Hispanics persists, even as the Hispanic population grows. Only 3.5 percent of prime time characters in 2010–2011 were Hispanic, compared to a population proportion of 16.3 percent. Although Hispanic roles are increasing in prime time, even as black roles are shrinking, the gap between the number of roles and the proportion of the population makes Hispanics the most underrepresented group on television. Representation of Asians has increased to 3.4 percent of roles, as the Asian demographic in America has increased to 4.8 percent. Native Americans, who comprise 0.9 percent of the population, are completely invisible on TV.

Hunt's study (2003) also includes an analysis of the types of roles played by different racial groups. He finds that Asians are more likely than all other

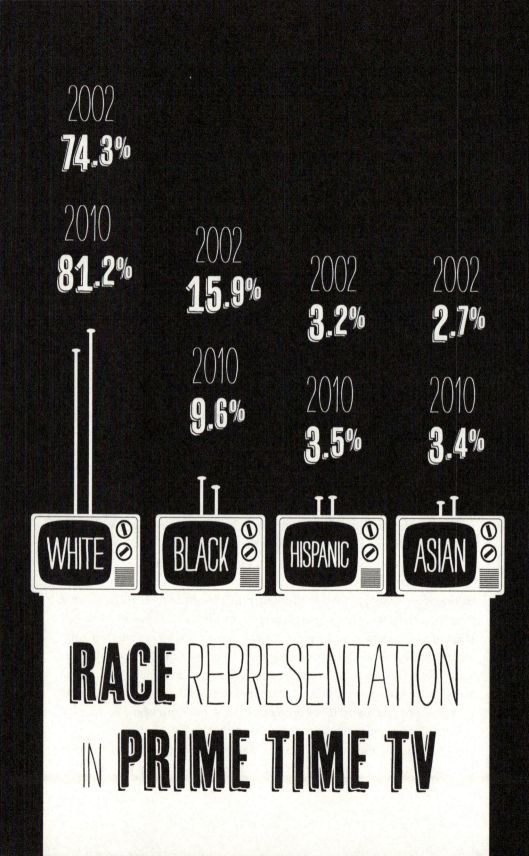

groups to appear as criminals; Asians and whites are more likely than other groups to appear as doctors; blacks are more likely than whites to appear as lawyers (but Latinos and Asians did not appear as lawyers at all in the year of his analysis); Latinos are more likely than all other groups to appear as students; and blacks and Latinos are more likely than other groups to appear as police officers. All racial groups are more likely to appear in dramas than sitcoms—dramas have larger casts and account for more programming—but a larger proportion of blacks and Hispanics had roles in sitcoms than whites or Asians.

Few demographic racial analyses have been conducted for music, which is odd, because it is quite easy to obtain annual lists of the Top 100 for various genres and for all genres. I conducted a simple coding of the performers of the Top 100 songs, across all genres, for 2010, using a list provided on *Billboard*'s website.* The performers were placed in the same racial codes that the census uses. If the song was performed by a pair or a group, then the first determination I made was whether the performers were racially homogenous. If so, then that song was placed under the racial category of those performers. If they were not racially homogenous, then the song was coded as mixed/other, meaning that the performers were a mixture of racial representations. I also placed one individual artist under mixed/other, who represented two of the songs on the chart (both Top 10). That artist is Taio Cruz, born in London to a Nigerian mother and Brazilian father. Cruz does not fit neatly into American census categories. "Racial Demographics of the Billboard Top 100 Hits" shows the breakdown. After I coded all one hundred songs, an interesting story emerged. White artists were responsible for forty-five of the songs, making them underrepresented. Black artists were responsible for thirty-six of the songs, making them significantly overrepresented. Hispanics produced only two of the songs, and Asians only one. Native Americans were not represented in the Top 100 songs of 2010. Sixteen of the songs fell into the mixed/other category. Some of these songs were made by racially mixed groups like the Black Eyed Peas. Many of the songs were made by a pairing of a white singer with a black rapper, or a white DJ (such as David Guetta) with a black rapper or singer.

These numbers, which I quickly tabulated on my computer, actually offer a window into a much broader story about the role of race in American music. The American recording industry has a long history of relying on black

---

* http://www.billboard.com/charts/year-end/2010/hot-100-songs.

RACIAL DEMOGRAPHICS OF THE BILLBOARD

2010

TOP 100 HITS

1 **WHITES** – 45 songs

2 **BLACKS** – 36 songs

3 **MIXED/OTHER** – 16 songs

4 **HISPANICS** – 2 songs

5 **ASIANS** – 1 song

musicians to produce much of its output. Johnny Cash discusses this openly in his autobiography, *Cash* (1997). He points to the important role played by Sam Phillips, the founder of Sun Records in Memphis, Tennessee, who discovered not only Johnny Cash but also Elvis Presley, Jerry Lee Lewis, and many others: "Sam Phillips was a man of genuine vision. He saw the big picture, which was that the white youth of the 1950s would go crazy for music that incorporated the rhythms and style of the 'race' records he produced for artists like Howlin' Wolf, Bobby Bland, B. B. King, Little Milton, James Cotton, Rufus Thomas, Junior Parker, and others" (Cash 1997, 79). From Cash's perspective, Phillips was a visionary, but he was also motivated by economic realities. Black performers could be paid much less than whites and, more important for American popular and country music, black songs could be purchased very cheaply to be recorded by white performers.

What of racial representations in literature? One of the best studies of children's books examines the inclusion of black characters throughout the twentieth century. Bernice A. Pescosolido, Elizabeth Grauerholz, and Melissa A. Milkie (1997) conducted a content analysis of children's picture books from 1937 to 1993. They divide these books into three types: (1) all winners of the prestigious Caldecott Medal (or Caldecott Honor), which are relatively expensive; (2) a sample of books listed in the *Children's Catalog*, a resource used mostly by children's librarians; and (3) all books in the Little Golden Books series, which are comparatively inexpensive. In total, the authors analyzed 2,448 children's picture books. Quantitatively, they calculated the percentage of books in each year that included at least one black character, as well as the percentage that featured only black characters. Qualitatively, they examined the prominence of the black characters, the types of roles they play, and the nature of their interactions with white characters. Their strongest finding is that black characters are shockingly underrepresented across the board. Across all years and all three types of books, only 15.1 percent of books had at least one black character, and only 3.3 percent had only black characters. Of course, many books have no human characters whatsoever, so the authors also calculated the percentages after subtracting the books that had no humans in them. In the resulting sample of 1,967 books, 18.4 percent had at least one black character, and 3.9 percent had only black characters.

The authors find that black representation has shifted in response to racial politics and does not reflect linear progress throughout the century. They divide the period of their analysis into four key epochs. The early years, 1937 through the mid-1950s, are marked by modest levels of black representation (between 10 and 20 percent of books in any given year included one or more black characters), confined mostly to surface contact interactions with whites (based on social roles, not relationships) or the inclusion of black characters in depictions of "all god's children," to use a phrase suggested by the authors. The late-1950s through the mid-1960s are characterized by significantly declining black representations. During this period, in any given year, only 5 percent or less of books included one or more black characters. Importantly, these were the years of the civil rights movement and of the highest levels of racial conflict in the United States, according to the authors' analysis of accounts in the *New York Times*. So it seems that the publishing industry was responding to racial conflict by removing black characters from children's books. The third period the authors identify, the mid-1960s through the mid-1970s, is characterized by a rapid increase in black characters, reaching a height of 30 percent of books having at least one black character. This increase would seem to mark the success of the civil rights movement. However, the quality of black representations during this period varies greatly. Many of the black characters in this time period are placed in African settings, which the authors refer to as safe and distant. The period following 1975 is identified as a stabilizing period, with higher levels of black representations than before, but still relatively few.

The comparison among the three types of books—Caldecott Medal books, *Children's Catalog* books, and Little Golden books—allows the authors to examine the important role played by **gatekeepers**, who are cultural leaders and institutions that mediate between cultural objects and their audiences. A DJ is a gatekeeper in the music world, just as a movie critic is a gatekeeper in the film world. Gatekeepers make careful selections from the range of cultural objects to curate a particular cultural experience. The three types of books that the authors examined reflect three different types of gatekeepers, with the Caldecott Award being the most prestigious and selective of the three. The Caldecott winners are most likely to feature black characters and to place them in American, not African, settings. The Caldecott books continued to increase in black representations, even during the period when representation was otherwise stabilizing for children's books overall in the 1980s.

The misrepresentation that we see today in the mass media is an extension of misrepresentations that date back at least to the early twentieth century. Sociologist Steven Dubin collected and analyzed mass culture objects that feature black characters such Aunt Jemima and Uncle Mose. Drawing on Pierre Bourdieu and Jean-Claude Passeron's (1977) concept of **symbolic violence**, Dubin (1987) refers to these objects as "symbolic slavery," arguing that they place black characters in positions of subservient work while juxtaposing humor and violence. Dubin's examples include a beanbag game that involved throwing bags at a board full of black faces, trying to get the bag through the mouth of a face. He also discusses "Niggerhead" golf tees, which came in a pack decorated with a black man's head that is pierced by a golf tee. These images, taken as a whole, constitute a profound world of imagery that attempts to render racial minorities powerless.

Methodology Moment
STUDYING CULTURAL EFFICACY

Media sociologist Michael Schudson (1989) suggests that one way we can study the social power of cultural objects is to look at their efficacy, or how they "work." To say that a piece of culture *works* can mean a variety of things. It could mean that the object is popular, like a blockbuster film, and reaches a wide audience. It could mean that the object is challenging, like the novel *Uncle Tom's Cabin* or the film *Precious*. It could mean that the object conveys a message very successfully, like a persuasive advertisement. Or it could mean that the object becomes a touchstone for a community, as the novels of Terry McMillan have done for black women.

Regardless of which meaning we associate with the term *work*, Schudson argues that we can explain this efficacy, or lack of it, by examining "Five Dimensions of Cultural Potency":

1. *Retrievability*. Can you get it? Is the object accessible to the audience? Objects that are highly retrievable are available in large quantities and very affordable. A film that plays at many cinemas is more retrievable than a film that plays only in a single art house cinema. A book that costs $20 is more retrievable than a book that costs $30. But the $30 book is more retrievable than a book that is out of print and only available in libraries. Retrievability can also be a matter of language. A popular French-language film is less retrievable by an American audience than an English-language film. Retrievability is measured both in the content of the object and in its relationship to an audience.
2. *Rhetorical force*. Is it powerful? Is there an aspect of the object that is striking and memorable? A catchy beat that you cannot get out of your head

continues

FIVE
DIMENSIONS OF
CULTURAL
POTENCY

1 RETRIEVABILITY:
CAN YOU GET IT?

2 RHETORICAL FORCE:
IS IT POWERFUL?

3 RESONANCE:
DOES IT FEEL FAMILIAR?

4 INSTITUTIONAL RETENTION:
DOES IT BECOME A NORM?

5 RESOLUTION:
DOES IT GIVE YOU SOMETHING TO DO?

is a sign of strong rhetorical force. Gil Scott-Heron's line "The revolution will not be televised" is a rhetorically forceful line. What if he had said, "The television is not going to provide anything that we can use for reorganizing racial reality in this country"? That just is not as striking. Listen to the song "Many Moons" by Janelle Monae. Throughout the song, we hear her sing a short phrase of "boo-doo-doo-doo-doo doo-doo-doo-doo-doo-doo doo-doo-doo-doo." Sound familiar? If you replace the boo and doos with the numbers one through twelve, you have a memorable song from the children's show *Sesame Street*. The song is called "12," and it plays during an animation of a pinball moving through a game. The song is catchy enough that many adults remember it years after learning their counting on *Sesame Street* as children, and its inclusion in Monae's song adds rhetorical force to her track. Rhetorical force is measured in the content of the cultural object itself.

3. *Resonance*. Does it feel familiar? Does the object tap into (resonate with) an ongoing conversation in society? A television episode in which the plot is "ripped from the headlines" is going to resonate with audiences who have been paying attention to those headlines and worrying about that issue. New genres often struggle to generate resonance and have to rely on other dimensions to succeed. Rap and hip-hop, in their early days, were often targets of anger and ridicule by people who just could not understand how these new musical forms could be called music. But now the musicality of these genres is taken for granted, and they resonate with wider audiences. The message of a cultural object is also important for measuring resonance. The message has to feel true. Resonance is measured in the relationship of the object to its audience.

4. *Institutional retention*. Does the object become a norm, institutionalized in society? Institutions can be formal or informal. Formal institutions play key roles in society, such as education, law, politics, and religion. Informal institutions are norms and expectations that take root in culture. Examples of a cultural object taking on formal institutional retention are novels that become part of the educational curriculum and websites that one is required to use for work. Examples of a cultural object taking on informal institutional retention are songs that become standards at weddings and television shows discussed so frequently that even if you do not watch them, you still need to follow them (often true of competitive reality television shows). Institutional retention is measured in the relationship between the cultural object

continues

and the social world and focuses less on audiences, although institutional retention can generate a larger audience for the object.

5. *Resolution.* Does it give you something to do? Is there a takeaway message? Cultural objects that give you something to do—some way to act—work better than cultural objects that do not. A television show with a cliffhanger demands that its audience return for the next episode, which means the audience gets hooked. A film with a powerful message about relationships, or family, or politics works better than a film that merely entertains. One form of resolution is consumption. Many objects encourage you to buy more. If you enjoyed this season of *Glee*, buy the DVD and the soundtrack and go see the concert and the concert movie. If you liked Janelle Monae's video for "Many Moons," go buy the album *Metropolis: The Chase Suite*. If you liked reading *Harry Potter and the Sorcerer's Stone*, read the rest of the books in the series, watch all of the films, and go to the theme park. Resolution is measured in the relationship between the cultural object and the audience, specifically how the audience is encouraged to act.

Although you can use these five measures to examine any piece of popular culture, it is especially interesting to use this method as a tool for comparison. Does *The New Normal* work better than *Modern Family* as a show that normalizes gay families? Does the *CSI* franchise work better, or just differently, than the *Law & Order* franchise? Does Jay-Z's music work better than Timbaland's music? At what? Why?

RACE IN PRODUCTION

What are the racial demographics of the labor force that produces popular culture? Who are the directors, writers, producers, editors, publishers, and so forth? We begin with film. Smith and Choueiti (2009) find that only six of the one hundred top-grossing films of 2008 had a black director, with one of those directors—Tyler Perry—working on two of the films. Only one of the black directors in the list of films is female: Gina Prince-Bythewood, who directed *The Secret Life of Bees*.

Does the race of the director matter for the content of the film? It does. Films with a black director have much higher black representation on-screen.

In the six films that Smith and Choueiti identified with a black director, 62.6 percent of the roles were played by blacks, compared to 10.9 percent in films without a black director (Smith and Choueiti 2009). This is further evidence that diversity in the labor force of the cultural industries is the most important way to generate diversity in on-screen representations.

The 1987 film *Hollywood Shuffle* offers a humorous but striking account of the way Hollywood treats black actors and the roles they play on-screen (Townsend 1987). Although the film is decades old, it still captures the relationship between race and film fairly accurately. The film was directed by Robert Townsend, a black filmmaker who also served as a writer and producer on the film, and as its star. Townsend plays Bobby Taylor, a young aspiring actor who is quickly dismayed by his prospects in Hollywood. In one scene, Bobby meets another actor, named Jesse Wilson, at an audition. Jesse warns Bobby not to "sell out" by accepting a role that is demeaning to black people: "The only role they gonna let us do is a slave, a butler, or some street hood or something." But when the casting agent calls Jesse's name, he changes his tune and even his speaking style and hurries off to audition. Bobby then has a fantasy about a black acting school where white instructors offer to teach black people how to talk jive and walk black and to play "TV pimps, movie muggers, and street punks."

In his book *Channeling Blackness*, Darnell Hunt examines the racial dynamics of the behind-the-scenes world of television, which he describes as follows: "Network television continues to be defined by a highly insular industry in which White decision makers typically reproduce themselves by hiring other Whites who share similar experiences and tastes" (Hunt 2005, 17). As evidence for this claim, Hunt examines various aspects of the storytelling process. He starts by looking at the "showrunner" position—the executive producers who are most in charge of what we actually see on television. The number of black showrunners in any given year can be counted on one hand, with the highest being five in 1990 (his analysis stopped with 2003).

In a review of the 2000–2001 television season, Hunt finds that minorities accounted for only 6 percent of directors on prime time television: 3 percent black, 2 percent Hispanic, and 1 percent Asian. Hunt then looks at the demographics of TV writers for 2002 and finds that only 13 percent were minorities. Many of these writers were working for the now-defunct UPN network. Most surprisingly, even on shows that targeted minority audiences, the majority of writers were white.

One issue that people often take for granted is the ownership of local television stations. Working at, and owning, local television stations is an important way that Americans participate in television production, especially given that so many television shows are made in southern California. The local television station makes TV more local and familiar than it would be otherwise. There are 1,349 television stations across America. A report from 2006 finds that minorities own only 3.26 percent of local television stations, compared to the 76.58 percent of stations owned by whites. Most of the remaining stations were owned by groups, with no one person maintaining a controlling interest. Hispanics, the second largest population in the United States, own just 1.11 percent of television stations. Blacks own 1.30 percent, Asians 0.44 percent, and Native Americans 0.37 percent (Turner and Cooper 2006).

These studies show again and again that racial minorities are significantly underrepresented in the production of popular culture, so it should come as little surprise that they are underrepresented in much of the content of popular culture. *In fact, minorities are actually better represented in popular culture content than they are in the production process.*

Methodology Moment
LABOR FORCE ANALYSIS

To understand the production of popular culture, it is important to look at the labor force that produces this culture. There are two major ways to do that. The first is to start with a particular cultural object or set of cultural objects and work backward to see who produced those objects. Smith and Choueiti's study of black film directors used this method. The researchers began with a list of the Top 100 grossing films of 2008 and then examined the race of the directors of each of these films. The website IMDb, or Internet Movie Database,* is a great tool for this kind of research for film and television. Although it provides the names of all of the actors and all of the crew members for any given film or television show, it does not explicitly identify their gender or race. Those details must be gathered through indirect means, such as examining their appearance or their names (for gender). IMDb does provide pictures of most of the people in the database, but not all. A researcher studying the influence of race and gender in the film or television industries, with a focus on the labor force, could use IMDb as an excellent starting point. Missing data, such as the race of someone who is named but not pictured or whose picture does not clearly indicate

---
* http://www.imdb.com.

continues

Methodology Moment: LABOR FORCE ANALYSIS *(continued)*

racial identity, can be gathered through Internet searches. One method is to search for images using Google's image search option. Another method is to perform a Web search on Google and read through the links that appear to see if any identifying information can be gleaned.

The second way to study the labor force for popular culture is to begin with the labor itself, rather than with the cultural object. The best source for this kind of information is the Bureau of Labor Statistics (BLS), especially its Occupation Employment Statistics (OES).* The most important section in the OES for this kind of research is the Occupational Profiles, found in the OES Tables. Within the profiles, the primary group from which we can gather information about the labor force for popular culture is category 27: arts, design, entertainment, sports, and media occupations. Clicking on this group provides a list of specific occupations in this field. Clicking on any one of these occupations leads to information about the number of people in this field, the industries in which they work, their wages, and the areas where they live. Although the wage information can be used as a proxy for class—telling us whether the average person in the field is rich or poor, or somewhere in the middle—this data source does not give us much more information related to identity. The BLS also issues reports, some of which have information that is more focused on identity, such as "Labor Force Characteristics by Race and Ethnicity, 2011." This report provides us with information about the racial proportions of various fields, including the broad category "Arts, design, entertainment, sports, and media occupations" and the specific occupations within that broad category.

* http://www.bls.gov.

HOW RACE SHAPES THE AUDIENCE EXPERIENCE

On the audience side, as with most aspects of reception, there is still much that we do not know. Perhaps the best examination of racial differences in film interpretation is JoEllen Shively's 1992 study of audience responses to the John Wayne Western *The Searchers*. Shively's analysis was sparked by her observation that many Native Americans love watching Westerns and her curiosity about whether Native Americans interpret the films the same way that whites do. She showed this film to a group of males who were all from the same town on a reservation. Half were Native American and half were white. After watching the film, the respondents completed a questionnaire and then participated in focus group discussions that were sorted by race. Although both groups loved the film, their reasons for loving it were very different, as were the messages they took from it. Both groups emphasized in roughly equal degrees the importance of both action and the landscape of the West. Both groups also ranked the film highly because of the presence of John Wayne and the fact that this was a "cowboys and Indians" movie, but the Native Americans actually placed more emphasis on this issue than the whites.

The biggest difference between the two groups in why they like this film comes down to two separate but linked issues: humor and authenticity. The white participants overwhelmingly emphasized the film's "authentic portrayal of the old West," something not mentioned at all by Native Americans. Instead of seeing the film as authentic, Native American participants thought the film was funny and ranked *humor* high among their reasons for liking it. Whites, by comparison, barely mentioned humor at all. (See Table 2.1.) Shively's study is important because it demonstrates that race can sharply impact the way that we interpret the movies we watch, even when a film is enjoyed equally by more than one racial group. Although race is a social construct, it is nevertheless a powerful social reality that organizes both life experiences and the ways that we make sense of the world around us, including the culture that we consume.

A different kind of racial analysis of film audiences is Matthew Hughey's 2010 study of reviewer responses to the 2007 film *Freedom Writers*. Hughey examines a very particular audience segment, film reviewers, that plays an important role in how wider audiences choose which films to see and how to make sense of those films. *Freedom Writers* tells the true story of Erin Gruwell, a young white teacher in a low-income school with largely nonwhite students who used writing, filmmaking, and the theme of tolerance to engage her students, with the result that all of them graduated—to the surprise of administrators. Hughey examines 119 reviews of the film and focuses on the kinds of frames that the reviews rely on for understanding Gruwell, her students, and the larger social structures that shaped their experience. He found a strong tendency for reviewers to pathologize the lives of low-income nonwhites. Nearly 91 percent of the reviews used pathological language with regard to the students, including terms like *dysfunctional, illiterate,* and *miscreants.* By comparison, only 13.5 percent of reviews used these kinds of frames to discuss Gruwell or the school administration. This may not seem surprising at

TABLE 2.I. Ranks of Reasons for Liking *The Searchers*, by Ethnicity			
	American Indians		
Reason	Ranked 1st	Ranked 2nd	Ranked 3rd	Weighted Sum of Ranks*
Action/fights	2	4	5	19
John Wayne	5	3	2	23
It had cowboys and Indians	6	5	3	31
Scenery/ landscape	6	3	2	26
Humor	1	5	6	19
Romance	0	0	1	1
Authentic portrayal of Old West	0	0	0	0
Other	0	0	1	1
	Anglos		
Reason	Ranked 1st	Ranked 2nd	Ranked 3rd	Weighted Sum of Ranks*
Action/fights	2	6	4	22
John Wayne	2	3	0	12
It had cowboys and Indians	3	2	5	18
Scenery/ landscape	3	5	6	25
Humor	0	1	1	3
Romance	0	0	1	1
Authentic portrayal of Old West	10	3	3	39
Other	0	0	0	0

*Ranks are weighted: 1st x 3; 2nd x 2; 3rd x 1.

(SOURCE: SHIVELY 1992.)

first, but in the film we find that Gruwell has many of the same traits as the families of her students. As Hughey explains: "She comes from a one-parent household, has an unsupportive father, and seems incredibly self-absorbed, and her marriage results in divorce" (Hughey 2010, 486). But these aspects of Gruwell's life go largely unnoticed in the reviews.

Freedom Writers falls into a category of film that is known to critics as "White Savior Films" (WSFs). In these films a lone white hero steps in to transform the lives of poor black and Hispanic people, usually young students. Some of the most prominent WSFs are *Dangerous Minds* (1995), *The Blind Side* (2009), *Finding Forrester* (2000), and *A Time to Kill* (1996). For *Freedom Writers*, 64.7 percent of the reviews chose to grapple with the issue of race, whereas 25.2 percent chose instead to present the film as a color-blind story. Hughey's study demonstrates that reviewers are part of an interpretive community that relies on a set of scripts and tropes for making claims about films. That claim challenges common assumptions that reviewers are isolated actors competing against one another for influence. Instead, Hughey finds that reviewers influence each other in many ways. Hughey explains how this new understanding of reviewers connects to the issue of race: "Customary practices of reviewing (racialized) films occur in concert with specific interpretive guidelines and become normalized in social space" (2010, 492). As Max Weber teaches us, human social life is not merely a world of objects and actions, because all objects and actions are thickly layered in meaning, much of which is taken for granted as mere common sense. The layers of meaning can be found in the films themselves and in the reviews of the film. Analyzing the frames used by reviewers reveals to us the kinds of "common sense" that are currently at play in how society grapples with issues of race and racial inequality.

When we turn to television, most of our knowledge about minorities is about black viewers. Nielsen has made public a significant amount of data about black audiences (Steadman 2005), while saying almost nothing about Hispanic or Asian audiences. The silence about Hispanics is especially striking, given that Hispanics represent a larger portion of the American population and, according to census data, have higher median household incomes than blacks.

One key fact reported by Nielsen about black audiences is that they watch more television than other groups. As "TV Viewership Time by Race" shows, for the overall population, the average daily household viewing time is eight hours and fifteen minutes. Removing black viewers reduces the average time to seven hours and fifty-two minutes. For black households, the average viewing

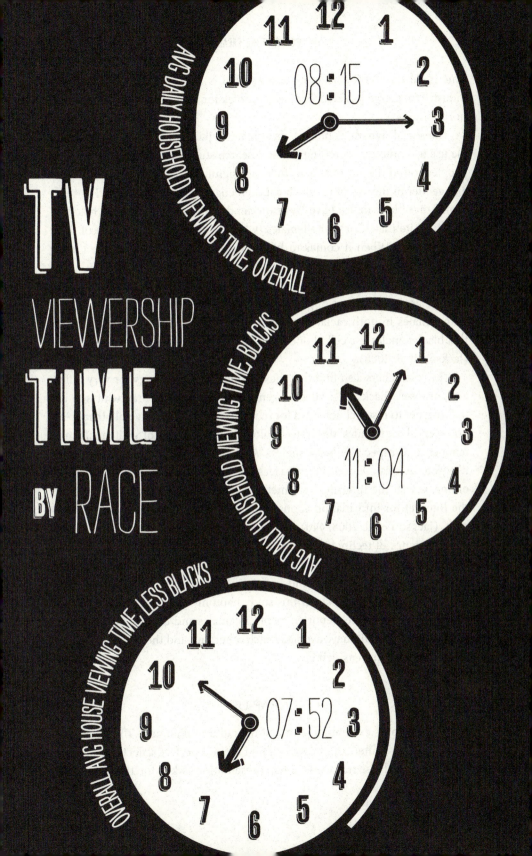

time is eleven hours and four minutes. That is a lot of black viewers for an industry that largely excludes minority professionals and rarely represents minority stories.

The social dynamics of race also create striking differences in how people use technology. According to one research study that surveyed 515 young people around the age of twelve, there are significant differences by both race and gender in the extent to which children engage with technology. The study found that black males have less experience with computers than black females, white males, or white females (who had the most experience of these four groups). When it comes to Internet use, black females reported using the Internet for longer than their counterparts in the other groups and using it more frequently. Black males reported using the Internet the least often of the four groups. In terms of playing video games, males reported higher rates than females in both racial categories. One of the most striking findings is that black females use cell phones at much higher rates than the other groups (Jackson et al. 2008).

The researchers also find that these groups use technology for very different purposes. Blacks, regardless of gender, are more likely than whites to use the Internet to research jobs and for religious purposes. In several other areas, however, black females' use of technology surpassed that of white males and females, and especially black males. "African American females were most likely and African American males least likely to surf the Web, buy something online, search the Internet for something needed for a school report, search the Internet for information about a hobby or interest, and use a search engine" (Jackson et al. 2008, 440). So race, along with gender, is clearly shaping the experience of technology users and Internet audiences. This study shows the important role of intersectional analysis, because it highlights the ways that race and gender work hand-in-hand while creating very different and somewhat surprising effects. If this study had only examined race, for many questions the high rates reported by black females and the low rates reported by black males would have averaged each other out, and the racial differences would not have been as striking.

WRAP-UP

Racial differences exist at all points of the cultural diamond. The differences in production, content, and consumption are not perfect reflections of racial differences in the social world. Misrepresentation is key for thinking about

Methodology Moment
AUDIENCE ETHNOGRAPHY

Ethnography is the study of people in their natural environments, as opposed to the unnatural environments of the research room where interviews and focus groups take place. Ethnography engages in participant observation, often with a focus on how culture is produced, negotiated, or set into action. It is more associated with anthropology than with sociology, because of the tendency for anthropologists to travel abroad to study various cultures. But sociologists often conduct ethnography as well.

For the study of popular culture, ethnography can take a number of forms. If we wanted to study movies ethnographically, we would go to movie theaters and watch the films alongside the audience, noting the types of moments that audiences react to visibly and audibly. The problem is that movie theaters are dark spaces in which there is an expectation of relative quiet. When I moved to Philadelphia several years ago, I was struck by how much more common it is for people there to talk during movies, sometimes reacting to the film and sometimes ignoring it. But in general, there is little to be gained from using ethnography to study typical audiences. Some films, however, generate atypical audiences that offer much to be studied. Certainly the annual Halloween screenings of *Rocky Horror Picture Show* could be an ethnographer's dream.

To use ethnography to study television consumption, we would need a way to examine groups who watch television together. John Fiske has done this in his study of college students watching the 1990s (and late 1980s) sitcom *Married . . . with Children* (Fiske 1992). Fiske refers to his approach as "audiencing," meaning that he is studying the audience as a social formation. In fact, Fiske presents audiencing as an alternative to **positivist** social science, because his method is better able to capture the fluidity of meanings. Positivist social science, he claims, is too caught up in generalizing: attempting to make broad claims that sweep across very different groups and experiences. In addition to college students watching TV together, ethnography can also be used to study families who gather around the television, groups of adults who meet up for their favorite shows (*Sex in the City* is one show that is known to have inspired a lot of group TV watching), or retirees watching TV together in common spaces at a retirement home.

Music offers an excellent ethnographic option: the concert. Concerts are social gatherings at which people with common musical tastes gather

continues

Methodology Moment: AUDIENCE ETHNOGRAPHY *(continued)*

not only to enjoy music together, but also to share meaningful experiences and produce a sense of solidarity in support of particular artists, genres, and musical cultures. The ethnographer can observe the preconcert activities, the ways the audience responds to the performers during the concert, and the ways that audience members engage with each other as they come down from the high of the show. Concerts provide an opportunity to look at audience diversity and interactions. How do white and black audience members respond to each other at predominantly white country music concerts or predominantly black rap shows? What role does gender play in shaping the concert experience?

We tend to think of books as something that we consume privately, in solitude, but there are a number of ways that ethnographers can study the experience of reading. For young children, the ethnographer can observe storytelling experiences. For adults, there are book groups and public readings. Reading does not only occur in isolation and privacy. We often read in public—from the businesswoman reading the *Wall Street Journal* on the train to the college student studying for an exam with a group of peers. It is important to think of reading as a social experience that produces shared meanings.

Social media are now creating new ways to engage in ethnographic research without the researcher even needing to be in the presence of the people being studied. On some level, every time we log onto Twitter, Facebook, or any of a number of social media outlets, we are engaging in a kind of ethnography, because we immediately begin to note (though perhaps not on paper) a wide range of comments, ideas, and experiences that our networks are tweeting about or posting updates about.

the relationship between race and popular culture. Racial minorities are underrepresented in the labor force for cultural production. This in turn seems to be at least one of the factors shaping the misrepresentation of many minority groups in cultural content. Intriguingly, blacks are overrepresented in popular music, and they were once overrepresented on television. Even overrepresentations tell a story of inequality, such as the exploitation of black artists in the music industry. In the area of consumption, social scientists have less demographic data and more qualitative data on the racially differing ways that people interpret the culture they consume.

The misrepresentation of racial and ethnic minorities goes hand-in-hand with the misrepresentation of whites. White characters in television, film, and literature live affluent lifestyles and are more likely to be represented in a predominantly positive way. They seem to always be the heroes, even when they are at their worst.

Despite underrepresentation, racial minorities are consuming popular culture at high rates, and they are doing some very interesting work to decide what it means and how they will use it in their everyday lives.

RESOURCES

Resources for Examining Race in the Social World

- US Census Bureau, Main Page on Race: http://www.census.gov/population/race.
- Video: *A Class Divided*. Frontline Special from PBS.

Resources for Examining Race in the Content of Popular Culture

- Video: *Hip-Hop, Beyond Beats and Rhymes*, from ITVS. Available in many libraries. Some clips can be found on YouTube.
- Video: *Hollywood Shuffle*, from Conquering Unicorn Films. Available in many libraries. Some clips can be found on YouTube.
- Website: Black Film Research Online, http://bfro.uchicago.edu.

3

Movin' on Up
CLASS PERSPECTIVES

Image 3.1. The Bunkers and neighbors in their home in Queens, from *All in the Family* (SOURCE: EVERETT COLLECTION).

TELEVISION'S CASTE SYSTEM

When George Jefferson struck it rich in the dry-cleaning business, he got to move into a New York City high-rise apartment. The theme song to *The Jeffersons* offers a concise summary of the achievement of the American dream in an urban setting:

> *Well we're movin on up,*
> *To the east side.*
> *To a deluxe apartment in the sky.*

. . .
Fish don't fry in the kitchen;
Beans don't burn on the grill.
Took a whole lotta tryin',
Just to get up that hill.

First things first. Fish don't fry in the kitchen? Beans don't burn on the grill? I always loved those lines, but what do they mean? They actually align very readily with the rest of the song, even though they seem so different. The basic message of the song is that everything used to be difficult, but now things are better, because we made it. In our old life, we fried fish and burned beans in our working-class kitchen. In our new life, a live-in maid cooks our food for us in our spacious penthouse. In our old life, we lived next door to racist Archie Bunker in working-class Queens (see Image 3.1). In our new life, we live on the Upper East Side of Manhattan. In our old life, we had to hustle to climb the hill. In our new life, we enjoy our piece of the pie and reap the rewards of our hard work.

The Jeffersons aired on CBS from 1975 through 1985 and was highly acclaimed. It was a spin-off of another CBS show, *All in the Family*, which aired from 1971 to 1979. Both shows were written by Norman Lear, whose television and film opus provides a powerful examination of the issues of class, race, and gender in the 1970s and early 1980s. One aspect of Lear's work that is strikingly different from other television shows is that his working-class people live working-class lives, from Archie Bunker's home in Queens to the high-rise housing project apartment occupied by the Evans family on *Good Times* (CBS, 1974–1979).

Of course, George and Louise Jefferson lived in a very nice apartment in Manhattan, but we the viewers were given an explicit explanation of how that happened. George Jefferson struck it rich in the dry-cleaning business. He opened his first store while the character was still on *All in the Family*, using the money he was awarded after his car was struck by a bus. By the end of the run of *The Jeffersons*, George had seven stores around New York City. The characters actually appeared years later in the series finale of *The Fresh Prince of Bel-Air*. George and Louise moved to Los Angeles and purchased the Bankses' family home—yet another step up in their affluent lifestyle.

Now fast-forward to 2009 and the debut of the ABC comedy *Modern Family*. We can compare the stories about class presented in *The Jeffersons* and *All in the Family* to those presented in this new show. *Modern Family* was created by Steven Levitan and Christopher Lloyd, who had previously worked together on shows like *Wings, Frasier, Out of Practice,* and *Back to You.* Levitan and Lloyd may not be as culturally prominent as Norman Lear, but they play an important role in writing the stories through which television tells us who we are, who we think we are, and who we want to be.

Modern Family is both critically acclaimed and a fan favorite. It has received consistently high ratings since it premiered in 2009. Even Norman Lear loves it: "The show is first-rate. I enjoy watching it every week with my wife [Lyn] and my 17-year-old twin daughters Madelaine and Brianna. We're always laughing. It's brilliantly written, and every member of the cast is terrific" (Lear 2012).

The show presents the day-to-day lives of three related nuclear families. Jay Pritchett is the patriarch of the family. He owns a construction business and is married to his second wife, Gloria Pritchett. Together they are raising Gloria's son from a previous relationship, Manny Delgado. Gloria is a homemaker. Jay is white, whereas Gloria and Manny are Hispanic, hailing from Colombia. Jay has two adult children, who each head up one of the other families on the show. Claire Dunphy, a homemaker, is Jay's oldest child. Before starting a family, she was a successful professional in the hospitality industry. She is married to a realtor named Phil Dunphy, and they have three children: Haley, Alex, and Luke. The entire Dunphy family is white. Claire's brother, Mitchell Pritchett, is an environmental lawyer. He and his partner, Cameron Tucker, are raising an adopted daughter named Lily. Cameron is a homemaker and a former clown, though he also cycles through jobs in a greeting card shop and as a music teacher. Mitchell and Cameron are white; their daughter is Asian, hailing from Vietnam.

All three families live in strikingly posh homes in southern California. Gloria and Jay's home is by far the largest and most impressive, presumably paid for by Jay's success in the construction industry. The Dunphy home has at least four bedrooms, with spacious living and dining rooms and large lawns in front and back. This lavish home is paid for, presumably, by Phil's career in real estate. But what is most striking here is that Phil is constantly represented as being quite bad at his job. He rarely seems to be working, and when he does work, he makes one blunder after the next. Yet Phil and Claire are never shown arguing about money.

Cameron, Mitchell, and their daughter Lily survive mostly on Mitchell's income as an environmental lawyer. Their enormous home might make sense if Cameron were a corporate attorney, but environmental attorneys make lower salaries. According to ehow.com, environmental lawyers in Los Angeles make an average salary of $117,500.* That salary is far above national per capita medians, but it is rather low for a lawyer and raises doubts about the family's capacity to own such an amazing home.

Let's examine the title of the show: *Modern Family*. Obviously it implies that the show focuses on how families live now, with a focus on family dynamics that are historically rather new. This includes blended families, gay families, second marriages, interracial marriage, and international adoption. The title is not *Modern Unusual Families* or *Modern Affluent Families*. It is just *Modern Family*, implying that the show tells us something about how most families live now. Each episode ends with one of the characters in voiceover delivering a key lesson as we watch scenes from the three families. The implied idea is that this is a show that we can all learn from, because it reflects back to us our own lives.

Class identity and class difference are established very quickly in the pilot episode of *Modern Family*. In the opening scene Claire and Phil are calling their children down for breakfast:

Phil: "Kids, get down here!"
Haley: "Why are you guys yelling at us? We were way upstairs, just text me."
Claire: "Alright, that's not going to happen."

This quote establishes both the size of the house and the taken-for-granted notion that three children would each have their own cell phones. The Dunphys are a financially privileged family.

In the next scene we meet Jay, Gloria, and Manny. In a cutaway to an interview with Gloria and Jay—a common aspect of the mockumentary style that is also used in *The Office, Parks & Recreation*, and other shows—Gloria helps to establish the vast class difference between herself and her husband.

Gloria: "We're very different, he's from the city, he has big big business and I come from a small village, very poor but very very beautiful. It is the number one village in all Colombia for all the, what's the word?"
Jay: "Murders."
Gloria: "Yes, the murders." (Levitan and Lloyd 2009)

---

* http://www.ehow.com/about_5510847_average-salary-environmental-lawyers.html.

In this case, class difference is intertwined with racial difference and nationality difference. Jay is a white American, and his financial success is explained by reference to his success in business. Gloria is Hispanic and from Colombia. The class character of her background could be signified sufficiently by the reference to her small village, but for comedic effect, the show's writers add that her village has the highest murder rate in Colombia. Of course in the context of the show, Gloria shares in her husband's affluence, living with him in his massive home.

Then we meet Cameron and Mitchell, returning home from adopting Lily in Vietnam. Initially we just see Mitchell on the plane with Lily, telling other passengers about the recent adoption. Then Cameron gets on the plane, and the other passengers realize that they are seated near a gay couple. Mitchell becomes conscious of judgmental reactions, right before a passenger walks by and notices Lily.

Passenger 3: "Look at that baby with those cream puffs."

Mitchell: "Okay. Excuse me. Excuse me. But this baby would've grown up in a crowded orphanage if it hadn't been for us 'cream puffs.' And you know what? Note to all of you who judge. . . ."

Cam: "Mitchell!"

Mitchell: "Hear this! Love knows no race, creed. . . ."

Cam: "Mitchell!"

Mitchell: "Or gender. And shame on you, you small-minded, ignorant few who. . . ."

Cam: "Mitchell! Mitchell!"

Mitchell: "What?"

Cam: "She's got the cream puffs!" [*pointing to actual cream puffs in Lily's hands*]

Mitchell: "Oh."

Cam (after a long pause): "We would like to pay for everyone's headsets."
(Levitan and Lloyd 2009)

Where is the class privilege in this scene? Is it the capacity for both members of a couple to travel internationally for an expensive adoption? Or is it just their ability to casually volunteer to pay for headsets for a plane full of people, immediately after that expensive adoption? The story told about family in *Modern Family* is also very much a story about class privilege that dismisses real issues of class inequality.

MARXISM, HOME, AND HABITUS

Why do contemporary television shows like *Modern Family* feature people who live affluent lifestyles without seeming to work for them, when older shows like *The Jeffersons* focused more on the traditional American dream story of rags-to-riches success? Is the American dream over? Or has it changed somehow?

The basic claim of the American dream is that class is a starting point, but not a life determinant. No matter what class you are born into, the dream claims, you can move up if you work hard and are a good person. You will succeed, and you can advance to a better financial position—just as George Jefferson did.

The fluidity of class implied by the American dream is very different from the caste system described in the work of Karl Marx, the father of class analysis. Any reader of Marx becomes quickly familiar with the two major classes that appear in his writings, the proletariat and the bourgeoisie. The proletariat is the working class, which provides the labor necessary for production within the capitalist economic system (these terms are specific to the capitalist mode of production). The proletariat's main contribution to the economic world is its labor power. It sells this labor power to the bourgeoisie, the wealthy class that owns the means of production: the land, the resources, the factories, the machines, and so forth.

What does Marx have to do with popular culture? As it turns out, quite a lot. First, popular culture is a form of capitalist production. If we want to understand cultural production, we need to examine it as part of the capitalist mode of production. Within Marx's notion of a two-class system—albeit with the nuance of a kind of middle class that he called the petite bourgeoisie—we have to think about who owns the means of production and who sells their labor for survival. Starving artists, struggling writers, camera technicians, and workers in the factories that make CDs, DVDs, and books are all members of the cultural proletariat. Who are the cultural bourgeoisie? It is tempting to name the executives, the directors, the producers, and maybe even the successful artists. But that would be a mistake. The question is: Who owns the means of cultural production? The answer to that question is the cultural oligopoly, a small handful of massive corporations that produce most of the commercial culture we consume. Where does that leave the directors and producers and executives? Marx's work may not fully answer that question for us. We could perhaps argue their way into the petite bourgeoisie, an under-theorized group in Marx's writings. But they are generally interpreted as small business owners, not wealthy leaders in the corporate system. So there is a lot of room within Marx's analyses to debate the role of these well-paid workers in the cultural economy.

Second, popular culture is a system of commodities. It could be described both as art transformed into commodity and as commodities that sell commodities. It is art turned into commodity because each of the genres of popular culture has it roots in long-standing artistic traditions. Obviously popular music developed out of much older musical traditions, and popular novels are the commercial variation of literature. Film and television are essentially commercial transformations of theater. Advertising images in the print media and online are commercial variations of fine art painting and photography. Walter Benjamin, the great aesthetician of the Frankfurt School, argued that art lost its "aura" because of the reproducibility made possible by technology and the system of mass production (Benjamin 1968). But this art that is turned into factory-produced commodity is also an advertisement for yet still more commodities. Television shows sell the products advertised, the market for the network, and the seasonal DVDs. Music sells the products advertised on the radio, the CDs and digital downloads from the artists, and concert tickets. Popular culture is art, transformed into commodity, working double-time as advertisement.

Commodities need values. Marx wrote about value at great length in *Capital* (Marx 1978). The use-value of a thing is the utility of that object in the day-to-day life of humans. To an individual human, the use-value of popular culture is the entertainment or pleasure that it brings to life. Surely some pleasure is necessary for human survival. We may not need much pleasure to get through the day, but more pleasure and more leisure are likely to lengthen one's lifespan. Leisure is likely also to make us more productive during working hours. Use-value does not get us far in determining how much a digital download should cost. We can consider the economic value in terms of the labor costs that go into the production of the object and the investment a consumer is willing to make to obtain it. Both of these determinations are difficult to calculate mathematically. If two books are priced the same at the bookstore, does that mean that they are of equal value to the reader? Does that mean that the exact same labor power went into producing them? If one book took twice as long to write as the other, should it cost twice as much?

Third, and finally, popular culture provides a symbol system that teaches audiences how to think about the economic world in which they live. Marx asserts in "The German Ideology": "The ideas of the ruling class are in every epoch the ruling ideas" (Marx 1978, 172). He is claiming that there is a dominant ideology in any era that is controlled by the ruling class. In the case of contemporary popular culture, that means that the ideas we consume are actually the ideas of the cultural oligopoly. "Wait," you say, "wouldn't it be the ideas of the rich people?" When it comes to the means of production for popular culture, as I have mentioned before, a set of corporations is in control, not a set of rich people. Some rich people benefit from these corporations very much, but it is the corporations that are in control and their ideas are the ideas of this epoch. Can corporations have ideas? Perhaps not in the usual sense, but they do have interests that differ from the interests of the people who work within them, and even from those of the people who run them.

Marx's writings about capitalism apply not only to how we think about class categories, but also to the other dimensions of identity explored in this book, because capitalism uses these identity systems as forms of the division of labor. So class stands alongside other identity categories—especially race and gender—as a system that influences the makeup of the labor force.

The American dream, as represented in *The Jeffersons*, suggests a corporate interest in promoting values of hard work. In the era of *The Jeffersons*, most of the work of making American goods still took place within the United States, and corporations needed hard-working Americans. The show encouraged this hard work by suggesting that it would be rewarded with affluence. Today the goods we consume are mostly made overseas. Corporations do not need hard-working Americans today as much as they need hard-spending Americans. The interests represented in *Modern Family* reflect the new American dream: affluent spending regardless of financial circumstances, devoid of hard work. The message in *Modern Family* is that you must be doing something wrong if you cannot afford to live like the Pritchett-Delgado-Dunphy-Tuckers, whether you are too poor or working too much to enjoy the wealth you ought to have.

What is it like to look at the world from the windows of the Dunphy house? The sociologist Pierre Bourdieu offers the concept of **habitus** to help us answer this question (Bourdieu 1977). *Habitus* refers to the structure of dispositions that we acquire from life, especially from our families. It is like the windows of our family home, through which we see the world. Bourdieu describes the concept as

systems of durable, transposable dispositions, structured structures pre-
disposed to function as structuring structures, that is, as principles which
generate and organize practices and representations that can be objectively
adapted to their outcomes without presupposing a conscious aiming at
ends or an express mastery of the operations necessary in order to attain
them. (53)

Structuring structures. Transposable dispositions. Conscious aiming. Oh my!
Bourdieu is arguing that although we do not arrive at each new situation that
we encounter as a blank slate, we also do not arrive as automatons acting out
a script written from before time began. Our habitus does not tell us what to
think or how to act, but it inclines us toward thinking and acting within certain boundaries.

The world looks very different from the Dunphys' window than from the
many other kinds of homes in which we might live: farmhouses, urban lofts,
low-income housing, suburban enclaves, and so forth. If you look at the world
from the Dunphys' windows, you can take it for granted that your parents might
text you to come down for breakfast, assume that your parents might have
plenty of time to come to all of your school events, celebrate your gay uncle's
adoption of a baby girl from Vietnam, and applaud your grandfather's marriage
to a young woman from Colombia. These are not taken-for-granted dispositions for people who grew up in different class backgrounds and different regions, with different values and beliefs. For me, growing up in rural Virginia,
none of these outlooks would have occurred to me as a young person. But television is increasingly becoming one of the windows through which we see the
world outside of our homes. We may all look at the same picture on the screen,
but the way we see that picture depends on the habitus we acquire from within
our homes and families. Our habitus is constructed by our class positions, as
well as by other factors such as our race, religion, and political ideology.

CLASS IN THE SOCIAL WORLD

Americans love the middle class. Politicians speak at length about how the
middle class suffers during difficult economic times, and they pander to perceived middle-class values—despite the fact that many of these politicians are
quite wealthy. But what *is* the middle class? I have asked my students for years
to tell me what they think the minimum income threshold is to be truly middle class, and I have heard a range of responses from $50,000 to $250,000. The

student who said $250,000 said he just did not believe people could thrive on anything less. To be sure, that was the highest amount ever suggested as a minimum threshold for the middle class. I have also asked what the ceiling is for the middle class. I've heard everything from $250,000 to $1 million. $1 million? As I discussed this with my students, they suggested that in an age with multimillionaires and billionaires, those with just a million dollars in income probably see themselves as right in the middle between the very rich and the very poor. During the 2012 presidential election season, $250,000 was often the magic upper threshold of middle incomes when taxes were being discussed.

Just focusing on money, what do we know about the incomes of Americans? According to 2011 data from the US Census Bureau, the median household income is $50,054. That is for all household types combined, and it marks a slight decline from the previous year, when median household income was $50,831. As Table 3.1 indicates, family households with married couples have much higher median incomes than single parent or single nonparent households.

Economically, the households in the middle of the American class system are making about $50,000 per year, with married couples, whites, Asians, men, and people who are not disabled generally fairing better than single people (parents and nonparents), blacks, Hispanics, women, and people who are disabled. The figures in Table 3.1 are for households, not individual incomes. The per capita numbers are much less than the household numbers. The median per capita income in the United States is $26,588. Does a person making $26,588 qualify as middle class? Does a family with an income of $50,054 qualify as middle class?

Class categories such as low, middle, and high—or poor, working, middle, and wealthy—are cultural categories more than official distinctions. There is no specific income structure that determines class identity. The lifestyle associated with any particular income level can vary widely depending on family size and how they live. Imagine a couple who both make $30,000 per year. By living together, their household income is $60,000, which could go quite far if they have no kids. They may have a neighbor, also making $30,000 per year, who is single and raising three kids. All three adults make the same amount of money, but the two households surely have very different economic experiences.

Beyond family structure and income, class is also heavily shaped by cultural patterns—what we might call taste. Herbert Gans has written one of the most compelling analyses of the American taste hierarchy, *Popular Culture*

TABLE 3.1. Median Household Incomes from the 2011 Current Population Survey

Household Type	Median Income
All	$50,054
Family: Married—couple	$74,130
Family: Female householder	$33,637
Family: Male householder	$49,567
Nonfamily: Female	$25,492
Nonfamily: Male	$35,482
White (non-Hispanic)	$55,412
Black	$32,229
Asian	$65,129
Hispanic	$38,624
Disabled Householder	$25,420
Nondisabled Householder	$59,411

(SOURCE: DeNavas-Walt, Proctor, and Smith 2012.)

and High Culture (Gans 1999). Gans identifies five "taste publics and cultures": high, upper-middle, lower-middle, low, and quasi-folk low. High culture is "serious" and focused on form, and its participants are usually highly educated. Upper-middle culture is somewhat less serious, and its participants reflect the new generations of college-educated people from the past few decades. They have money and are more concerned with making their financial means visible to others and less concerned with issues of form. Lower-middle culture is the numerically dominant culture; it is overwhelmed by commercial production. According to Gans, lower-middle culture is romantic and focused on representation, and it is less tolerant of abstraction than upper-middle and high culture. Low culture is more traditional and more conservative than the other forms and tends to treat the idea of culture as effeminate and immoral. It is more likely to maintain strong gender distinctions. Gans points to action movies as the epitome of male low culture. Finally, quasi-folk low culture refers to groups isolated by poverty from mainstream American culture. Gans notes urban graffiti and Mexican telenovelas as examples. Gans first identified these taste cultures in 1974, in the first edition of his book. When he revised the book in 1999, he maintained the focus on these five categories, while also acknowledging some convergence among them and the proliferation of new ones. Overall, though, he insists that the relationship between culture and class persists.

BROADCASTING CLASS

Talking about class is difficult in contemporary America, whether focusing on the media or on everyday life. The concept of class implies clear categorical differences between groups within a hierarchy. In contemporary America, those categories are impossible to discern, even though we have extreme inequality, with the gap between the rich and the poor the greatest it has ever been. Class is further complicated by the number of variables that seem to shape our experience and position within social hierarchies. Income and wealth are the most significant factors, but education, race, culture, household size, and region are all relevant as well.

Class becomes even more difficult to discern when we move into the largely fictional space of television content. On prime time, television sitcoms tend to celebrate the lives of the comfortable middle class in forms like suburban home life, the urban single dating scene, and the office workplace. Dramas have a tendency to feature middle- and upper-class professionals such as police, lawyers, and doctors, whose jobs bring them into interaction with the working class and the nonworking poor. But the lower-class roles on dramas tend to be one-off characters rather than parts of the regular cast. These roles are generally criminals, victims, and medical patients.

Reality television has a mixed relationship with class. Shows like *Cops* offer a voyeuristic glimpse into the lives of the poor, while celebrating middle-class police professionals. But reality competition shows are more likely to feature middle- and upper-class contestants who have sufficient leisure time—they can leave work for a series of weeks to appear on television.

Even as television offers varied representations of class experience, it also distorts them. One of the most discussed examples of this is the apartment that was featured on the NBC sitcom *Friends*. The characters, only two of whom lived in the apartment for most of the series, were young, middle-class professionals. During the course of the show they aged from their late twenties into their midthirties. But the New York apartment they lived in had a sprawling living room, a large kitchen, a balcony, and two large bedrooms. Any New York resident would insist that these characters could not afford that apartment.

Shifting from the small screen to the big screen, invisibility is the key to understanding how film treats the issue of social class and economic inequality. I am not referring to the invisibility of any one class group. There are certainly films about the poor and films about the working class. And many films feature middle-class and wealthy characters. I am referring to the invisibility of class as a concept, as a shaper of life experiences, and as a point of conflict in human social life. I am referring to the invisibility of the relationship between economic power and social or political power. In the absence of class as an operating principle, poverty is depicted as a function of race, culture, bad values, criminality, or bad parenting. For example, in the 2010 film *Winter's Bone*, the poverty of the main character is explained through her father's drug abuse and her mother's mental illness, without any reference to the local economic conditions or the history of industrial transformation in the rural Ozark mountain town in which the film is set. Even films that feature middle-class characters depict their economic lives as simply normal and natural, without much reference to fluctuations or the levels of privilege and opportunity necessary for maintaining even a middle-class existence in American society.

Why is class invisible in American film? Historian Steven Ross (1998) explains that early films actually focused quite heavily on economic disparities and on the issue of labor. This was before the First World War, before the film industry was fully defined and became centered in Hollywood. In those days the union movement used silent films as an organizing tool. But fear of the radical ideas of unions led to a postwar burgeoning of censorship, which coincided with the solidification of a tightly controlled studio system rooted in Hollywood. The development of large and beautiful movie theaters also helped to transform film into a middle-class endeavor.

As film became more middle class, more commercial, and more centrally controlled, images of class conflict largely disappeared. Linda Holtzman, in *Media Messages*, examined a list of the all-time Top 100 box office successes in the United States.* She found that only nine of those one hundred films focused on class themes. The fact that ninety-one of the Top 100 grossing films do not contain class themes illustrates the invisibility of class in American film (Holtzman 2000).

What do films tell us about class on the rare occasions when it is made visible? (See "Class Themes in Film.") Holtzman argues that two sorts of messages

---

* That list is constantly updated and is available at http://www.filmsite.org.

predominate in films about class, both within and beyond the films in the Top 100. The first message is that "true love conquers all" in cross-class romantic relationships. This theme is perhaps better labeled "true love conquers class." She found that seven of the nine films about class from the Top 100 featured this message: *Gone with the Wind* (1939), *Titanic* (1997), *Love Story* (1970), *My Fair Lady* (1964), *Aladdin* (1992), *Funny Girl* (1968), and *Pretty Woman* (1990). In these films, an aristocrat falls in love with someone from a lower class. Class initially acts as a barrier to the success of the relationship, but that barrier is ultimately overcome. The couples do not always live together happily ever after, but in the final analysis of the film, the romance is judged a worthy success. These films obscure the fact that cross-class relationships are rare and rarely succeed—particularly when the higher-class person is a female. Moreover, the films obscure the realities of class position and class conflict by reducing class to a mere romantic obstacle.

The second message that Holtzman finds in class-themed films is the "American dream" narrative that we can all succeed if we work hard, even (perhaps especially) those who begin in poverty or other difficult circumstances. This theme, though common in much of American culture, appeared in only two of the nine class-themed films from the Top 100 list: *Rocky* (1976) and *Funny Girl* (1968). In both films, the protagonist begins in meager circumstances, but with a dream. When that dream is combined with hard work and tenacity, the end result is tremendous success. If we internalize the message of these films, we then have to explain the millions of Americans living in poverty by concluding that they simply are not working hard enough. This ignores not only the barriers they face to attaining class mobility, but also the tremendous ways that they work very hard in their homes, families, occupations, and communities.

One last class-themed film that Holtzman finds in the Top 100 list is *West Side Story* (1961). In this musical we discover two individuals from two different cultural groups—Italian and Puerto Rican—living in New York City. Both groups are living in poverty, but they are divided against each other by ethnic tensions. The film does not hide the class dimensions of their lives. Instead, it shows how class creates common ground for the two sides, though ethnicity prevents them from building on it. We could call this theme "Ethnic Division Trumps Class Unity."

Where does class appear in popular music, and how would we even measure it? Consider the following ways that we can approach the subject of class in music:

CLASS THEMES ɪɴ FILM

FROM THE TOP 100 BOX OFFICE SUCCESSES

TRUE LOVE CONQUERS CLASS

GONE WITH THE WIND (1939)
MY FAIR LADY (1964)
FUNNY GIRL (1968)
LOVE STORY (1970)
PRETTY WOMAN (1990)
ALADDIN (1992)
TITANIC (1997)

AMERICAN DREAM

FUNNY GIRL (1968)
ROCKY (1976)

ETHNIC DIVISION TRUMPS CLASS UNITY

WEST SIDE STORY (1961)

CLASS INVISIBILITY

MOST AMERICAN FILMS

1. The class background of the artists.
2. The frequency of messages that are about class, as compared with messages focused on relationships, dancing, and so forth.
3. The quality of class references. Do they demonize the working class or the wealthy? Do they rely on stereotypes?
4. The frequency and type of references to work and labor.
5. The frequency and type of references to consumption.
6. The frequency and type of references to home life, family, and upbringing.

As an experiment, I analyzed the Top 10 songs from 2010 using this protocol. I obtained the list of songs from *Billboard*'s website.* This is obviously a very small sample, but as the Top 10 songs of the year, these songs reached the largest audience. These ten songs were performed by three female performers, four male performers, and two bands. One male performer, Taio Cruz, performed two of the ten songs. Information about the performers' backgrounds was obtained from Wikipedia. (I discuss the merits of using Wikipedia below.)

1. "Tik Tok," by Ke$ha (Ke$ha 2010a). Ke$ha was raised by a single mother who was a songwriter, living first in LA and then in Nashville, and occasionally received support through welfare programs. The song explicitly references both an aspirational affluence and lower economic position. She sings: "Ain't got no money but I'm already here." The protagonist is young and driven by a desire to party, as indicated by frequent comments directed to the DJ. The aspirational affluence is indicated by references to pedicures, clothes, phones, and CDs.
2. "Need You Now," by Lady Antebellum (Lady Antebellum 2010). This band consists of Hillary Scott, Charles Kelley, and Dave Heywood. All three seem to be from upper-middle-class backgrounds, although that was difficult to ascertain through Wikipedia. Hillary Scott was raised in Nashville by parents from the country music industry. Her mother, Linda Davis, is a country singer. Charles Kelley and Dave Heywood were both raised in Augusta, Georgia. Charles Kelley's brother is a pop

---

* http://www.billboard.com/charts/year-end/2010/hot-100-songs.

singer who is married to the actress Katherine Heigl. Dave Heywood is the son of a teacher and a dentist. The song is not by any means about class; it is a song about being drunk late at night and wanting the company of a former lover.

3. "Hey, Soul Sister," by Train (Train 2009). This band consists of Patrick Monahan, Jimmy Stafford, and Scott Underwood. The lead singer, Monahan, is the only member to have his own Wikipedia page. He was raised in Erie, Pennsylvania, by a father who owned a clothing store. He went to Edinboro University of Pennsylvania. The song is about causing a woman to swoon through music and dance and makes several references to pop music. There are no particular references to class.

4. "California Gurls," by Katy Perry (Perry 2010). Perry's parents were both pastors in Santa Barbara, California. Besides that information, little is mentioned that indicates their class position. The song is a celebration of California women that says very little about class. Although it does make reference to a leisurely life—"sippin' gin and juice, layin' underneath the palm trees"—these particular lines could refer to anyone's vacation or even just a day off, regardless of class. There is some reference to consumption in the lines "white sand in our stilettos, we freak in my jeep."

5. "OMG," by Usher (Usher 2010). Usher was born in Dallas and raised in Chattanooga and then Atlanta. His father left when he was very young. His mother remarried. Wikipedia says nothing about their jobs or economic position. The song is not about class at all and is instead about falling for a woman at a dance club.

6. "Airplanes," by B.o.B. (B.o.B. 2010). This artist was born in Winston-Salem, North Carolina, and raised in Decatur, Georgia. His father is a pastor. This song has the most explicit references to class and to labor. The song is a cautionary tale about the American dream deferred, about a creative and aspiring musician whose creativity was eaten up and spit out by the culture industry. The singer is pining for the time before he found the success he foolishly thought he wanted:

> Yeah, somebody take me back to the days
> Before this was a job, before I got paid,
> Before it ever mattered what I had in my bank.
> Yeah, back when I was tryin' to get a tip at Subway.

The song offers an excellent Marxist illustration of the alienation that artists feel as laborers and as cogs in the wheel of the culture industry machine.

7. "Love the Way You Lie," by Eminem (Eminem 2010). Eminem was born in Saint Joseph, Missouri, and moved to Detroit in his teens. In his music and public life, he is heavily associated with Detroit. His mother was fifteen when he was born, and his father abandoned them soon after. The song is not about class; it is about a relationship falling apart, largely due to domestic violence.

8. "Bad Romance," by Lady Gaga (Lady Gaga 2009). This artist was raised in affluence on the upper west side of New York City by parents who worked in the communications industry. The song is not about class and says nothing about consumption, although it is known for a striking music video in which a number of products were placed quite prominently.

9. "Dynamite," by Taio Cruz (Cruz 2009a). Cruz was born in London to immigrant parents. His father was from Nigeria and his mother was from Brazil. Wikipedia makes no mention of his parents' jobs or class position, but it does say he attended a private prep school. The song is strictly about dancing and having a good time. The only reference to consumption is found in the line "I'm wearing all my favorite brands, brands, brands."

10. "Break Your Heart," by Taio Cruz (Cruz 2009b). This song is a warning to a potential lover that he will only hurt her. There is no reference to class.

Of these ten songs, not a single one refers to family life and upbringing. Only one song, "Airplanes," discusses labor. In "Airplanes," B.o.B. talks very clearly about the labor of being an artist and the relationship that he has to the owners of the means of production. "California Gurls" and "Dynamite" both make very light references to consumption. "Tik tok" makes much more frequent references to consumption, as does "Airplanes." But in "Airplanes," consumption is clearly associated with the alienated labor that the singer wishes to leave behind.

This simple analysis of ten songs is meant to offer a sample of the ways that we could analyze class issues in popular culture if we only tried to get over the hurdles created by the ambiguities of class.

Can Wikipedia be trusted as a resource? The answer is yes *and* no, which happens to be true of many other sources. Wikipedia is an open access encyclopedia. Anyone with the right Internet access can edit the content of a Wikipedia page. This means that wrong information can be added very easily, either intentionally or unintentionally. But it also means that wrong information is often corrected quite quickly. Wikipedia editors—a term that refers not to staff members but rather to the volunteers from all over the world who create and edit Wikipedia pages—are expected to include citations for the information they present, and noncited material is flagged, though not usually removed. For the information that I provided above, I cross-checked the claims on Wikipedia with the cited sources and with other online searches. But Wikipedia remained the consistent centralized starting point for all the information I gathered.

Many college professors do not allow their students to use Wikipedia, and with good reason. But many of those same professors use Wikipedia themselves when they are preparing lecture slides for their classes or gathering information for their research. Wikipedia is simply too big, too easily available, and too widely used to ignore at this point. But is it any more flawed than other sources we might use, such as scholarly journals? We know that articles in scholarly journals are peer reviewed by scholars from the field. But those scholars do not always function as fact checkers. They often focus on how accurately the scholar engages with his method or how successfully she deploys a particular theory. If a wrong fact sneaks in along the way, the peer reviewers can easily miss it. Once it is published in a peer-reviewed scholarly journal, that factual error appears to have an authoritative stamp of approval. Scholarly journals are much less likely than newspapers to solicit and publish letters from readers, which is one way that factual errors are sometimes corrected, and few journals include a regular errata section in which they acknowledge mistakes in recent issues. By comparison, the open access nature of Wikipedia means that (1) readers are unlikely to see it as having an authoritative stamp of approval, and (2) factual errors are likely to be corrected fairly quickly when the topic is of broad interest.

When we are gathering data, it is best to neither ignore any particular source nor to trust any source too much. The safest method is to cross-check with other sources.

CLASS AND THE MODES OF CULTURAL PRODUCTION

Class is tricky off-screen, too. We tend to think of actors and directors as highly paid professionals who lead lives of privilege. But that is only true of a handful of the most successful. Most television and film professionals make middle to low incomes, and many have to supplement their film-related income with work in other fields. The Bureau of Labor Statistics (BLS) does not even

Methodology Moment
QUALITATIVE CONTENT ANALYSIS

What are the dominant messages about class (or race, gender, etc.) in the popular culture that we consume? What are the nondominant messages—the countertrends and alternatives? Open-ended questions like these often call for a qualitative method with a focus on discovery. Qualitative content analysis allows us to answer these broad questions about media messages.

A qualitative analysis should begin with a very clear research question, such as: What are the dominant messages about class in television? Notice the open-ended character of the question. We are not testing a hypothesis about a relationship when we ask this kind of question. Consider the following alternative question: What is the relationship between the class background of a show's writers and the class identities of the show's characters? To answer this second question, we would need quantitative data about both writers and characters. Gathering the data about characters would require content analysis, but that would be quantitative content analysis.

Wait, wait, wait. Isn't television content qualitative data, as compared to median incomes or multiple choice survey responses? As *data*, television may seem qualitative, but like all data, we can examine it with both quantitative and qualitative analyses. In this section I focus on the qualitative analysis of cultural content.

One of the best overviews of this approach is the aptly titled *Qualitative Media Analysis* by David L. Altheide and Christopher J. Schneider (2013). These authors argue specifically for what they call *ethnographic content analysis*, which is the combination of participant observation with the typically more quantitative objective content analysis. The logic of this approach is based on the cultural character of the objects of study: "Culture is difficult to study because its most significant features are subtle, taken for granted, and enacted in everyday life routines" (6). The fact that culture's most important features are so subtle means that they are also often difficult to quantify. The scholar, like the audience member, perceives something through a kind of trained intuition—not unlike a habitus—that falls beyond the clear classifications of our quantitative codes, but is nevertheless not only *real* but also *vitally important*. It may be a pause after a striking comment, or the raise of an eyebrow, that suddenly inverts the meaning of the cultural moment.

A researcher conducting qualitative content analysis needs to proceed with a very clear method, outlined in a protocol. The protocol establishes the

continues

unit of analysis, provides key identifying information about each unit, and lists the major areas for analysis. It functions as a kind of worksheet that is completed for each unit that is studied. For example, if we were examining class messages on television, the protocol might look like Table 3.2.

TABLE 3.2. Research Protocol, Class Analysis of Television		
Show Title:	Episode Title:	Air Date:
Season/Episode #:	Night:	Time Slot:
18–49 Ratings/Share:	Number Viewers:	Network:
Overview of class position of each major character, including a) income representations, b) educational attainment, c) class background, and d) class culture.		
Overview of each discussion of class that occurs in the episode, including a) context of the discussion, b) focus of the discussion, c) variety of messages that are presented, and d) the overall message or the stance the show seems to take.		

With just these few protocol items, we could conduct a rich qualitative analysis. This protocol treats the episode as the unit of analysis. We still have to address questions of sampling. How big will our sample be? Will all channels, cable and broadcast, be included? Will all genres be included? How many shows? How many episodes? As Altheide and Schneider point out, sampling for qualitative content analyses is typically purposive rather than random. It is common to focus just on the prime time hours of the major broadcast networks, as these shows have the largest audiences. But if we made our question more specific, we might have good reason just to focus on daytime or just to focus on cable channels. Conducting a qualitative analysis of every episode of any given show, let alone an array of shows, is very time consuming and may be costly if it is necessary to keep recordings of the shows. A smaller sampling of episodes could be just as effective.

The outcome of the qualitative content analyses is that we can discover what exactly is happening in the cultural objects we consume. Because the universe of popular culture is so large and growing so fast, there are many questions that have not yet been methodically addressed. Those questions that have been asked before may need to be asked again to account for changes over time. So there is tremendous room to use this approach to produce an expansive amount of new information about the cultural universe.

calculate average annual salaries for actors because of how highly variable their employment terms are. Actors work on a contingent basis, sometimes for years and sometimes just for an hour. The BLS indicates that the median hourly wage of actors is $19.14,* based on 2011 data. That is well above minimum wage, but hardly in the ranks of the rich. If we calculate using a forty-hour workweek and a fifty-week work year, that is an annual salary of just $38,280. "Show Me the Money" summarizes the average annual wages for various occupations in the culture industries.

Most of the actors we see on television and in film never become famous enough to garner the high wages associated with celebrities. Directors fare better than actors, but again, they are not overwhelmingly rich. The median annual wage for producers and directors is $70,660, again based on 2011 data.† This is well above the 2011 median per capita income of $27,554, as reported by the US Census Bureau,‡ but it places most directors and producers

---

* http://www.bls.gov/oes/current/oes272011.htm.

† http://www.bls.gov/oes/current/oes272012.htm.

‡ http://www.census.gov/hhes/http://www/income/data/historical/people.

SHOW ME THE MONEY

ANNUAL WAGES FOR VARIOUS OCCUPATIONS ASSOCIATED WITH THE CULTURE INDUSTRIES, 2011.

◯ = $3,000

| MEDIAN PER CAPITA IN THE US $27,554 | ACTORS $38,280 | PRODUCERS & DIRECTORS $70,660 | FILM & VIDEO EDITORS $52,940 | CAMERA OPERATORS $40,170 |

in the upper middle class. Remember, $70,660 is a median, not a mean, so 50 percent of directors and producers make less than that amount, and some make quite a bit less.

Working in film or television, whether as an actor or a writer, camera tecÚician, set designer, or in any other role, involves a tremendous amount of uncertainty and potentially sets up the laborer to be exploited heavily. To mitigate this uncertainty, the labor market in Hollywood has constructed a series of unions and other forms of labor protection. For example, the Screen Actors Guild (SAG) relies heavily on its members' adherence to Global Rule One: "No member shall work as a performer or make an agreement to work as a performer for any producer who has not executed a basic minimum agreement with the Guild which is in full force and effect."* This rule can limit the options of an actor in SAG, but it helps to promote both the vitality of the union itself and its capacity to protect the working conditions of the actor. Those protections may seem silly when we are focused on a famous millionaire actress like Angelina Jolie, but the great majority of actors in the film industry have no such wealth.

---

* http://www.sagaftra.org/production-center/globalruleone.

REPORTERS & CORRESPONDENTS	MUSICIANS & SINGERS	EDITORS (PUBLISHING)	WRITERS & AUTHORS	ATHLETES	FASHION DESIGNERS	SOFTWARE DEVELOPERS
$34,870	$45,980	$52,380	$55,870	$39,670	$64,960	$89,280

Methodology Moment
PRODUCTION ETHNOGRAPHY

What does it look like to be on the inside of the production of popular culture? What do writers, directors, and publishing executives talk about? How do they make decisions? What roles do cameramen (they are mostly men), set designers, and typesetters play in the creative process? Apart from actually becoming a creative professional, it can be quite difficult to answer these questions, especially if we do not live in one of the epicenters of cultural production like Los Angeles, New York, or Nashville. But if we want to observe the production process, one of the best research methods we can employ is ethnography.

Ethnography is a form of observation. It means stepping into a particular social process to observe how it happens and identify its basic mechanisms. An ethnography may be as simple as going to a concert to observe how audiences engage with the music and interact with one another, although that would not be a production ethnography. A *production ethnography* requires observing the behind-the-scenes processes to see how they shape the final content of the cultural object.

Very few ethnographies of cultural production have been conducted by sociologists, because it can be very difficult to gain access to the private world of the mass media corporation. Two of the best studies of production are about the same type of cultural object: the TV talk show. Joshua Gamson published *Freaks Talk Back* in 1998, and Laura Grindstaff followed a few years later with *The Money Shot* (2002). Although Gamson focuses much more on sexuality than does Grindstaff, both scholars pay significant attention to the issue of class.

Gamson's method combined interviewing with aspects of ethnography. He interviewed both production staff and guests, conducted content analyses of many episodes of several talk shows, and used focus groups to access audience perspectives. In addition, he attended several show tapings as an audience member. These tapings allowed him to conduct ethnographic analysis of some of the production process. He explains this in the methodological appendix to his book:

> The interviews certainly provided me with a good deal of information about how producers do and think about their work, but I also wanted to see it in action. Since access to production meetings and other

continues

behind-the-scenes activity was restricted, I attended tapings of most of the New York City–area talk shows (and sat in the control room with producers during one other taping) over the course of the 1995–96 season. The object here was both to witness key pieces of the production process as they were taking place (especially the management of the audience and the guests), and to experience the role of audience member from the inside. I treated the tapings as an anthropologist treats the ethnographic encounter with cultural ritual, taking extensive, detailed field notes for later analysis. (Gamson 1998, 228)

Gamson does not say specifically what he watched for during these ethnographic moments. On the one hand, it can be very helpful to have a protocol, so that the researcher knows what to pay attention to. On the other hand, such a protocol can distract the researcher from making other valuable observations. Some balance can be found by using a very limited protocol.

Although Gamson's overall method is quite extensive, his ethnographic work is very limited, precisely because it is so difficult to access the private aspects of the production process. Laura Grindstaff was actually able to access many of these private aspects by using a much more intensive ethnographic approach. She secured internships on two talk shows, which she refers to with the pseudonyms Diana and Randy, during the 1995–1996 television season. These internships, which were obtained through existing institutional partnerships, allowed her to not only witness, but also even participate in, the very decisions she sought to study. Grindstaff approached her work through a feminist lens, which resulted in a closing chapter on feminist fieldwork. Of central concern in this chapter is an issue that is also central to her book—the ways that producers manipulated guests to capture a particularly powerful moment, the "money shot." As researchers, we have a responsibility to disclose important and sensitive information to our research subjects. This placed Grindstaff in a tricky position with relation to the shows' producers:

The difference between me and producers here is not so much that I was willing to admit to deception and they were not, or that I was personally troubled by its use and they were not, or even that academic

continues

Methodology Moment: **PRODUCTION ETHNOGRAPHY** (*continued*)

institutions frown on deception and the television industry does not. The difference was that my backdoor method of entry and the gradual nature of my coming out deeply upset my feminist sensibilities and that, at some point, I began to connect my anxiety over these issues specifically with my identity as a feminist. (Grindstaff 2002, 286)

Grindstaff explains that she increasingly saw the similarities between herself and these producers, and between academic work and cultural production. Both practices are ultimately forms of representation that are deeply infused with questions of power at all levels. The central issue is that when we contend with other humans—their lives, identities, and relationships—we have to grapple with the tremendous responsibilities that come with treating people as the objects of research.

So if the story that gets told most about Hollywood is that it is a rich white man's game—and it is—we still need to wonder about the prospects for everyone who falls outside of that identity. Their stories are not getting told.

THE STRATIFICATION OF RECEPTION

Examinations of television audiences that focus on class are also scarce, at least in the American context. In Britain, where class identity is more salient, cultural studies scholars have paid a lot of attention to how class shapes audience experiences with television. In America, one of the best of studies in this field is seemingly about another topic altogether. Andrea Press's *Women Watching Television* (1991) appears on the surface to be an analysis of gender. But Press's method, interviewing women about the shows they watch and the ways they evaluate those shows, makes it impossible for her to make claims about how gender works. Her approach accomplishes an important feminist task of placing women at the center of analysis. Although it reveals a lot about women, it does not reveal much about gender, because it makes no comparisons to men. Her interviewees were twenty working-class women and twenty middle-class women. Her findings about how these groups make sense of the TV they watch may also hold true for men, but we cannot know that without conducting a similar analysis of men.

Press offers a tremendous amount of insight into the ways that class led her two groups of interviewees in very different directions as they formulated a relationship with television. The most important finding is that middle-class women view television primarily through a gendered lens, whereas working-class women view television primarily through a class-based lens. Working-class women tend to evaluate a show primarily in terms of how realistic it seems to be. They are highly critical of shows that get the working-class experience wrong. At the same time, they often believe that television's depiction of the middle class is accurate.

Middle-class women have lower expectations of television's capacity to be accurate. If anything, they approach television with a high degree of cynicism. But they still invest a lot in television content. Their investment is more focused on how women are depicted in interpersonal relationships with spouses, children, coworkers, and bosses. Middle-class women expressed particular interest in the ways that TV grapples with the tension between work and home that many women, particularly middle-class women, struggle with.

Two particular comparisons are striking in Press's analysis. First, when asked about the show *I Love Lucy*, middle-class women tended to view the lead character as a powerful feminist who undermined gendered hegemony both at work and at home. Working-class women were far more critical of Lucy and tended to characterize her as manipulative or stupid. Second, when asked about the movie starlet Ginger on *Gilligan's Island*, middle-class women viewed Ginger's sexiness and glamour as a form of feminist strength, defining sexuality on her own terms. Working-class women were critical of Ginger's sexuality and expressed greater comfort with another character, Mary Ann. Mary Ann is portrayed as simpler and more modest than Ginger. Mary Ann struck working-class women as more real than Ginger, whereas middle-class women saw Ginger's character as something worth aspiring to.

Of course class impacts the audience of film as well. The great theorist of the culture/class relationship is Pierre Bourdieu, whose cultural capital model indicates that upper-class people buttress their position not only with economic power but also by demonstrating their ease with "legitimate" culture. Cultural performance—demonstrating that one has the necessary level of cultural capital—becomes a way of legitimizing economic power.

If we take this theory at face value, we might surmise that wealthier people tend to watch art films and that poorer people prefer Hollywood blockbusters. Sociologists Lisa Barnett and Michael Patrick Allen (2000) tested this notion by surveying upper-middle-class and lower-middle-class people to determine what kinds of films they watch, and how they watch them. Do members of the upper middle class watch more art films than members of the lower middle class? Yes. But they also watch more classic films and more blockbusters than members of the lower middle class, simply because they consume more films overall. Upper-middle-class people visit the cinema more often than do lower-middle-class people, and they watch films at home more often. However, the authors also found that lower-middle-class people watch more films on television than upper-class people do. This study was published in 2000, so the class patterns may have adjusted somewhat as new technologies have

Methodology Moment
AUDIENCE SURVEYS

To capture audience perspectives on popular culture, one of the most effective methods is the audience survey. Depending on how they are constructed and carried out, surveys can be very cost effective and easy to conduct. Historically, surveys were conducted face-to-face or over the phone, but today many survey methodologists are able to utilize the Web and related technologies to gather data. Sites like SurveyMonkey are now being used to conduct some fairly large sociological research projects.

Surveys allow us to address a limited set of questions to a potentially quite large set of respondents. The limitation on a survey is that we do not get the opportunity to ask follow-up questions, to clarify the meaning of our questions, or to clarify the meaning of the responses we receive. The conversational element that makes interviews so powerful is lost in the anonymity of the survey. That means that the information we get from a survey may not be as *intensive* as the information we would get from interviews, but it is usually much more *extensive* because of the large number of respondents.

Some survey results are available to the public, which allows researchers to conduct secondary analysis of these data. The General Social Survey (GSS) is a large national survey that has been conducted frequently since 1972—almost annually until 1994 and every second year since then. Some of the questions asked in the GSS have been repeated every year or

continues

Methodology Moment: **Audience Surveys** *(continued)*

at least in multiple years, whereas others have been asked only once as distinct units to explore a particular topic. The data can be obtained online* and in other formats. The questions that have been asked in the GSS are presented in the GSS Codebook, which lists all of the variable names for those items. The GSS has asked questions about film attendance, television viewership, and a number of other activities that relate to popular culture. Unfortunately these questions about culture have not been asked often, so there is limited information on cultural consumption patterns over time.

Researchers who are unhappy with the limitations of the GSS and other existing available data sets may choose to conduct their own surveys. An excellent example of recent audience survey work is Katherine Sender's (2012) analysis of the audience for reality television shows in *The Makeover*. Sender was specifically interested in the audience for makeover shows and how audiences use the content of these shows in their own lives. Through SurveyMonkey, she created four surveys, one each for four television shows: *The Biggest Loser*, *Queer Eye for the Straight Guy*, *Starting Over*, and *What Not to Wear*. She used online message boards for these shows to recruit her participants. Each survey consisted of forty questions: twenty-three about the show, five general questions about reality television, and twelve background questions about the participants. To keep the data manageable, Sender primarily used closed questions that could be answered in a multiple-choice format. But she also posed a few open-ended questions, such as: "What tips or advice have you picked up?" These open-ended questions allow her to make a deeper analysis than she might have with only multiple-choice questions. However, asking too many open-ended questions results in the information quickly becoming unmanageable. New advances in qualitative analytical software help to mitigate this problem, but only to a degree.

Surveys like any research involving human participants, are subject to the oversight of an institutional review board, which examines and approves all research on human subjects to ensure the application of appropriate ethical standards.

---

* http://www3.norc.org/gss+website.

allowed easier home access to films, but that access is still influenced by income and other factors related to class. It is unlikely that the class patterns for cinema attendance have shifted much in that time.

WRAP-UP

Studying class is a tricky business, to say the least. For starters, *class* is an increasingly vague concept, even as economic inequality is increasingly important for understanding the social order. Other categories of identity—gender, race, disability, or sexuality—carry a great deal of ambiguity and arbitrariness as well, but we have found ways to make sense of them nonetheless. I know very few people who do not have an idea of what their race, gender, sexuality, or disability status is. But I find that many people are unsure of what their class is or how to figure it out. Is it a matter of income, education, or lifestyle? When does your parents' class cease to determine your own? When class is so ambiguous in the social world, how do we even begin to examine it in the representational spaces of television, film, music, novels, or the Internet?

My discomfort with class stems from more than just the ambiguity of class as a concept. I am also concerned that the patterns for class may differ from the patterns for other kinds of identity. Specifically, where are the class freaks? If women, trans people, racial minorities, disabled people, and queer people are appropriating popular culture to carve out spaces for their own unique identities over and against a culture that is tremendously homogenizing, where are the poor and working-class people who are also using popular culture in this way?

The problem is that although the culture industries can abide, and even profit from, a proliferation of identities, precisely by transforming them into niche markets, it cannot abide an identity that does not aspire to spend. So the poor and working classes are encountered by the culture industries as aspirants to the middle class and are told that their best chance for entry into the middle class is not through a redistribution of wealth, or political action, or organized labor (unions), or increased education or occupational attainment; their best chance for entry into the middle class is through consumption. If they spend like they belong, then they really will. The alienation that Marx describes is perfected by the culture industries, which abstract production away from daily life and transform the lives of the laborer into lives defined by consumption. The habitus and the home of the contemporary human is increasingly one built and mediated by commercial culture.

RESOURCES

Resources for Examining Class in the Social World

- Video: *People Like Us*, from PBS. Available in many libraries. Some clips can be found on YouTube. Resources available online at http://www.pbs .org/peoplelikeus.
- Class Matters: a special section of the *New York Times*: http://www .nytimes.com/national/class.
- US Census Bureau, data on poverty: http://www.census.gov/hhes/http:// www/poverty.
- US Census Bureau, data on income: http://www.census.gov/hhes/http:// www/income.

Resources for Examining Class in Popular Culture

- Video: *Class Dismissed*, from the Media Education Foundation.
- Website: Unions in Hollywood, http://tvtropes.org/pmwiki/pmwiki .php/Main/UnionsInHollywood.

4

Men Are from Marlboro Country, Women Are from Wisteria Lane
GENDER PERSPECTIVES

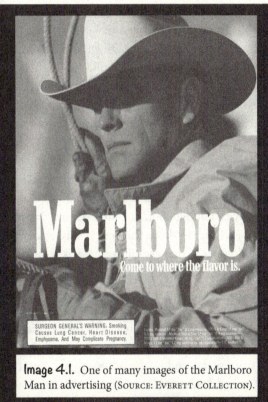

Image 4.1. One of many images of the Marlboro Man in advertising (SOURCE: EVERETT COLLECTION).

GENDER NEVER GOES DOWN SMOOTHLY

Have you ever been in a conversation about a work of art, a song, or a poem, and heard someone say something like "meaning is open to interpretation; it could mean anything depending on the observer"? There is a common perception about cultural objects that they have no inherent meaning, that the meaning is always open. Let's ponder that in the context of a Belvedere vodka ad that appeared online in March 2012. The ad shows a smiling man holding onto a woman from behind, as the woman, with eyes opened wide, eyebrows raised, and mouth open in an O shape, leaps away.* The caption above the photo reads, "Unlike some people," and the copy overlaid on the photo says, "Belvedere always goes down smoothly." Aside from some blinds and wood paneling behind the two figures, there's nothing else recognizable in the image. If I told you that this ad, as described, is a social commentary on globalization, I think you would raise your eyebrows. If I told you that this ad depicts two puppies playing in the park, you would think me crazy. But if I said that I saw this image, with the accompanying text, as an offensive joke about rape, I think people's reactions would vary. Some might quickly agree, whereas others would say that I am reading too much into an advertising image. In either case, people are not likely to think that I am insane, as perhaps they would if I said this image displays puppies or globalization. In other words, the possibility that I could interpret this image as an offensive rape joke is structured into the content. A man is grabbing a woman from behind; she looks frightened or alarmed as she tries to get away. He is smiling in a way that might be taken as sinister; the text implies that she is the kind of person who does not go down smoothly. Clearly, in this ad, going down smoothly is preferable to the kind of refusal that she is making. "Going down smoothly" is a common way of talking about alcohol. "Going down" is a common way of talking about oral sex. In short, this image tells a story about a man who is pulling a woman into a sexual assault, and she is refusing. He would get less resistance from his glass of vodka than he is getting from this assault victim. It is not irrelevant that alcohol is estimated to be a factor in two-thirds of sexual assaults and date rapes among adolescents and college students.

Are there other ways that we can read this image? Maybe they were watching a movie, cuddled next to one another during a date, when she reacted with fear to a scary scene, and he is comforting her. But if that is the case, the line about not going down smoothly does not fit. The line implies that there are people who do not go down smoothly, so an alternative explanation would have to make clear what such a person would be (outside of the context of a rape joke) and how such a person figures into this image. Maybe we are meant

---

* The ad is easy to find online, using search phrases such as "Belvedere vodka ad controversy."

to interpret this male as creepy, and therefore as someone who does not go down smoothly, so we should identify with this woman and choose a glass of vodka instead of this creepy guy. Maybe that's what Belvedere intended, or maybe now we are reading that into the image in an attempt to let Belvedere off the hook for an offensive ad.

The ad was only on Belvedere's Facebook page for one hour before it was pulled down. The company apologized and promised an investigation. And that is where the story gets even more interesting. The image was created by an ad agency called Last Exit, which was hired to spur Belvedere's online and social media promotions. The image used in the ad was actually stolen from a user-generated video called "AWKWARD MOMENTS: The Baby Picture," posted to the website Funny or Die, a popular site for watching short humorous videos, many of which feature celebrities. But users can also post their own videos. "AWKWARD MOMENTS" was posted by an actress named Alicyn Packard, who does voice work for Cartoon Network programs, and it features Packard and her boyfriend acting out a comedic sketch in which a woman's parents pressure her to reenact a scene from a baby picture (Gardner 2012). To do this, she has to climb onto her boyfriend's lap. The video implies that he develops an erection, which he claims is really just his cell phone. In the climactic moment of the video, just as the parents snap the photo, she jumps in response to something that she feels beneath her. That's the moment that they make the very faces we see in the Belvedere ad. The boyfriend then apologizes, saying, "Sorry, that was my voicemail," to which she replies, "Why is your voicemail wet?" Packard has since sued for damages in response to the theft of the video still.

It is tempting to dismiss the Belvedere vodka ad. A rogue midlevel advertising executive stole an image, gave it a whole new and very disturbing context, and released it in an ad for his client. Belvedere isn't the problem; advertising isn't the problem; it was just a "bad apple," which was handled appropriately with an apology and a retraction. Problem solved.

But the problem is not solved if the Belvedere ad is indicative of the kinds of images that we see in advertising across the board. Consider the ways that women are typically posed in advertising (see Image 4.2). Again, the meaning is open to multiple interpretations, but it is difficult to avoid recognizing that women are often placed in vulnerable poses in which they are sexualized and objectified. These kinds of images appear again and again across advertising and throughout popular culture. Jean Kilbourne explains why this matters in the documentary *Killing Us Softly 4*:

We all grow up in a culture in which women's bodies are constantly turned into things and objects, here she's become the bottle of Michelob. In this ad she becomes part of a video game. And this is everywhere, in all kinds of advertising. Women's bodies are turned into things and objects. Now of course this affects female self-esteem. It also does something even more insidious—it creates a climate of widespread violence against women. I'm not at all saying that an ad like this directly causes violence, it's not that simple, but turning a human being into a thing is almost always the first step towards justifying violence against that person. We see this with racism, we see it with homophobia, we see it with terrorism. It's always the same process. The person is dehumanized and violence becomes inevitable. And that step is already and constantly taken against women. (Kilbourne 2010)

The goal of this chapter is to explore the ways that gender impacts the production, content, and audience of popular culture. Popular culture tells many stories about women and men, including many different kinds of women and many different kinds of men.

CULTURE AND THE AWAKENING OF GENDER

Why is popular culture so full of disparaging images of women—images that belittle, berate, and sexualize women? To answer this question, I turn first to Beatrice Potter Webb, whose work spanned from the late nineteenth century into the twentieth. Webb was a self-taught sociologist who was deeply connected to the reform movements of her time. She published her own analysis of gender relations in 1913, in the introduction to a special issue of *The New Statesman*, a magazine that she founded along with her husband, Sydney Webb. The special issue was entitled "The Awakening of Women," and it sought to understand the development of the women's movement of the time. In her introduction, Webb argues that the women's movement developed hand-in-hand with both the labor movement and the movement of "subject peoples" seeking liberation from their oppressors. She asserts that movements of liberation advance out of deep intersections of race, class, and gender. Her explanation for these forms of oppression, and for the growing movements against them, is largely economic:

For good or for evil, the capitalist system has forced millions of women out of a position of economic dependence on husband or father into the position

Image 4.2. A selection of ways that women are portrayed in advertising in popular magazines.

of independent wage-earners, often responsible for the livelihood not of themselves alone, but also of family dependents. The tragedy of the situation is that, whilst we have forced these millions of women to walk along the wage-earning road, we have not unbound their feet! (Webb 1998, 304)

Webb's observation is that the economic situation had changed, pushing more women into the economic realm through work and making them major and even primary breadwinners for their families.

But even as this economic change occurred, the cultural system lagged behind by devaluing the status of women:

By continuing to brand the woman as the social inferior of the man, unworthy of any share in the direction of the country, upon the economic development of which we have made her directly dependent; by providing for her much less technical training and higher education than for the boy; by

telling her that she has slighter faculties and smaller needs, and that nothing
but toil of routine character is expected from her. (Webb 1998, 304)

Webb wrote this essay a century ago, yet many of her claims still seem to describe the relations of women and men in the twenty-first century. Women
are still branded as the social inferiors of men in many ways, and most of
that branding happens through the mechanism of popular culture. Every female and every male whom we see on television, in film, in music, in books,
and on the Internet presents us with a story about gender. There are currents
and countercurrents in this ocean of stories, but when they are all added up,
we find that women are overwhelmingly presented as *less than*, whether it is
through sexual objectification, stereotypes, or underrepresentation.

Contemporary sociologist Judith Lorber helps to explain the powerful and
persisting role of culture in *Paradoxes of Gender* (1994), which focuses on the
ways that gender is socially constructed. The idea that gender is a social construction pushes against deep-seated and taken for granted ideas that gender
is simply the mechanical outcome of divergent human biologies. Lorber provides two useful axioms for understanding the social construction of gender.
First, "for individuals, gender means sameness." For men, the multitude of differences between all of the males in the world is collapsed, so that the category
"male" can invoke one list of meanings for all of those men. That's the sameness involved. Gender implies that all men are somehow the same as all other
men, and that all women are somehow the same as all other women. Lorber
explains that studying the effect of gender on individuals means studying sex
categories, gender identities, gendered marital and procreative statuses, gendered sexual orientations, gendered personalities, gendered processes, gender
beliefs, and gender displays.

Second, Lorber says that "for society, gender means difference." As gender
collapses individual differences into two categories of sameness, it also marks
those categories as fundamentally different, with a gulf between them that
cannot be bridged. Woman is "night to his day" to use Lorber's phrase. Or as
the popular author John Gray says, "Men are from Mars and women are from
Venus." That phrase implies that men and women are alien to one another and
come from radically different parts of the solar system. That extreme level of
difference cannot be rooted in biology, because men and women are the same
species and share the same DNA. The idea that men and women are fundamentally and radically different from each other is a cultural phenomenon.

It is part of the beliefs of contemporary American society, and in one way or another, it has been part of the beliefs of nearly all human societies in history. In many societies this idea is undergoing some renegotiation, but it is far from disappearing. According to Lorber, studying gender's effects on society means examining gender statuses, the gendered division of labor, gendered kinship, gendered sexual scripts, gendered personalities, gendered social control, gender ideology, and gender imagery. This chapter looks primarily at gender imagery and the ways that this imagery is used to construct gender ideology and gendered sexual scripts. But it also examines the division of labor as it pertains to the production of popular culture.

GENDER IN THE SOCIAL WORLD

The majority of Americans are female. According to the US Census, 50.8 percent of Americans are "female persons."* When discussing gender in the contemporary United States, we often draw on the same language we use to discuss minorities—racial minorities, ethnic minorities, sexual minorities, and so forth—but women are not a minority. They may have a minority of the available social **power**, but in terms of numbers, women are a majority.

The **privilege** that men receive in this country is of course not new, and it is not unique across the planet. But the exact character of male privilege does vary across time and among societies. Understanding how male privilege is maintained, negotiated, and reproduced seems especially relevant when examining a society like the contemporary United States, where in some ways we have attempted to unpack that privilege. First-wave feminism produced the women's suffrage movement and led to women receiving the right to vote in 1920. Second-wave feminism focused on educational and occupational equality, emboldened by the inclusion of gender discrimination in the Civil Rights Act of 1964, as well as Betty Friedan's discussion of "the problem that has no name" in her famous *The Feminine Mystique* (1963). Third-wave feminism has brought greater attention to women of color, poor women, queer women, and the diverse experiences of women around the globe. And yet men still dominate in many occupational spheres, outnumber women in the political arena, and make more money than women for doing the same work with the same level of experience.

---

* http://quickfacts.census.gov/qfd/states/00000.html.

GENDER DEMOGRAPHICS IN THE MASS MEDIA

Despite comprising just over half of the population, women are underrepresented on television. Martha Lauzen's report on prime time television analyzes women's representation on TV from a number of years. In the 1995–1996 television season, female characters comprised only 37 percent of prime time television roles. This percentage rose steadily, eventually reaching 43 percent for 2007–2008 (Lauzen 2008). My own analysis of the 2010–2011 season found that women characters comprised only 39.4 percent of credited roles on prime time for the major broadcast networks.

We do not see a lot of trans men and women in popular culture, except as rare one-off characters who are often the butt of the joke. But that is changing. When Mac, on *It's Always Sunny in Philadelphia*, met a trans woman named Carmen, it initially seemed that the story would be used solely for goofball humor. But things became more interesting as Mac started dating Carmen and struggled with the tension between his feelings of attraction and the pressures he felt from his friends to reject her.

I really enjoyed the character Alexis on the show *Ugly Betty*, played by Rebecca Romijn. The show only occasionally focused on her identity as a trans woman and did not hesitate to make her beautiful and powerful. It did explore her dating life in one episode, as well as her friendships with other women, but in a fairly nuanced and interesting way. She felt three-dimensional in ways that other trans characters do not. Her gender identity was only one aspect of her role on the show, and her status as a professional in a family company trumped the issue of gender.

However, trans characters make very few appearances on television or in other forms of popular culture. Some trans representation has occurred regularly since news coverage in the 1950s of the Christine Jorgensen story, about a woman who returned from Denmark after undergoing surgery to reassign her to a female gender (now referred to as gender confirmation surgery). We really cannot say that the frequency of trans representation has increased significantly, but the quality of trans representations may be improving.

Comparing gender representations by genre, for 2010–2011, as shown in "Gender Representations in Prime Time Television," I found that reality TV offered the most gender parity, 51 percent of roles going to men and 49 percent to women. That is not to say that reality TV is especially progressive when it comes to gender. On the contrary, the major reason for the even split in gender roles is that reality television remains deeply committed to gender

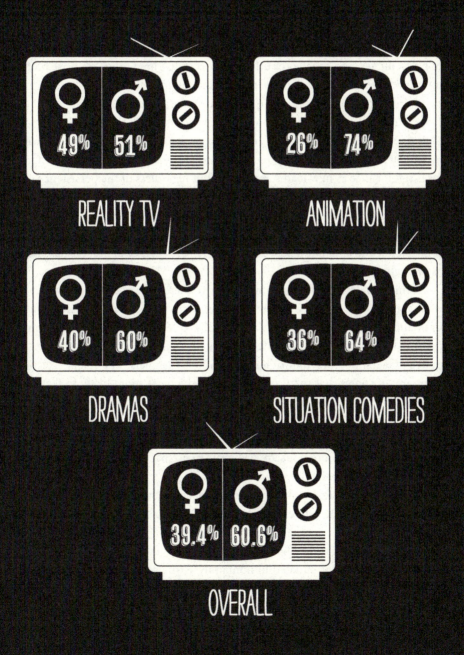

GENDER REPRESENTATION ON PRIME TIME TV

REALITY TV
49% 51%

ANIMATION
26% 74%

DRAMAS
40% 60%

SITUATION COMEDIES
36% 64%

OVERALL
39.4% 60.6%

divisions, demonstrating this by frequently pitting men against women for at least a portion of the season. Shows like *The Biggest Loser*, *The Apprentice*, *Hell's Kitchen*, and *So You Think You Can Dance* usually begin their seasons with even numbers of male and female contestants. On other shows, the contestants are made up of either all men (*The Bachelorette*) or all women (*America's Next Top Model*). These single-gender shows roughly balance each other out. So the gender parity in reality television is actually quite carefully constructed in a way that tends to affirm, rather than challenge, gender divisions. In addition to the contestants, a small number of roles on each show are given to hosts, judges, and coaches or other support staff. These roles comprise both men and women, with a slight overrepresentation of men.

Shifting from quantitative to qualitative analysis, we could argue that the *types* of roles played by women are in fact progressive. There is seemingly no logical reason for contestants on *Hell's Kitchen*, a cooking show, to be divided by gender—and as the show progresses into the season, the gender division loses significance as new teams are forged. But regardless of the persistence of gender division, the show still presents a model of women as successful chefs, and in a way that makes their success look no different from the success that men have in the same field. Other programs demonstrate that women excel in professional and amateur fields, or that women are capable of great feats, such as dramatic weight loss.

Turning to dramas, we find a world where there is less gender parity than on reality TV but also less gender division. Only 40 percent of prime time dramatic roles are performed by women. Despite the underrepresentation, many of these women are presented in roles very similar to the men's: lawyers, police officers, doctors, and other types of professionals. The major exceptions are on shows that focus on the home, which are more likely to feature women who are "housewives," desperate or otherwise. Although women are presented as powerful and respected in occupational dramas, their numbers are usually well below those of men. So the story told about these settings indicates that these occupations are primarily male spaces that accommodate a limited number of women.

Women are even less visible in the genre of situation comedies, where they comprise just over 36 percent of characters. This may seem surprising, because many sitcoms over the years have focused on family settings, in which women would seem to be about half of the characters. An increasing number of sitcoms are now situated in nonfamily settings, focusing on particular workplaces (*The Office*, *30 Rock*) or on groups of young singles (*How I Met*

Your Mother, Big Bang Theory). Though women play key roles in these newer types of shows, they are nevertheless a numerical minority in most cases. On *30 Rock*, Tina Fey's character Liz Lemon offers a model of a successful and creative woman working in the television industry. She is the star of the show, but she is surrounded by several men and very few women. Although we might *perceive* that shows like *30 Rock* offer heightened visibility for women in strong roles, as women move to the central roles on these shows, they are surrounded by an ever-growing gaggle of men.

Animation, the sitcom's little cousin, is the most masculine space on broadcast television. Less than 26 percent of characters on animated prime time shows are women. At first glance these shows appear to focus on families, like *The Simpsons*, where men and women are roughly equal in number. But the patriarch in these families—Homer Simpson, Peter Griffin, Cleveland Brown—dominates the story lines, which means we meet far more of his male friends than his wife's female friends.

We find a similar picture when we shift our attention to the cineplex. Many popular films, from comedies to dramas, focus on heterosexual relationships, which would seem to require a male and a female lead, and perhaps some gender parity for supporting roles as well. Many action movies, including the buddy cop genre, tend to feature only male leads and present environments that are predominantly male. These films are balanced, though, by "chick flicks," which focus more on female leads and female environments. In sum, we might expect that the content of films would be a 50/50 split between male and female characters.

Not so, says the research on film characters. Consider the evidence from reports by lead author Stacy L. Smith, a scholar at the University of Southern California's Annenberg School of Communication. Smith and her coauthor examined the one hundred top-grossing films of 2009 and found that only 32.8 percent of speaking characters were female (Smith and Choueiti 2010), as shown in "Percentage of On-screen Roles Held by Women." This is the same percentage of women characters they found in a study of 2008 films, and it is only slightly higher than their findings from 2007, when 29.9 percent of film characters were women. The authors also counted the number of films that had gender parity in 2009. These are films in which girls or women appear in 45–54.9 percent of the speaking roles. They found that only 17 percent of 2009 films achieved this gender parity.

The authors compared male and female characters in terms of the quality of their characterizations. They found that women are frequently sexualized in

PERCENTAGE OF

ON-SCREEN ROLES

HELD BY **WOMEN**

FOR TOP 100 FILMS

2007	2008	2009
29.9%	32.8%	32.8%

these roles, much more so than men. Of female characters, 25.8 percent were shown in "sexy attire," compared to only 4.7 percent of male characters. Some 23.6 percent of female characters were shown at least partially naked, compared to only 7.4 percent of male characters. Finally, 10.9 percent of female characters were explicitly identified by other characters as attractive, compared to 2.5 percent of male characters. That 10.9 may seem like a small percentage, but most characters are presented as attractive in ways that do not involve having another character state the attractiveness. In addition, female characters are more likely than male characters to be shown in a committed relationship, conveying a message that women's identity is more dependent than men's on romance and monogamy. Women's roles cluster more toward the lower end of the age spectrum than men's roles do. Although young adulthood is the most common character age for both genders—48.7 percent of males and 56.6 percent of females—women begin to disappear in older age groups. More than a third of male characters, 35.2 percent, are aged forty to sixty-four, compared to only 22.2 percent of female characters. At the other end of the spectrum, 10.7 percent of female characters are teenagers (ages thirteen to twenty), compared to only 6.4 percent of male characters. A smaller number of male and female roles are preteens, and an even smaller number are elderly, but women outnumber men in the preteen category, and men outnumber women in the elderly category. This is especially interesting because men typically die at younger ages than women, and women outnumber men among the elderly in the real world.

One of the most popular mechanisms for analyzing women's relevance to the world of film was developed not by a sociologist, but by a cartoonist. Alison Bechdel presented the **Bechdel test** in her 1986 comic book *Dykes to Watch Out For* (Bechdel 1986). A film has to meet three criteria to pass the Bechdel test, which only moderately certifies the film as progressive on gender. The film must have (1) at least two or more female characters who (2) have names and (3) talk to each other about something other than men.* This seems very simple and in many ways outdated, but Hollywood is still struggling to produce films that pass this test. Anita Sarkeesian, a media critic who runs the blog Feminist Frequency, ran the Bechdel test on the 2011 Best Picture Oscar nominees:†

---

* The rule about the characters needing to have names is not actually in the original comic book presentation of the test, which is discussed by an unnamed character. The name rule was added in popular use at some point thereafter and has stuck.

† Available online at http://www.feministfrequency.com/2012/02/the-2012-oscars-and -the-bechdel-test.

The Descendants: Passes the test because a few named female characters do have some limited conversations.

Money Ball: Fails the test because there is never a moment when two female characters speak to each other.

The Tree of Life: Fails the test because in the only scene of two women speaking to each other, they are speaking about the death of a male.

Hugo: The test is inconclusive. There is a very brief (five-second) scene of two females talking about film, but otherwise the females only speak to each other about males.

Extremely Loud and Incredibly Close: Fails the test because the women characters only speak to each other about a male character.

Midnight in Paris: Fails the test. Although there is a scene of two women speaking to each other about a possible furniture purchase, there are also two men involved in that discussion. Even the presence of poet Gertrude Stein as a character in the film does not manage to help the film pass the test.

War Horse: Fails the test because it centers on male characters.

The Help: Passes the test and features many conversations between women about topics other than men. However, it has been criticized for its treatment of race.

The Artist: Fails the test. This is a silent film, so Sarkeesian looked for any nonverbal communication between women about something other than a man, but could not find any.

Out of nine films nominated for the 2011 Best Picture Oscar, only two passed the test, and only one of those films is actually focused on female characters. As Sarkeesian points out, many excellent films may fail the test, which is why the test is best administered on a grouping of films such as award nominees or box office hits.

Beyond the quantitative demographics, we can find some consistencies in the depictions of gender in American films. In 1987 sociologist Stanford M. Lyman published a qualitative analysis of major American films released in the years 1930–1980, focusing on the types of roles played by women and men and the ways their characters develop. He found that the purposes of women characters are largely presented as conquering and taming men, undermining men's individuality, and knitting rebellious men back into the social fabric. "Women chasten misanthropic men, repair their social, psychic, and self-or-war-inflicted wounds, and wind them back to the world of everyday American reality—that world of competitive coexistence, compulsive conformity and driving incentives to success" (Lyman 1987). What is most striking about Lyman's observation is that women are defined entirely in terms of men, not on their own terms. Obviously this does not account for all films. It is simply a generalization about the overall pattern in American film. By comparison, the story presented about men in American film is that their "true traits of masculinity" emerge only when they reject society and escape into the wilds (the desert, the ocean, outer space). In many films, some balance is forged when men rebel and conquer and then marry. The man must leave society to conquer it, but he is restored to the perfected society through marriage to a woman.

Lyman's interpretation of gender in American films can also be used to analyze gender in advertising images. Historically, advertising's archetype of the powerful, solitary male is the Marlboro Man, a rugged, cigarette-smoking cowboy. The Marlboro Man defines life on his own terms and cannot be tamed by women or society. More recently, some images of men have poked fun at what we might call **hypermasculinity** (see Image 4.3). For example, Old Spice has run a series of very popular ads featuring Isaiah Mustafa declaring to women: "Anything is possible when your man smells like Old Spice and not a lady." The line, and the ads, are so over the top that most viewers laugh. But the Old Spice man is still a masculine man who is selling a product. As one commenter warns: "The commercials in effect say, 'Isn't it silly how we pull stunts to get you to buy our product? Silly, but still—buy it'" (Sherwood 2010). Susan Bordo reviews the changing images of men in advertising in *The Male Body* (Bordo 1999). She suggests that images of men have experienced a bifurcation in recent years, as increasingly male bodies have become elements of spectacle. She refers to the two leading images as "rocks" and "leaners." Rocks are active, muscular, and powerful men. They are like the Marlboro Man if he were to rip off his shirt and reveal six-pack abs and intimidating biceps. Leaners are feminized, more passive, more inviting to the viewer. They are posed in ways that have been more common for women for decades. Their bodies are less muscular but very lean.

The leaner is a profoundly new image of men, but it is not a profoundly new image. Women have been posed this way in advertising for years. As Bordo explains, leaners are not the result of feminism, and these images are not the result of new attention to male desire; quite the contrary. Gay men have taken on powerful roles in both advertising and fashion and have found a space in which they are able to express their own desires through advertising

Image 4.3. A selection of ways that men are portrayed in advertising in popular magazines.

imagery without ever having to deeply discuss the sexual politics behind the image. But surprisingly, as a result some men are now subjected to the same kinds of sexual objectification that has typically been targeted only to women.

If we turn to the world of books, we find that the best demographic work has focused on children's books. A team of authors led by Janice McCabe published a study looking at gender in children's books throughout the twentieth century (McCabe et al. 2011). The first important point to understand about gender in children's books is that many children's books have no human characters. Many nonhuman characters, such as animals, *are* gendered, but some are not. McCabe and her coauthors analyzed 5,618 children's books across a span of 101 years, divided into three categories: all Caldecott Award winners, all Little Golden Books (from the main series, but ignoring those in side series), and all books listed in the *Children's Catalog*. Of these, only about half had gendered characters, either human or animal.

How do representations of females compare to those for males? The analysis of the titles of books is shown in "Male and Female Characters in Children's

MALE AND FEMALE CHARACTERS IN CHILDREN'S BOOKS

Male and Female Characters in Major Children's Books

5,618 TOTAL NUMBER OF BOOKS

36.5% WITH MALE IN TITLE

17.5% WITH FEMALE IN TITLE

26.4% WITH BOY CHARACTERS

19.0% WITH GIRL CHARACTERS

23.2% WITH MALE ANIMALS

7.5% WITH FEMALE ANIMALS

56.9% WITH MALE CENTRAL CHARACTERS

30.8% WITH FEMALE CENTRAL CHARACTERS

Books." The authors find that males appear in titles about twice as often as females. On average, 36.5 percent of books include a male in the title, compared to only 17.5 percent that include a female. Focusing on the actual characters, the authors find that the gender pattern depends on the type of character in question. When the type of character is human children, boys outnumber girls, but not by much, appearing in 26.4 percent of books compared to girls at 19 percent. Animals show the least amount of gender parity. Male animals appear in 23.2 percent of the books analyzed, compared to female animals appearing in only 7.5 percent. This study indicates that from a very young age, boys and girls are presented with a cultural landscape that "symbolically annihilates" women.

As boys and girls become older, their attention may shift from books to music and music videos. Sut Jhally's documentary series *Dreamworlds* offers a gendered critique of music videos from the perspective of cultural studies. *Cultural studies* is an interdisciplinary field of academic scholarship that draws on the methods of textual analysis long used by literary scholars and historians and applies them to a wide variety of texts that were previously ignored by these disciplines. A growing number of sociologists engage in cultural studies as well, but the method is quite different from other sociological practices because of the focus on tracing narratives across cultural texts rather than relying on strict sampling methods. In *Dreamworlds*, Jhally never tells us how or why he chooses the videos that he discusses, but it is presumably because of the way these videos allow him to tell a very particular story about the presentation of women's bodies. Had he conducted a random sample of music videos, he likely would not have been able to present the same narrative. Jhally made the first *Dreamworlds* documentary in 1990. He was threatened with legal action by MTV but managed to avoid it by insisting that his clips were within the realm of fair use laws. He released a second version in 1995 and a third in 2007. Jhally claims that music videos systematically reduce women's lives to the roles they play in men's sexuality. He points to videos in which women seem disabled by the absence of men and driven by their sexual need for them. Jhally concludes that is not a problem of too *much* sex in music videos, but rather of too *little*: only one story about women's sexuality is told in these videos, while many alternative stories are suppressed.

Jhally's claims are supported by a 2011 analysis by Cara Wallis (2011). She compares the behaviors of male and female performers in music videos. She finds that women are much more likely than men to childishly suck on their fingers, to touch themselves delicately, to give sultry looks, and to touch their hair. A similar study of music was performed a few years earlier by Rana A.

Emerson (2002), who looked specifically at black women's performances in music videos. Emerson offers neither a comparison to white women, nor a comparison to men. Instead, she engages in a descriptive analysis that focused on discovering how black women are presented, and present themselves, in music videos. She divides her findings into three categories: (1) stereotypes and controlling images, (2) counter-controlling images, and (3) images of ambivalence or contradiction. The term *controlling images* refers to the work of Patricia Hill Collins, who has a chapter titled "Mammies, Matriarchs, and Other Controlling Images" in her book *Black Feminist Thought* (1990). Emerson's goal is to identify the controlling images in music videos, as well as the alternatives to those controlling images. The main controlling images that she finds are the focus on women's bodies, the reduction of women's lives to a one-dimensional need for men and romance, and the presentation of female performers as the protégées of male producers and DJs. The counterimages she discusses include videos that focus on blackness as a marker of empowerment, that feature sisterhood and black women working together, and that focus on women's independence. Emerson also examines a set of videos that seem to fall between the two extremes of controlling and counter-controlling images. These ambivalent videos may focus on male/female collaboration in music production, women objectifying and sexualizing male bodies, or women who sing about autonomy even as the visual aspect of the video continues to objectify their bodies.

Methodology Moment
DESCRIPTIVE ANALYSIS

The world of popular culture can present an incredibly large universe for asking social science questions. Although this book demonstrates that a wealth of social scientific inquiry has already analyzed many corners of the pop culture universe, there is still far more that we need to explore. It can be difficult to ask precise questions about the social world if the specific territory that we are examining has not been mapped out carefully. When we turn our attention to an understudied topic, we often need to begin with projects focused on descriptive analysis.

Descriptive analysis is a form of inquiry that allows the researcher to map out the prominent landmarks of a given social world. Although it is

continues

important to read as much relevant literature on the topic as possible, with descriptive analysis the literature review would not yield a set of hypotheses, because such hypotheses can bias us toward seeing patterns that may not actually be present or are present but not significant. Rana Emerson's study of how black women are presented in music videos is an excellent example of descriptive analysis. Emerson describes her research as follows: "This study explores Black women's representation in music video through the analysis of a sample of videos by African American women singers, rappers, and musicians produced and distributed at the end of the 1990s." The key word here is *explore*. Descriptive analysis is a kind of exploratory study. Emerson was turning her scholarly gaze on a subject—black women in music videos—that had been theorized and discussed, but not empirically researched. She knew from her examination of the existing literature on cultural representations that both controlling images and counterimages are important focal points for analysis, and she added some question about videos that might be positioned between those two extremes, which she calls ambivalent images. What she did not know going into the study is what it actually looks like to fit into any of these three types of images. Her exploration allowed her see what kinds of controlling images appear in music videos, what kinds of counterimages appear, and what kinds of ambivalent images appear. Although she lacked a detailed map of the territory when she began, she at least had some guideposts based on the work of previous scholars studying similar topics.

Beginning a descriptive analysis requires asking an exploratory question that focuses on a sociological issue. Consider the following question: *What is happening on reality television*? I hear that question often from folks who are dismayed or overwhelmed by the seeming bizarreness of reality TV. Although it is an interesting question, it is not sufficiently sociological. A stronger version might be: *How do depictions of men compare to depictions of women in reality TV?* Now we have a thematic focus for the question that is social in nature. We could perhaps start with the kinds of depictions in which men and women are presented as the same, and compare those moments to depictions of men and women as dramatically different. That would give us some sense of how reality television draws lines of humanity (male and female), femininity, and masculinity. We would then choose a sample of shows to see what kinds of depictions we find when keeping our attention trained on this question about gender.

GENDERED PRODUCTION

To understand the representations of women and men in the content of popular culture, it is important to look behind the scenes to see how gender shapes the workforce of the culture industries. Here we find that women are even more underrepresented than they are in the content.

Martha Lauzen (2012) has studied the role of women in television production for several years. Examining the 2010–2011 TV season, she found that only 25 percent of behind-the-scenes professionals on prime time shows were women. There is significant variation by the type of work performed, but women are underrepresented in all occupations. Lauzen's findings paint a bleak picture for women's involvement in television (see Table 4.1).

These numbers highlight the fact that television is an overwhelmingly male field, even more off-screen than on. Women's voices, visions, and interests are underrepresented across the scope of television production. These numbers suggest that most female characters on television are authored, framed, and photographed by men. Many of the women we see on TV are actually voicing the imaginations of men, rather than offering new visibility for women's perspectives.

Lauzen and her colleague David Dozier have studied the relationship between television content and women's participation in televisual storytelling from a number of angles. One study in 2004 compared shows made by all-male teams to shows made by mixed-gender teams, finding that when women are involved in the storytelling process, the stories told on TV are more likely to show

TABLE 4.1. Percentage of Women-Held Occupations on Prime Time TV Shows, 2010–2011 Season*

Occupation	Percent
Producers	37
Executive Producers	22
Editors	20
Creators	18
Writers	15
Directors	11
Directors of Photography	4

*On the major broadcast networks
(SOURCE: LAUZEN 2012.)

equity between men and women (Lauzen and Dozier 2004). By comparison, when the story is told only by men, the male characters have much higher levels of power and occupational prestige than the female characters. Another analysis by the same authors in 2006 found that on scripted shows, women's involvement behind the scenes has the effect of increasing women's numerical representation and their likelihood of being featured in moments of conflict and resolution (Lauzen and Dozier 2006). Conflicts are an important marker of the centrality of a character, because conflict so often drives plot. But surprisingly, this pattern does not hold up when the authors turn to reality television. Reality, which has more gender parity than any other genre, is less likely to feature women characters, including within central conflicts, when women are involved in the storytelling process. Lauzen and Dozier can only speculate about this anomaly:

> Perhaps the often-macho environs of reality programs, which often include the mean streets of large metropolitan areas on crime shows (e.g., *Cops*), the rugged settings of survival contests (e.g., *Survivor*), and the base contests pursued on "can-you-top-this" gross out programs (e.g., *Fear Factor*) attract women storytellers who hold more traditional perceptions of appropriate gendered behavior. (2006, 453)

The gendered patterns for scenes of conflict and resolution are given more detail in a 2008 report, which found that women's involvement off-screen decreases male-male physical conflicts, but has no significant effect on mixed-gender or female-female physical conflicts. These physical confrontations are then compared to "verbally competitive interactions" (arguments) and "verbally cooperative interactions" (debates/discussions). For most forms, there is no significant difference between all-male storytelling teams and mixed-gender teams. But mixed-gender teams do feature significantly more use of male-male arguments and fewer male-male debates (Lauzen and Dozier 2008).

Two other patterns are worth noting. First, when women are involved behind the scenes, female characters are more likely to "break the fourth wall" by speaking to the camera (Lauzen and Diess 2009). Overall, men dominate this unusual but powerful storytelling technique, but the involvement of women makes it more likely that female characters will employ this convention as well. When female characters break the fourth wall on shows that have female involvement off-screen, they are more likely than male characters to use that moment to comment on issues of competition, as compared to shows with all-male storytellers. Second, when women are involved off-screen, male and female characters are both more likely to be featured in interpersonal settings and roles, rather than in work roles, than in shows with all-male storytellers (Lauzen, Dozier, and Horan 2008). The inverse is also true: when women are not present off-screen, both male and female characters are more likely to be featured in work roles, rather than in interpersonal roles. Overall, men are more likely to dominate work roles, whereas women dominate interpersonal roles.

We return to the work of Stacy L. Smith to examine the influence of gender in the film industry. Smith and her coauthor look at the demographics behind the camera and find that, for the one hundred top-grossing films of 2009, only 3.6 percent of directors, 13.5 percent of writers, and 21.6 percent of producers are female (Smith and Choueiti 2010). (See Table 4.2.) Most films are crafted almost entirely by men, who seem unlikely to give many roles to women or to reduce the stereotypical ways that women are portrayed. When women *are* involved behind the scenes, the number of on-screen roles for women increases. Whereas films with no female writer presented women in only 29.8 percent of on-screen roles, films with a female writer (even when she was just one among several men) featured women in 40.0 percent of on-screen roles. Films with no female director presented women in only 32.2 percent of on-screen roles, compared to films with a female director, which featured women in 47.7 percent of on-screen roles. However, the authors are quick to point out that only four films in 2009 had female directors, so we cannot conclude much from this finding. In a study published in 1996, Denise Bielby and William Bielby found that women writers in the film industry experience a cumulative disadvantage whereby the gap between their incomes and those of men grows across the span of their careers, so that men benefit financially from accumulating experience far more than women do. Similarly, sociologists Anne E. Lincoln and Michael Patrick Allen (2004) have found that women suffer more from the detrimental effect of age on acting careers than do men. They also demonstrate that although the gender gap in the number of film roles is lessening, the presence of women as prominent cast members still lags behind men in significant ways.

TABLE 4.2. Percentage of Women-Held Off-screen Occupations for Top 100 Films

Year	2007	2008	2009
Off-screen Occupations	16.7%	17.0%	18.1%

(Source: Smith and Choueiti 2010.)

Male privilege also permeates the music industry, at least as much as it does the other segments of the mass media. In 2003 *Rolling Stone* magazine formulated a list of the top 500 albums of all time by surveying music professionals and critics. The compilation of this list created an opportunity for two sociologists—Vaughn Schmutz and Alison Faupel—to examine the dynamics of what they call "cultural consecration," the process by which certain cultural objects are given a privileged status. Schmutz and Faupel (2010) used a mixed-method approach to answer the question of why so few women made the list. Only 38 (7.6 percent) of the 500 consecrated albums were made by female solo performers or all-female performing groups, compared to 415 albums by male individuals and groups (the remaining 47 albums were by mixed-gender groups). The authors question whether album sales, Grammy awards, and critical reviews offer any predictors of consecration and use logistic regression analysis to find that positive critical recognition is the best predictor. Female musicians are actually more likely to achieve popular success or to receive a Grammy than they are to receive positive recognition from critics. So the most important predictor of consecration is also the professional tool that is least available to women. The authors turn to qualitative methods to see if the reviews that accompany the *Rolling Stone* list reveal any important patterns of gender difference. They find that reviews of male artists tend to focus on the performer's role in history, artistic vision, and solitary creativity. Women, by contrast, are discussed in terms of their authenticity, honesty, emotionality, and placement in extended social networks. Unlike men, who are described as singularly following their visions to achieve artistic success, women are presented as dependent on the fortune of relationships, often with men (fathers, husbands, producers), to secure professional success.

Methodology Moment
INTERVIEWING CREATORS

The best way to find out why culture looks the way it does is to ask the very people who create it. Surprisingly, we have very few studies that do just that. There are a number of reasons for this lack. First, for most of us the production of popular culture happens in far away places like Hollywood, New York, or Nashville. Second, as we saw in Chapter 1, the bulk of popular culture is produced within massive private corporations that are very

continues

protective of their products and their production processes. Third, many researchers (myself included) succumb to the ease with which we can study cultural content, rather than cultural production, because the content is usually freely available and we need no special permissions to study it. Whatever the reason, many sociologists of popular culture have chosen not to go to the source of those cultural goods to find out why the content is what it is.

An important exception to this quandary is Todd Gitlin's groundbreaking work on the production of prime time television (Gitlin 1983). Gitlin began with a question about how television handles power, politics, and social issues. Initially, his inquiry started with an examination of television itself, but then, he explains, "It began to dawn on me that I could not hope to understand why network television was what it was unless I understood who put the images on the small screen and for what reasons" (13). As a result of this realization, Gitlin shifted his attention to interviewing the folks who create prime time television. That forced him to take the bold step of reaching out to the executives who seemed to be locked away inside corporate studios. Luckily for Gitlin, he was able to live in Los Angeles during the time the interviews were conducted.

Beginning the process of interviewing cultural creators can be challenging, as Gitlin explains:

> I had started cold, with a University of California, Berkeley, letterhead and the names of a few friends of friends and onetime colleagues of colleagues. One name led to another. . . . From January through July 1981, some 200 industry people were decent enough to let me interview them about why they do what they do. Only half a dozen refused outright to speak to me, all of them high-level. (1983, 13)

Because Gitlin actually accomplished this feat of speaking to network executives, many of whom he discovered were only too eager to talk about what they do, he was able to discover that they operate in a field of tremendous uncertainty, not knowing how their newest projects are likely to fare. He calls this "the problem of knowing."

Reaching out to network TV executives was not easy, but Gitlin tried it, and it paid off. A lot of important sociological knowledge has never been gathered simply because no researcher has been bold enough to reach out and ask the questions of the right people.

GENDERED AUDIENCES

One final issue to consider is how gender shapes cultural consumption. This actually opens up a host of important questions. Do men and women watch television and film differently? Do they prefer different types of shows? Do they have comparable tastes in music? Do they use the Internet for the same reasons and at the same rates? Why do they align with different genres of literature?

Unfortunately our knowledge of audiences is quite limited, and gender-specific information is even more limited. For television, Nielsen collects data on audiences by gender, but their data are not publicly available. Scholars who study audiences primarily do so through focus groups, interviews, or ethnographies, which are quite time consuming and typically involve very small sample sizes. Cultural studies scholars, particularly in Great Britain, have given more attention to audience analyses than American sociologists, but their findings on gender are still quite limited.

David Morley (1992) has produced some of the best television audience research in England. One of his major assertions is that television watching should be analyzed in terms of household patterns rather than individual patterns. Unlike cell phones or laptops, televisions are used collectively by entire households, particularly by families. Morley's research examines the way that gendered family roles shape television watching patterns. For example, he finds that fathers typically control the television remote, giving them control of what the family watches, when, and for how long. He also finds that men think of television as a focused individual experience, even when they watch TV with their families. So they tend to prefer watching in silence, and they are more likely to change channels without any discussion. Women, he finds, view TV watching more as a social experience and are more interested in processing what they watch through conversation. He notes that mothers will sometimes watch programs they have no interest in simply as a way to connect with their children. Women also report talking about their viewing experiences with their peers, whereas men are much less likely to do so. Finally, he also notes that the television set is often viewed as an appliance and is therefore coded as masculine. There is an expectation for men to understand the mechanics of television setup and to show an interest in television technology.

Regarding film, the Motion Picture Association of America claims that half of all movie tickets are purchased by women. On average, women go to the movies 4.0 times per year, compared to a slightly higher number for men,

TABLE 4.3. Genres and Subgenres by Association with Gendered Audiences

	Male Audiences	Female Audiences	No Strong Gender Association
Main Genres	Action Adventure Comedy Crime & Gangster Horror Science Fiction War Westerns	Dramas Musicals/Dance	Epics/Historical
Subgenres	Disaster Fantasy Guy Films Road Films Sports Films Supernatural Thriller/Suspense	Chick Flicks Melodramas & Weepers Romance	Biopics Detective & Mystery Film Noir

The main genres and subgenres are found at http://www.filmsite.org/genres.html and http://www.filmsite .org/subgenres.html. The claims of gendered audience association are purely my own.

4.2.* Surprisingly, we have very little data on how men and women interpret the films they consume, so we do not really know whether there are key gender differences in film reception. Clearly, many genres include some subtle gender coding. Drawing from the genre list on filmsite.org,† as well as the associated list of subgenres,‡ I code "chick flicks," dramas, melodramas, and romance films as all associated primarily with women—highlighting the ways that female representations in popular culture emphasize women's need for relationships. The list of genres associated with men is much longer: action, adventure, comedy, crime and gangster, horror, science fiction, war films, Westerns, disaster films, guy films, road films, sports films, and thriller and suspense. But the female audience for male-associated films is very high, whereas the male audience for female-associated films is quite low. (See Table 4.3.)

---

* MPAA (2012).

† http://www.filmsite.org/genres.html.

‡ http://www.filmsite.org/subgenres.html.

How does gender influence the consumption of popular music? According to a study by Gregory T. Toney and James B. Weaver III (1994), men and women have very different reactions to music and music videos. These authors showed a series of popular rock videos to a sample of sixty-nine females and ninety-six males, then asked the participants to complete a survey about their reactions to those videos. The survey questions included indicators of how much the participants *enjoyed* each video as well indicators of how much they found the video to be *disturbing*. For women, there was an inverse relationship between disturbance and enjoyment. The more disturbing the women found the video, the less they enjoyed it. The less disturbing they found the video, the more they enjoyed it. For men, the researchers found there was a direct relationship between disturbance and enjoyment, because men actually linked disturbance to enjoyment. The more disturbing they found the video, the more they enjoyed it. The less disturbing they found the video, the less they enjoyed it. According to these findings, it seems clear that gender plays a shaping role in the experience of musical consumption. From a sociological perspective, that is unlikely to be a result of biological differences and instead is probably a consequence of very different socialization experiences as well as differing social roles, norms, and expectations.

Gender can function not just as a standpoint from which we consume culture, but also as a set of **interpretive strategies**, mechanisms by which we make meaning out of the culture we consume. *Interpretive strategies* is a social science concept that in many ways parallels the humanities notion of aesthetics. Both concepts refer to the ways that we make judgments about cultural objects. Whereas aesthetics pays more attention to the nature of the object itself, the concept of interpretive strategies focuses more on how we incorporate cultural objects into social action. Sarah M. Corse and Saundra Davis Westervelt (2002) have demonstrated the ways that changing ideologies about gender have in turn changed the ways that society critiques popular literature. They focus their analysis on the critical reception of the Kate Chopin novel *The Awakening*. Chopin's novel was published in 1899 and followed another successful novel and two books of short stories, but *The Awakening* was received less favorably. Corse and Westervelt examine critical reviews of the novel in three historical periods: (1) the initial release of the novel, characterized by unfavorable reviews; (2) the years 1950–1979, described as a liminal period for the novel, with somewhat improved reviews; and (3) the years 1980–1994, in which the novel was presented as a taken-for-granted member of the American literary canon. How does a novel go from being ridiculed as immoral and poorly written to becoming canonized? Corse and Westervelt use the term *valorization* to describe this process of a cultural object moving upward through the cultural stratification system. They find that the growing influence of feminism as an interpretive strategy is the best way to explain the valorization of *The Awakening*. Some feminist analysis began to appear in the middle period, but the feminist perspective was largely taken for granted by the later period. This raises questions about how contemporary social movements may one day lead to a reevaluation of the culture we currently consume or reject.

Feminism is just one of many ways that gender can construct interpretive lenses through which we might make sense of culture. The cultural studies scholar Janice Radway discovered this in her ethnographic study of women who read romance novels (Radway 1984). Romances have often been critiqued by feminists as mechanisms that celebrate and reproduce patriarchy by glorifying the story of the damsel in distress. But Radway discovered that romance readers can be far more discerning than feminist scholars might suspect and are making careful choices about the kinds of romance novels they read. She asked her forty-two participants, a semi-organized group of women in the pseudonymous town of Smithton, to identify their three main reasons for reading romance novels from a list of eight possible reasons. She combined the top three choices to get the rankings shown in Table 4.4.

What do these numbers tell us? First and foremost, they reveal that neither the romance nor the men are the main draw of these novels. Instead, the books provide a refuge for these women. Reading relaxes them and provides

TABLE 4.4. Combined 1st, 2nd, and 3rd Choice Responses

Question: Which of the following best describes why you read romances?	
a. To escape my daily problems	13
b. To learn about faraway places and times	19
c. For simple relaxation	33
d. Because I wish I had a romance like the heroine's	5
e. Because reading is just for me; it is my time	28
f. Because I like to read about the strong, virile heroes	4
g. Because reading is at least better than other forms of escape	5
h. Because romantic stories are never sad or depressing	10

(SOURCE: RADWAY 1984, 61.)

them with a way to carve out time to focus on themselves. In addition, the historical settings of the books can also provide an educational experience. Radway demonstrates that romance readers are not mere pawns of a patriarchal publishing system. They make their own demands upon the text, even if these demands do little to transform the patriarchal world in which these women live. As Radway explains:

> When the act of romance reading is viewed as it is by the readers themselves, from within a belief system that accepts as given the institutions of heterosexuality and monogamous marriage, it can be conceived as an activity of mild protest and longing for reform necessitated by those institutions' failure to satisfy the emotional needs of women. . . . When viewed from the vantage point of a feminism that would like to see the women's oppositional impulse lead to real social change, romance reading can also be seen as an activity that could potentially disarm that impulse. (1984, 213)

The centerpiece of Radway's argument is that we must study audiences ethnographically to understand how they consume cultural objects and put them into play in social action.

Gender also influences the ways that we engage with the Internet and social media. Eszter Hargittai and Gina Walejko (2008) refer to this difference as the *participation divide*, a play on the more established notion of the **digital divide**. The concept of the *digital divide* refers to perceived and real differences—by class, race, and gender in particular—in the extent to which people have access to computers, the Internet, and the skills needed to succeed with these digital tools. Hargittai and Walejko's concept of a participation divide shifts attention to the capacity for Internet and social media users to go beyond accessing culture into actually creating it. They surveyed 1,060 first-year college students about their creation of content using digital tools as well as their experience with sharing their self-produced content online. Initially, it appears that men and women create content at similar rates: 62.3 percent of men and 60.0 percent of women claim to have made content in the form of music, artistic photography, poetry/fiction, or film/video. But disparities arise when we focus on each of the specific types of content. In the sample, 42.6 percent of men have created musical content, compared to only 27.4 percent of women. Men also surpass women in creation of film and video: 26.6 percent of men in the survey claim to have made film or video, compared to 16.9 percent of women. Women surpass men in creation of artistic photography and poetry/fiction: 29.6 percent of women in the sample have created artistic photography, compared to 25.2 percent of men, and 30.3 percent of women in the sample have created poetry/fiction, compared to only 20.5 percent of men. So men and women create different kinds of cultural content, but they are equally involved in cultural creation overall. When it comes to hitting the "publish" button and uploading that content online, another disparity emerges: 60.3 percent of men say that they share the cultural content they create online, compared to only 50.6 percent of women. If we shift the focus to the specific type of content—music, artistic photography, poetry/fiction, or

Methodology Moment
STUDYING CONTROVERSY

Culture causes wars. The stories that we tell ourselves through the culture that we produce and consume are sometimes heavily disputed. Across the territories of popular culture we can find a number of war-torn frontlines, and culture that addresses issues of identity and inequality is usually the ground zero for these conflicts. The term *culture war* has been coined to describe these spaces in which symbolic battles are being fought over notions of national identity, public policy, and shared morality. James Davison Hunter's book *Culture Wars* (1991) explores five major fields in which such wars are taking place: the family institution, education, the legal system, electoral politics, and media and the arts. I have written about the culture war of the arts in a book published in 2010, *Legislating Creativity* (Kidd 2010). In that book I define a culture war as "a media-grabbing multi-vocal conflict within and across institutions that has consequences for the kinds of demands that institutions make on public policy" (147). Recent battlegrounds in the culture wars range from the uproar over the 2004 Super Bowl incident in which Justin Timberlake ripped open Janet Jackson's shirt, exposing her breast, to the 2012 election discussions of PBS and *Sesame Street*, resulting in the Million Puppet March on Washington.

Studying controversy is a kind of *ethnomethodology*, which is the study of everyday folkways, and it is most associated with the sociologist Harold Garfinkel, who published *Studies in Ethnomethodology* in 1967. Folkways

continues

Methodology Moment: STUDYING CONTROVERSY *(continued)*

are everyday norms and practices that we take for granted. These norms are brought to the surface and made visible when they are violated, such as when introductory sociology students are asked to breach a norm as a class assignment. Folkways exist at all levels of society. Cultural controversies reveal the folkways of major institutions, from art worlds to politics to the media.

One of the most striking battles in the culture war over gender centers on the underreported controversy over Sarah Jones's song-poem "Your Revolution." Inspired by Gil Scott-Heron's "The Revolution Will Not Be Televised," Jones crafted a performance poem around the line "Your revolution will not happen between these thighs." Her poem is a lament that many men in the hip-hop world are making music about dominating and belittling women, rather than focusing on racial revolution. She takes the actual lyrics of these male performers and spins them on their heads:

> With LL, hard as hell, you know doin' it and doin' it and doin' it well,
> Doin' it and doin' it and doin' it well, nah come on now.
> Your revolution will not be you smacking it up, flipping it, or
>   rubbing it down
> Nor will it take you downtown or humpin around
> Because that revolution will not happen between these thighs.
>   (Jones 2000)

Just in this short selection of lyrics, Jones draws from LL Cool Jay's song "Doin' It," Bell Biv DeVoe's "Do Me," and Bobby Brown's "Humping Around." Jones's goal is not to verbally assault black male artists, but rather to hold some artists accountable for the choices they have made and to turn the attention of artists and audiences back to the issue of revolution.

Jones performed "Your Revolution" on HBO's *Def Poetry Jam* to great acclaim and then worked with DJ Vadim to craft a more musical version of the poem. When Portland, Oregon, radio station KBOO played "Your Revolution" in May 2001, the Federal Communications Commission levied a $7,000 fine for the airing of a song with "indecent content." Once that fine was imposed, no other station would touch "Your Revolution." The indecent content stems entirely from the lyrics that Jones quotes from songs by men—songs that have all played on the airwaves without dissent from the FCC. With the help of People for the American Way, Jones sued the FCC.

continues

Methodology Moment: **STUDYING CONTROVERSY** (*continued*)

Initially the suit was thrown out of a federal court for lack of jurisdiction, but Jones appealed. While awaiting the appeal, which some commentators thought she would win,* the FCC reversed its ruling and declared that "Your Revolution" is not indecent. The conflict over "Your Revolution" became a battle over gender, corporate versus artistic authority in the hip-hop world, and the legitimacy of external regulation of creative content.

---

*See Marjorie Heins (2003), "The Strange Case of Sarah Jones," on the Web site for the Free Expression Policy Project: http://www.fepproject.org/commentaries/sarah jones.html.

film/video—men outpace women in sharing for all types. This is even true for the types that are produced at greater rates by women.

WRAP-UP

The term *annihilation* might be the best way to make sense of how gender works in popular culture. Gender's influence is to symbolically annihilate women and girls from children's books, television, and film. Women's bodies are annihilated in advertising images that use sexual assault as a comedic premise to sell liquor. Women's multidimensional identities are annihilated in music videos that reduce women's lives to the need for romance and sex from men. Some women are annihilated more than others. Women of color, lesbians, trans women, poor women, and older women seem to be particularly at risk, as are political women, tough women, and radical women.

Male privilege, a key aspect of how gender works in the social world, is produced in part by the mechanisms of popular culture. Men—or at least *some* men—can take for granted that when they turn on their televisions or open their books they will see people like themselves who are empowered and successful, in a variety of possible life outcomes. Men can assume that other men are the authors of the stories that are told about men and about human life in general. Male privilege is particularly beneficial to wealthy and upper-middle-class men, white men, and straight men, as well as manly men, strong men, and men with guns.

RESOURCES

Resources for Examining Gender in the Social World

- US Census Bureau, Main Page on Age and Sex: https://http://www.census.gov/population/age.

Resources for Examining Gender in Popular Culture

- Video: *Killing Us Softly 4*, from the Media Education Foundation.
- Video: *Tough Guide*, from the Media Education Foundation.
- Video: *Dreamworlds 3*, from the Media Education Foundation.

5

Not That There's Anything Wrong with That
SEXUALITY PERSPECTIVES

Image 5.1. Logo for the It Gets Better Project, which began in 2010 as a campaign to reduce suicide among LGBT teens. (Courtesy of It Gets Better Project.)

WE LOST A LITTLE MONSTER THIS WEEK

On May 4, 2011, fourteen-year-old Jamey Rodemeyer took to his YouTube video blog* to send an important message to the world. Jamey was an openly bisexual student who faced constant bullying in his school for his sexuality. He knew that many other teens faced the same problem, and he wanted to inspire them to persist and survive:

_____

* http://www.youtube.com/user/xgothemo99xx.

Hi, this is Jamey from Buffalo, New York and I'm just here to tell you that it does get better. Here's a little bit of my story. December 2010 I thought I was bi and then I always got made fun of because I virtually have no guy friends and I only have friends that are girls and it bothered me because they would be like "faggot that" and they caught me in the hallways and I felt like I could never escape it. And I made a Formspring, which I shouldn't have done, and people would just constantly send me hate telling me that gay people would go to hell.

And I just want to tell you that it does get better because when I came out for being bi I got so much support from my friends and it made me feel so secure. If your friends or family isn't even there for you I look up to one of the most supporting people of the gay community that I think of, that I know, Lady Gaga. She makes me so happy and she lets me know that I was born this way and that's my advice to you from her. You were born this way, now all you have to do is hold your head up and you'll go far because that's all you have to do is just love yourself and you're set. And, I promise you it will get better.

I have so much support from people I don't even know online. I know that sounds creepy but they are so nice and caring and they don't ever want me to die and it's just so, so much support for me. So, just listen here, it gets better. And look at me I'm doing better, I went to the Monster Ball and now I'm liberated so it gets better.*

Jamey titled the video "It Gets Better, I Promise!" It was his contribution to the It Gets Better Project (see Image 5.1), a YouTube-based initiative that was started in 2010 by the columnist Dan Savage in response to a slew of suicides by lesbian, gay, bisexual, and transgender (LGBT) teens.†

Savage's column Savage Love has provided weekly sex advice to readers of the Seattle-based weekly, *The Stranger*, since 1991, and to the many readers who follow the syndicated column in other outlets across the country. His podcast has offered similar advice since 2006. When the media began to pay particular attention to LGBT suicides in 2010, Savage decided to address what seemed to be a growing problem by sending a message to LGBT teens that they are not alone and their lives are going to get better. Savage and his

---

* Jamey Rodemeyer's video can be found on YouTube at http://www.youtube.com /watch?v=-Pb1CaGMdWk.

†http://www.itgetsbetter.org.

partner Terry Miller posted one of the first It Gets Better videos on YouTube and began recruiting other celebrities to do the same. They also invited noncelebrities to upload their own It Gets Better videos. In their video, Savage and Miller talk about how difficult their own childhoods were as gay youths whose sexuality was not accepted by their parents and peers. But their families came around in time, they both found success in their careers, they met each other and fell in love, and they started a family with the adoption of their son. Things started out rough, but they got better.

It Gets Better videos have been posted by nearly three thousand people and groups, including Barack Obama, Perez Hilton, Ellen Degeneres, Hillary Clinton, and Google.

And Jamey Rodemeyer. Four months after posting his video, Jamey Rodemeyer took his own life. He hung himself outside his suburban Buffalo home, a day after sending his last message to the world via Twitter: "@ladygaga bye mother monster, thank you for all you have done, paws up forever." "Mother monster" is a term of endearment for the pop singer Lady Gaga, who calls her fans Little Monsters. The word *monster* highlights the way that fans of Lady Gaga see themselves as freaks and misfits, even as they find community and solidarity with one another. The limited release Super Deluxe version of her album *Fame Monster* included an art book stating the Manifesto of Little Monsters:

There's something heroic about the way my fans operate their cameras. So precisely and intricately, so proudly, and so methodically. Like Kings writing the history of their people. It's their prolific nature that both creates and procures what will later be perceived as the "kingdom." So, the real truth about Lady Gaga fans lies in this sentiment: They are the kings. They are the queens. They write the history of the kingdom, while I am something of a devoted Jester.

It is in the theory of perception that we have established our bond. Or, the lie, I should say, for which we kill. We are nothing without our image. Without our projection. Without the spiritual hologram of who we perceive ourselves to be, or rather to become, in the future.

When you're lonely,
I'll be lonely too,
And this is the fame.*

---

* http://ladygaga.wikia.com/wiki/Manifesto_of_Little_Monsters.

A week after Rodemeyer's death, Lady Gaga took to the stage at the iHeart-Radio music festival in Las Vegas and dedicated her song "Hair" to him, saying, "We lost a little monster this week," and posting a photograph of Jamey on a large screen for the audience to see. "I wrote this record about how your identity is really all you've got when you're in school . . . so tonight, Jamey, I know you're up there looking at us, and you're not a victim . . . you're a lesson to all of us."* The song "Hair" (Lady Gaga 2011b) is about a seemingly rebellious teenager who wants to express himself (or herself) through his hair, and how he wants to be loved for being who he is. The central message of the song is "I am as free as my hair. I am my hair."† After Jamey's death, even as messages of sadness and support came pouring in to Jamey's family, his parents went on the *Today* show to ask that cyber bullies stop posting hateful messages online about their son.

SEXUALITY, SUICIDE, AND POWER

Why do LGBT youths turn to the Internet to share their voices, at the risk of providing more ammunition to bullies? Why do adult leaders in the LGBT community turn to YouTube to try to stop teen suicide and the bullying of LGBT youths? Why do kids like Jamey Rodemeyer take pop stars like Lady Gaga so seriously? It is not just the Internet or Lady Gaga; LGBT activists are increasingly focusing their attention on cultural outlets like television and film as driving forces for change, rather than just focusing on the political system. This gives us the opportunity to explore the functions that popular culture serves in contemporary society.

Emile Durkheim, one of the early founders of sociology in Europe, might seem an odd person to turn to at this point. He certainly is not known as a theorist of sexuality; rather, his theories are much more general and can be used to understand all sorts of social boundaries and the mechanisms that we use to construct them. Durkheim is well known for his study *Suicide* (1951), which presents a sociological perspective on suicide rates. We typically think of suicide in psychological terms. A person experiences depression or loss and cannot cope, and a suicide may result. But Durkheim takes the stance that suicide *rates* are social facts, which vary from one society to the next and

---

* http://www.youtube.com/watch?v=MpHSWMQwovA.

† The song stands in contrast to India.Arie's song "I Am Not My Hair," (India.Arie 2006), even though both songs present messages of liberation and self-acceptance.

from one time period to the next and tell us something about the social world. Durkheim argues that suicide tends to increase during periods of **anomie**, or normlessness. If society is in flux—economically, politically, culturally—then people may feel disconnected from it or uncertain of how to live, and this in turn can lead to an increase in suicide. According to Durkheim, two factors are important for reducing anomie: integration and regulation. Individuals must be woven into the fabric of society—through relationships, contracts, associations, and so forth—and society must provide some moral authority that gives its members a sense of direction and purpose. That moral authority can be the church or pop music, as long as it is a strong authority.

Durkheim turned to the question of social functions in *The Rules of Sociological Method* (1938). Despite the perception that all crime is bad, Durkheim took the stance that crime is normal, is unavoidable, and serves positive functions for society. Today, popular culture performs many of the functions that Durkheim attributed to crime. Crime and its punishments have become so routinized and obscured from public observation that they simply are unable to play the same role that they did when trials were held in the public square and executions were spectator events. Occasionally a major hearing, such as the trial of O. J. Simpson, will capture public attention, but that is only because of the mediating role of commercial media. I contend that popular culture serves five major social functions.*

First, popular culture generates basic social norms. Although no American consumes all of American popular culture, most Americans consume quite a lot of it. In *The Dominant Ideology Thesis*, Nicholas Abercrombie, Stephen Hill, and Bryan Turner (1980) identify popular culture as the key means by which the ideas of the dominant classes might be transmitted to the whole of society in the era of late capitalism. Today, in the realm of sexuality, popular culture is becoming a vehicle for new ways to think about sexual orientation. The new visibility of gay characters and artists is providing LGBT youths with more images of people like them. When Joe Biden stated his support for gay marriage, he cited *Will and Grace* as an important factor in changing American minds about gay people.

Second, popular culture produces social boundaries. The clothing we wear, the music we listen to, and the television we watch not only constitute our identities, but also help to separate our identity categories from others'. My

---

* For an expansion on this discussion, see Kidd (2007).

love of Willie Nelson and Emmylou Harris helps me to find others who are "like me." People who listen to Billy Ray Cyrus or Eminem are not "like me," at least not musically. Maybe there is an Eminem fan who really should be my friend; fashion, television, film, and literature may yet bring us together.

Paul Willis (1977) finds that popular culture in the form of fashion is an important tool for boundary maintenance among working-class adolescent males in Britain. In *Learning to Labor*, Willis takes as his subject population a group called the "lads," who actively resist the authority of the school system. The lads define their identities in contrast to the "ear'oles," who embrace school culture, and in contrast to the school itself:

> As the most visible, personalised and instantly understood element of resistance to staff and ascendancy over "ear'oles," clothes have great importance to "the lads." The first sign of a lad "coming out" is a fairly rapid change in his clothes and hairstyle. The particular form of this alternative dress is determined by outside influences, especially fashions current in the wider symbolic system of youth culture. (1977, 17)

Fashion is a shorthand for a distinctive set of values, goals, and practices. Willis uses the phrase "coming out" in a generic way, not in reference to gay kids acknowledging their sexual orientation. But it is also true that young people often use fashion as a marker of coming out of the closet and embracing gay identity. There is no inherent reason for gay youths to change their hair, clothes, or appearance. But as Lady Gaga says in her manifesto and in her song "Hair," these are among the few tools that young people have to declare their individuality.

Third, popular culture produces rituals that generate social solidarity. People who share identity categories have solidarity with one another, thanks to the rituals of popular culture. Teenagers are united by rhythms at the rave and the club; college students come together to watch "Must See TV" on NBC; Harry Potter fans become friends at book release parties or while standing in line for the movies. As a college student in the 1990s in the small-town South, I used to go to The Round Up on Friday nights for line dancing with the locals. These rituals produce feelings of shared sentiment—the excitement and love for Lady Gaga as a role model and mother figure, for example—and these feelings produce social cohesion by bonding members of society together in relationships of trust and shared purpose. When Lady Gaga declared, "*We* lost a little monster," her fans took it as a very personal loss to their community.

Why does solidarity matter? Based on the work of Durkheim, it is clear that solidarity is the basis of social cohesion; the sense of trust that solidarity engenders is a necessary precondition before members of society will take the risky step of investing their resources, time, and selves in their societies. Without solidarity, humans are purely biological—and not social—entities. In contemporary capitalist societies, popular culture is one of the most important sources of the rituals that produce solidarity, because of its widespread and frequent consumption.

Fourth, popular culture generates innovation. It is an outcome of technical innovations, such as the printing press and photography. But the market value of popular culture has produced a race for new technologies whose benefits extend beyond the realms of the popular and the cultural. Arguably the most important area of technological progress as a consequence of popular culture is the Internet. The World Wide Web is largely driven by one of the most financially successful areas of popular culture: pornography. We can thank the porn industry for such important technological advances as e-commerce and streaming videos (Barss 2010). These technologies are now widely used for nonpornographic purposes of business and leisure. Americans consume pornography at very high rates, and many Americans spend a fair amount of money on it. The financial stakes have allowed pornography to take risks in technological advancements that have offered tremendous benefits to the rest of the online commerce world.

Fifth, and finally, popular culture generates social progress. Books in particular have been very important. Upton Sinclair's *The Jungle* (1906) led to significant reforms in the American food industry. Harriet Beecher Stowe's 1852 publication of *Uncle Tom's Cabin* prepared America for massive reorganization of its racial structure and is credited as at least a partial cause of the Civil War. Contemporary spaces of popular culture that lead, or may lead, to social change are numerous and varied. Dan Savage's It Gets Better project is a prime example of using the Internet to effect social change—not just a decline in suicide rates among LGBT youths, but also a transformation in how Americans treat gay people. The weighty role that popular culture performs in social change makes it an important element in the dynamics of contemporary social life.

This extension of Durkheim's functionalism helps us understand some of the roles that popular culture plays in contemporary social structure. But Durkheim offers us very little when it comes to accounting for **power**. I turn now to the work of Michel Foucault, who wrote very explicitly about power and its relationship to sexuality. Foucault's definition of power differs substantially from the top-down model that most other scholars use:

> It seems to me that power must be understood in the first instance as the multiplicity of force relations immanent in the sphere in which they operate and which constitute their own organization; as the process which, through ceaseless struggles and confrontations, transforms, strengthens, or reverses them; as the support which these force relations find in one another, thus forming a chain or system, or on the contrary, the disjunctions and contradictions which isolate them from one another; and lastly, as the strategies in which they take effect, whose general design or institutional crystallization is embodied in the state apparatus, in the formulation of the law, in the various social hegemonies. (1990, 92–93)

This is not an easy statement to follow, to be sure. But Foucault's influence on theories of both power and sexuality is enormous, and this statement captures much of his position on the topic, so it is worth spending some time to unpack what he says. Foucault's approach to power is rooted in microlevel relationships. Every relationship is a power relationship. From Foucault's perspective, there are no powerless people. Every person who has one or more relationships contends with power. But power is not something held by individual people; it is a property of the relationship itself. Power is found both in the prevalent patterns of society *and* in the counterpatterns that push against the current. Laws and "social hegemonies" like racism, homophobia, and sexism are crystallizations of power relationships.

Applying power to the story of Jamey Rodemeyer's life and tragic death, we may be tempted to focus on the power that Jamey's bullies seem to hold. But Foucault would instead have us focus on the relationship between Jamey and his bullies, not just on the bullies themselves. They were engaged in a sort of "ceaseless struggle" that is actually very common in American middle and high schools. Bullying is a relationship of power that is often linked to other power relationships in the bully's past. Many bullies were themselves the victims of bullying, and still others come from abusive homes. Moreover, bullies often target kids who are subject to discrimination in the larger social world. In Jamey's case, a homophobic culture made him seem like a legitimate target to the bullies in his school. Those bullies were not acting in isolation; they took their cues from the "social hegemonies." Jamey was not a powerless victim. His video blog gave him a voice to speak against his bullies and to speak

CHAIN OF POWER RELATIONS

THE CHAIN OF POWER RELATIONS
SURROUNDING THE LIFE OF JAMEY RODEMEYER.

JAMEY'S LAW
◆
PRESIDENT
BARACK OBAMA
◆
LADY GAGA
◆
2 MILLION VIEWERS
ON THE INTERNET
◆
JAMEY RODEMEYER
◆
BULLIES
◆
CULTURE OF
HOMOPHOBIA

up for kids like himself. His video "It Gets Better, I Promise!" has received nearly two million views. Jamey was active in confronting and transforming the multiplicity of force relations that were immanent in his own life. The actions of a seemingly powerless fourteen-year-old boy influenced a wealthy and powerful pop singer, Lady Gaga, to arrange a meeting with President Barack Obama to begin a discussion about crafting federal antibullying legislation. As of this writing, that legislation has not passed, but it is still being debated, and it is generally referred to as Jamey's Law. From Foucault's perspective, we have a "Chain of Power Relations."

SEXUALITY IN THE SOCIAL WORLD

We are only beginning to learn to measure sexual identity. One measure of sexuality is offered in the Centers for Disease Control and Prevention's (CDC) report *Sexual Behavior and Selected Health Measures* (Mosher, Chandra, and Jones 2005). In this study, just over 90 percent of men and women identify as heterosexual. (See "Sexual Demographic of the United States.") But that does not mean that nearly 10 percent are gay or lesbian. For men, 2.3 percent identify as homosexual, 1.8 percent identify as bisexual, 3.9 percent identify as "something else," and 1.8 percent did not report their sexual identity. The respondents who did not report, or chose "something else," are not necessarily queer. We simply do not know what their sexualities look like. They may be straight people who have internalized a message that sexual categories are limiting or socially constructed. So only 4.1 percent of men in the study identified themselves as gay or bisexual. For women, the numbers are similar: 1.3 percent identify as homosexual, 2.8 percent identify as bisexual, 3.8 percent identify as "something else," and 1.8 percent did not report. Although queer women were more likely than queer men to identify as bisexual, we still find a total of 4.1 percent of women claiming a lesbian or bisexual identity.

WARNING: SEXUAL CONTENT

The metaphor of the closet, out of which gay people must emerge to reveal their sexuality in a world that presupposes straightness, has been adapted for the film industry as the celluloid closet, referring to the compound that was used to capture early films. Film historian Vito Russo coined this term in a book of the same name (Russo 1987). The "closet" that gays come out of is of course a metaphorical and symbolic closet, which begs the question of

SEXUAL DEMOGRAPHICS OF THE UNITED STATES

HETEROSEXUAL
90.2% MEN
90.3% WOMEN

HOMOSEXUAL
2.3% MEN
1.3% WOMEN

DID NOT REPORT
1.8% MEN
1.8% WOMEN

BISEXUAL
1.8% MEN
2.8% WOMEN

SOMETHING ELSE
3.9% MEN
3.8% WOMEN

how exactly it is constructed as a kind of psychic structure, not only for gay people—many of whom find the idea ridiculous—but also for an entire society that struggles with comprehending the emergence of sexual identity. The notion of a *celluloid* closet highlights both the deep-seated though surprising homophobia of the film world and the role that film plays in forcing many gays and lesbians into hiding an important part of their identities.

It is not uncommon to associate Hollywood with gay people. The world of theater has often been a refuge for young gay people who felt rejected in other career paths or found that acting gave them a valuable way of exploring sexuality and identity and of passing in a world that rejected them. Certainly there have always been gay people involved in the film industry, at all levels. But Hollywood has its own closets, and the film industry has to be responsive to moviegoers and theater owners all across the country.

Consider the case of *Brokeback Mountain*, the 2005 film by director Ang Lee. The movie was considered "groundbreaking"—a term used in reviews in the *LA Times*, the *New York Times*, and many other outlets—because of its mainstream presentation of same-sex romance between two male sheepherders. The film's director is a straight man, it was adapted from a short story written by a straight woman (Annie Proulx), and its lead male and female actors were all straight. The film appeared on 2,089 cinema screens and made just over $83 million in domestic gross receipts, making it the twenty-second highest grossing film of 2005. This was thirty-six years after the Stonewall Riots. Though many gay historians dispute using the Stonewall Riots of 1969 as the opening of the gay liberation movement, no one argues that it started later than that. So if Hollywood's groundbreaking moment came thirty-six years after the latest possible start of the political organization of gays and lesbians in the United States, then we can hardly say that film is leading the way for progress. Indeed, we have to recognize that film is often far behind the political currents of society.

Russo's *Celluloid Closet* examines why and how Hollywood has lagged behind for so long. The book offers close readings of a slew of films with important, if coded, messages about sexuality, as well as an analysis of the industry itself and its off-screen aspects that account for the on-screen lag. In Russo's estimation, even when Hollywood has shown queer characters, those characters have been far removed from the realities of gays and lesbians. He distinguishes the bulk of Hollywood images as films about homosexuality, not films about gay people. He appeals for change in the afterword of his revised edition: "So no more films about homosexuality. Instead, more films that explore people who happen to be gay in America and how their lives intersect with the dominant culture" (1987, 326).

One of Russo's chapters is subtitled "The Invisible Years," referring to the earliest years of film, up to the 1960s. Are gays and lesbians still invisible in film today? The issue can be considered in many ways. How many gay characters appear in film? How many gay-themed films reach the cinema screens? How large is the audience for gay-themed films? I address this last question by looking at Box Office Mojo's list of the Top 100 gay/lesbian movies, which is ranked in order of the lifetime gross of each film.* The number 1 film on this list is *The Birdcage* (1996), which has grossed over $124 million. When we scroll down to the number 10 film on the list, *To Wong Foo, Thanks for Everything, Julie Newmar* (1995), the gross drops tremendously, to $36 million. The number 20 spot is held by *The Kids Are All Right* (2010), which comes in at just under $21 million. Jumping all the way down to 50, we find *Personal Best* (1982), coming in at $5.6 million. The last film on the list, *My Summer of Love* (2005), has made only $1 million. Based on this list, even with what seems like a recent explosion of gay films, we have to conclude that broad audiences simply are not seeing many gay-themed films. None of the Top 100 gay/lesbian films has earned enough to make it into the Top 100 US films.

Turning to the small screen, one of the largest demographic changes on television in recent history is the emergence of many characters who are gay, lesbian, or bisexual. Shows like *Ellen* and later *Will and Grace* gave heightened visibility to this American demographic. This is not the first time that queer characters have appeared on television. Steven Capsuto's historical analysis of television, *Alternate Channels* (2000), finds that the earliest acknowledgments of homosexuality came in the form of unscripted programs like sports and news. Wrestling's Gorgeous George was an implied gay character in the late 1940s, though the sportsman behind the character, George Wagner, was a married heterosexual. In the 1950s, variety and news shows took an interest in Christine Jorgensen, a transsexual woman who had returned from sex re-assignment surgery in Denmark. When the McCarthy hearings of 1954 added homosexual "perverts" to their list of targets alongside communists, the news media were forced to at least acknowledge gay sexuality on television.

In the many years since then, televisual portrayals of queer identities have transformed from one decade to the next, with a focus on gay politics in the

---

* http://boxofficemojo.com/genres/chart/?id=gay.htm.

1960s, disco in the 1970s, AIDS in the 1980s, gay mainstream visibility in the 1990s, and gay civil rights in the first decade of the twenty-first century.*

The most consistent analysis of LGBT representations on television is conducted by the Gay and Lesbian Alliance Against Defamation (GLAAD), which publishes two annual reports that assess the presence of queer roles on TV. "Where Are We on TV?" reviews the new television lineup every fall, as announced by the networks (Gay and Lesbian Alliance Against Defamation 2011a). The "Network Responsibility Index" (NRI) provides a follow-up to "Where Are We on TV?" by looking back at the preceding year of television and grading networks on their inclusion of queer characters and themes (Gay and Lesbian Alliance Against Defamation 2011b).

The 2011 NRI looked back at the 2010–2011 television season, examining any programming that aired between June 1, 2010, and May 31, 2011. The NRI counts hours of LGBT impressions. If an hour of television includes a major character who is queer, that hour counts as one major impression. If the hour includes only a discussion of gay issues or the presence of a minor character who is queer, that hour counts as a minor impression. The main goal of the NRI is to compare networks, and from year to year. Networks are given one of four grades, based on the percentage of LGBT-inclusive hours of programming, as well as the quality of the representations that are offered and the diversity of those representations: excellent, good, adequate, or failing. For 2010–2011, GLAAD ranked the broadcast networks as follows:

1. The CW: Good (33% of prime time hours LGBT-inclusive)
2. Fox: Good (29% of prime time hours LGBT-inclusive)
3. ABC: Good (23% of prime time hours LGBT-inclusive)
4. NBC: Adequate (15% of prime time hours LGBT-inclusive)
5. CBS: Adequate (10% of prime time hours LGBT-inclusive)

In terms of racial diversity among LGBT characters, GLAAD's NRI found that black LGBT characters were the most underrepresented group in number of programming hours (not in number of characters). Hispanic and Asian LGBT characters fared better than blacks, but still had quite limited representation compared to whites.

---

* These eras are covered in detail in the Media Education Foundation documentary *Off the Straight and Narrow*.

Most LGBT impressions on TV are of gay men. Lesbians are significantly underrepresented, and queer women are more likely to be presented as bisexual than lesbian.

In my own analysis of the same season—shown in "Sexual Demographics in Television"—which focuses on characters rather than hours of programming, I found that lesbian, gay, and bisexual characters accounted for 5.1 percent of prime time characters whose sexuality was clearly identified. (Many characters are never identified sexually, either because of their age or because of the small scope of their roles.) That leaves 94.9 percent of sexually identified characters as straight. The characters who are queer are mostly gay males: 3.6 percent, compared to 0.7 percent lesbians, 0.2 percent bisexual males, and 0.6 percent bisexual females. In other words, 70.1 percent of queer characters are gay males. Also, 82 percent of queer characters are white; 3.3 percent are Asian, 8.2 percent are Hispanic, and 6.5 percent are black. Some 93.5 percent of queer men on prime time TV are gay, whereas 6.5 percent are bisexual. By comparison, 53.3 percent of queer women on prime time TV are lesbian, and 46.7 percent are bisexual.

Comparing queer representation across genres, we should first start with the special case of animation. Animation on prime time for the major broadcast networks really just means Fox on Sunday evenings. It is a very small subset of prime time television. At first glance, animation appears to be quite progressive when it comes to sexuality, given that 16.9 percent of animated characters in 2010–2011 were queer. That is much higher than the overall average of 5.1 percent. But many of these characters are minor, and they often serve as the butt of jokes. As GLAAD points out, "FOX's greatest problems with LGBT representation have typically been during their Sunday animation block" (Gay and Lesbian Alliance Against Defamation 2011b, 12). On sitcoms, queer roles constitute 6.1 percent of sexually identified characters, compared to 4.7 percent of characters on reality shows and 3.6 percent of characters on dramas. Across all genres, gay white men occupy most of the queer roles.

In the world of music we find a very different pattern. Although there are some prominent gay men in the popular music industry—Elton John, George Michael, Ricky Martin—nearly all avoided coming out until after their fame was well established. The same has been true for lesbians in the music industry, with some of the most prominent being Melissa Etheridge, The Indigo Girls, and K. D. Lang.* But unlike men, many women in music have become very successful while identifying as bisexual. A review of the *Billboard* Top 100 from 2010

---

* http://lesbianlife.about.com/od/lesbianmusicians/a/TopLesbianBands.htm.

SEXUAL DEMOGRAPHICS IN TELEVISION

94.9%

HETEROSEXUALS

3.6%

GAY MALES

0.6%

LESBIANS

0.2%

BISEXUAL MALES

0.6%

BISEXUAL FEMALES

reveals that two bisexual women—Lady Gaga and Ke$ha—each had four hits on that year's Top 100 list.* Katy Perry, who does not identify as bisexual but hit fame with the bisexually charged "I Kissed a Girl," had two of the Top 100 songs of 2010. There are no lesbian women in the Top 100 from that year, and there is only one gay male: Adam Lambert. Lambert has one song in the Top 100, which we can combine with the four each from Lady Gaga and Ke$ha to conclude that 9 percent of songs in the 2010 Top 100 are by queer performers. Not bad, but that's only three different performers. It is true that there is some fluidity to sexual identity, especially in a world where queer people are pressured to stay in the closet and may only come out later in their careers or never at all. What I analyze here in the case of musicians refers to the *public* sexual identity, which tells us something about how these performers are understood by audiences.

The field of literature would seem to be the richest space for research on gay representations. Thus far, however, sociologists have largely left that work to their colleagues in the English department. Although literary analyses of gay characters can help us to better understand the role of sexuality in literary history, we need to apply the methods of sociology to really make claims about the frequency of different types of representations, the practices through which these representations are produced, and the deployment of these representations by audiences engaged in the process of meaning-making.

Neil Shyminsky (2011) offers a queer analysis of comic book heroes and their sidekicks. He begins with the premise that the many male superheroes are gay enough that they produce queer anxiety, from their S&M-themed costumes to the superpowers that make them mutants and freaks. But the superhero must be affirmed as the very model of modern masculinity, which is where his sidekick comes in. Although the sidekick creates an ambiguous homosocial relationship, he also serves as a foil for the failed masculinity of the superhero. The ambiguity of the superhero/sidekick relationship is comedically celebrated and mocked by the *Saturday Night Live* animated shorts "The Ambiguously Gay Duo." Shyminsky pays particular attention to the relationships between Superman/Clark Kent and his "cub reporter" sidekick Jimmy Olsen, and between Batman and the three men who stepped into the Robin role over the years of that comic. Both Jimmy and Robin are presented as feminized men, which allows them to affirm the masculinity of the superheroes they serve. Jimmy Olsen

---

* http://www.billboard.com/charts-year-end/hot-100-songs?year=2010#/charts
-year-end/hot-100-songs?year=2010.

Image 5.2. Batman and his sidekick Robin both dressed in unusual ways, but we could argue that Robin is significantly more flamboyant than the superhero he assists (Source: Everett Collection).

frequently wears drag to go undercover to investigate a story, but just as frequently puts himself in danger's way and needs Superman to save him. Robin foolishly wears the flamboyantly red, green, and yellow costume and arrogantly thinks he can take down the villains on his own (see Image 5.2). The role of Robin, the sidekick, has been played by three alter egos over the years since he was first created in 1940. The original Robin, Dick Grayson, eventually went to college. The second Robin, Jason Todd, was killed by the Joker. The most recent Robin is Tim Drake, who operates as the Red Robin. According to Shyminsky, these sidekicks serve as the less ambiguous half of the gay superhero/sidekick duos, distracting queer anxiety from the superhero.

GAY HOLLYWOOD

We know very little about queer participation in the production of television behind the cameras. Unlike gender and race, sexuality is not a category for

Methodology Moment
QUANTITATIVE CONTENT ANALYSIS

Quantitative content analysis is the act of counting characters, plot elements, and other kinds of representations in a carefully chosen sample. It allows us to make very broad, but often not very deep, claims about the kinds of representations that appear in cultural content. Quantitative content analysis allows for breadth because, when carefully made, a coding sheet facilitates most analyses happening relatively quickly, so that a larger sample can be reviewed. It does not allow for depth, because it usually separates specific representations from the context in which they occur. For example, I stated previously that 5.1 percent of sexually identified characters in the 2010 season of prime time programming on the major broadcast networks are gay, lesbian, or bisexual. If you were to ask me whether those representations were largely positive or negative, or what kinds of jobs the characters had, or how multidimensional their lives are, I could not tell you, because none of those were codes in my analysis. I can certainly add codes, but there will always be layers of meaning that are missed in a quantitative content analysis. By comparison, if you asked Neil Shyminsky (cited in reference to comic book characters) to comment in depth about Jimmy Olsen or Robin, he certainly could. But if you asked him what percentage of superheroes have sidekicks, or how many sidekicks serve as gay foils, he certainly could not answer that question based on the research he conducted for the article I cited. That article offered a deep analysis of the meaningful relationships within a small handful of comics, whereas my study offered a broad overview of television representations. Although deep issues of meaning are tremendously important, it is just as important to examine the broad context of cultural representations. I like to think of qualitative content analyses as landscape paintings of one particular perspective from within a scenic location, and of quantitative content analyses as maps drawn from above.

Quantitative content analyses need to begin with a research question. *What is the racial breakdown of prime time television? What is the ratio of men to women in film? How many television programming hours include gay characters? How many children's book characters are disabled?* The research question should help to determine what the unit of analysis needs to be. If the question is about characters, then the unit of analysis is each individual

continues

character (perhaps limited to speaking roles). If the question is about programming hours, then the unit of analysis is an hour of television programming. An hour of television programming should not be confused for an individual television program, as many programs are only thirty minutes long, and others (such as movies, extended episodes, and sporting events) last longer than an hour. In a study of music, a research question about songs has a different unit of analysis than a question about albums.

The research question should also clarify the important variables being counted, such as the race of an author, the gender of a singer, or the sexuality of a character. Of course we also have to determine how we will know the answer to this question. This can actually be quite tricky. How would we know if a television character is gay? Do we presume the character is straight until there is an indication otherwise? If a character is shown in a same-sex relationship, do we presume he is gay or she is lesbian? How would we know the character is not bisexual? Identifying the sexuality of nonfictional people is hard enough. When the person is fictional, it becomes even tougher.

Here is how I answer those questions. I argue that a character has no more substance than what the creator of the character has actually shown. The creator has the right to reveal more later, but until that time all we have is what has been shown. If a character explicitly states his sexuality, then we have to assume that the statement is accurate until we are given some indication otherwise. If a male character dates a female, but then declares to her that he is gay, then we have to code him as gay in our analysis, even though we've only seen him in a straight relationship. If a character does not identify his own sexuality, then we have to look to his relationships for an indication. So a character in a straight relationship would be coded as straight, up until the specific episode when he declared his gay identity. A character having relationships with both men and women would be coded as bisexual until a moment when the character declares otherwise. Any character who is not shown in a relationship or with an interest in a relationship, and who does not declare her or his sexuality, must be coded as "unknown," meaning the character's sexuality has not been identified.

The process for making each determination is written up in a codebook, which is a set of protocols used in completing each coding sheet. We start to see quite quickly that quantitative content analysis can offer a number of difficult research complexities. The best resource for anyone preparing to engage in quantitative content analysis is Kimberly A. Neuendorf's *The Content Analysis Guidebook* (2002).

which we regularly collect labor market data. So we know nothing about the percentages of actors, writers, directors, producers, or camera technicians who are gay.

Given the possibility of sexual nondisclosure, we should assume that gender patterns influence the opportunities faced by queer men and women in television production. That pattern means that gay men are likely to have many more opportunities off-screen than are lesbian women. Gay men have played key roles as creators, producers, and directors for some of the most watched shows. Key figures in this list are Greg Berlanti (*Dawson's Creek*; *Dirty, Sexy Money*; *Brothers and Sisters*), Ryan Murphy (*Glee*; *Nip/Tuck*), and Andy Cohen (*The Real Housewives* series; *Project Runway*). These prominent gay men have few lesbian counterparts. Lesbian women *are* working in television—Allison Adler's work on *Chuck* and *Glee* is an example—but they are fewer and less prominent.

Gay actors report having a very difficult time breaking into and succeeding in the film industry, although that is starting to change. In the essay "'I Saw You Naked': 'Hard' Acting in 'Gay' Movies," the actor Christopher Bradley discusses his struggles as a gay actor in the 1990s. His concerns were brought into focus one evening while he was working as a waiter at an event and was recognized by someone who remembered a nude scene that he had been in:

> I thought about the huge risk I'd taken in making that movie—being gay and starring in a gay independent film, something that just wasn't done at that time. A film with a nude love scene, no less. There were casting directors over the years who had refused to call me in just because they'd heard that I *might* be gay. If this risk didn't pay off, things were going to be far worse in that regard.
>
> I thought about the cover story interview I'd done for *Genre* magazine in which I'd spoken openly about being gay, when everyone would have understood (and even supported me) if I'd lied and said I had a girlfriend. How many actors have taken that route over the years? I thought about how my agent told me not to do *Leather Jacket Love Story* because it would ruin my career, and how I'd refused to budge. I thought about my bold plan to be the first gay actor to make it big while telling the truth right from the start, rather than after years of lying. (Bradley 2009, 42)

Although Bradley made a choice to be out and may have paid a price for it, many other gay and lesbian actors choose to keep quiet about their sexuality or to come out only after achieving significant success. In 2012 Matt Bomer and Jim Parsons, who both act on TV and in films, acknowledged their sexuality publicly. In both cases, the actors were said to have "come out," even though both were already open about their sexuality with their friends and families. The coming out in question was a matter of media acknowledgment, which also means standing up publicly as a gay figure. Christopher Bradley says things have become much easier in the new millennium: "I told this new manager I wasn't going to lie about it. She looked at me with some confusion and said, 'No one cares about that anymore.' Thirty years of tightness went out of my body" (2009, 52).

The emergence of gay- and lesbian-themed culture happened much earlier in the music industry, even if that industry still struggles to bring queer culture into the mainstream. Before the small art house music studios were swept up by the massive culture industry conglomerates, some gay and lesbian artists found safe havens in boutique recording studios. One such studio was Folkways Records, founded in New York City in 1948 by the recording engineer Moses Asch. As Cindy Boucher (2008) documents, Folkways produced four important gay- and lesbian-themed albums in the 1970s. Boucher argues that these albums were able to emerge in the 1970s, and not sooner, because of how the politics of the 1969 Stonewall Riots and the creation of the Gay Liberation Front helped to solidify queer community in America. Prior to the coming out of queer politics, gay and lesbian musicians hid their sexuality in innuendo and double entendre. Although other minority groups, from African Americans to working-class whites, were making protest songs several decades earlier, the only openly gay music existed in camp and parody songs, many produced in the 1960s by a company called Camp Records. But many of the musicians on Camp Records albums did not reveal their identities, which allowed the sexuality of the music to be out of the closet although the singer stayed in.

By contrast, the Folkways albums of the 1970s were openly gay, and most of them clearly identified the artists involved. The first was Michael Cohen's 1973 album *What Did You Expect? . . . Songs About the Experiences of Being Gay.* That is about as clear as an album title can be. The album is a mix of songs about gay romance and dating as well as protest songs against repressive Christianity. The 1979 Kathy Fire album *Songs of Fire: Songs of a Lesbian Anarchist* was even more radical and political, with songs like "Mother Rage" about lesbian pride and community among women. The other two albums were collaborations. *Walls to Roses: Songs of Changing Men* (Various Artists 1979) was an exploration of new ideas about masculinity, including many gay-themed songs such as the opening track, "Gay Spirit." *Gay and Straight Together* (Various Artists 1980) seemed to anticipate the creation of the national version of Parents and Friends of Lesbians and Gays (PFLAG) just one year later, as Boucher points out.*

If gay and lesbian artists in the 1970s had small labels like Folkways Records to find a voice, where do gay musicians turn today? Some go mainstream, usually hiding their sexuality until their careers are established. Others find a home in the dance music industry. The gay hip-hop artist Cazwell has been with the dance label West End Records since 2006. In comparison to the protest songs of the Folkways Records albums, Cazwell's songs tend to be more sexually charged and kitschy, such as his 2006 debut song "All Over Your Face" and his 2010 song "Ice Cream Truck." Cazwell has largely relied on YouTube to make his music videos available to his audience.

Although a number of artists have been out in the world of pop music, we are only now beginning to see more artists coming out in both hip-hop and country. Country singer Chely Wright came out in 2010. She was the first major country star to come out since K. D. Lang did so in 1992, and her experience is chronicled in the documentary *Wish Me Away* (Birleffi and Kopf 2011). In 2012 hip-hop artist Frank Ocean released a letter on his Tumblr account that detailed a same-sex relationship that had influenced his music, essentially revealing himself as gay or bisexual.† Ocean received more open support from the hip-hop community than Wright did from the country music community.

On rare occasions the corporations of the culture industry play a direct role in identity politics. Google is one company that has chosen to weigh in on gay politics, at the risk of alienating more conservative customers. It issued its position statement, "Legalize Love," in the summer of 2012.‡ The statement not only boasts of Google's sponsorship of gay pride events around the world, but also features a discussion of Gayglers, Google's network for LGBT

---

* Three of the four Folkway Records albums discussed here can be found on Spotify. Only Kathy Fire's is not available there. Some of her songs can be found on YouTube.

† http://frankocean.tumblr.com/post/26473798723.

‡ http://www.google.com/diversity/legalise-love.html.

Methodology Moment
PRODUCTION SURVEYS

Surveys allow us to ask important questions of a broad spectrum of people. Whereas interviews require sitting down with one person at a time, which also means adding in travel time and interview transcription time, surveys can often be conducted with far less human resource time, especially when done online. Very few surveys have been conducted that focus specifically on creative workers in the culture industries of film, television, publishing, music, and the Internet. This is because of the sense that workers in these industries are difficult to access, being geographically isolated in a small handful of cities and working for private corporations that do not make a lot of employee information publicly available. By comparison, most employees in small nonprofits are named on their organizations' websites, usually with contact information.

When it comes to issues of identity and inequality, there are two ways to approach conducting a survey of workplace experiences. The first is to survey a broad sample of workers, using demographic variables as a tool for comparing the experiences of different groups. For example, a survey researcher who is interested in how sexuality impacts job satisfaction may ask respondents to identify their sexual orientation in a set of demographic questions, perhaps along with age and race, then ask a series of questions about workplace experiences. This would allow for a comparison between straight employees and LGBT employees. The downside of this type of survey is that it does not allow us to find out much about a specific minority group, and often that group will represent only a small proportion of respondents. If gays, lesbians, and bisexuals only represent 5 percent of the population, then a survey of one hundred workers in a given industry may only have five respondents from the gay community. The data from those five respondents will be far less useful than the data from ninety-five straight respondents. Also, if we are asking gay and straight people to answer the same questions, then we have to account for the different ways they experience their sexual identity and the intervening role of privilege.

It may seem valid to ask a gay person: "What is it like to be lesbian, gay, or bisexual in your industry?" But a straight person could only speculate. The question is worded in a way that presumes a gay respondent. We could reword the question to make it more neutral: "How well does your industry handle issues of sexual identity diversity?" But heterosexual priv-

continues

ilege is likely to yield very different perceptions. Those differences are very interesting, but if most respondents are heterosexual, then their responses may skew the kind of conclusions reached by the survey.

The alternative approach is to design a survey about the experiences of the minority group within the industry. To continue the example at hand, that could be a survey about gay, lesbian, and bisexual experiences in an industry, or even a survey that just targeted one of those groups. This approach offers the possibility of building a sample that is entirely made up of the minority group, although it may also be quite difficult to build a large sample of an underrepresented group. It also offers the opportunity to ask a particular group detailed questions that would be irrelevant to the larger population. For example, you can ask gay people about their experience revealing their sexual identity to coworkers, but heterosexual people do not have to "come out" to coworkers. The pitfall of this approach is losing the chance to make comparisons between groups, such as comparing gay and straight workers.

One major survey that examines issues of sexuality in the workplace is the Out & Equal Workplace Survey, conducted collaboratively by Out & Equal Workplace Advocates, Witeck-Combs Communications, and Harris Interactive.* The survey follows the first approach discussed here, asking neutral questions of both straight and gay respondents, and the data are summarized in an online press release. They survey 2,775 workers, only 362 of whom identify as lesbian, gay, or bisexual. At 13 percent of respondents, gay people are actually overrepresented. They find important differences between gays and straights on a number of issues, including the importance given to nondiscrimination policies, the role of diversity in recruitment, and the extent of belief that employees are entitled to equal benefits regardless of sexuality. Just to highlight one of their findings, 92 percent of LGBT respondents agree with this statement: "How an employee does his or her job should be the standard for judging an employee, not their sexual orientation." By contrast, 78 percent of straight respondents agree with that statement. To be clear, a majority of both groups agree that performance matters in employee assessment, not sexuality, but many more LGBT people agree. So that is an interesting difference in worker perceptions.

---

* http://www.harrisinteractive.com/NewsRoom/PressReleases/tabid/446/ctl/Read Custom%20Default/mid/1506/ArticleId/577/Default.aspx.

continues

Methodology Moment: **PRODUCTION SURVEYS** *(continued)*

The Out & Equal Workplace Survey does not focus on a particular industry. If we were to focus a survey on creative workers within the culture industries, we would have the opportunity to expand our questions beyond workplace experience to broader questions about the influence of sexual identity on the process of creative production. How often do gay writers get the opportunity to include gay characters in their scripts? How much do gay songwriters think about the opinions of fans when deciding what kinds of songs to write or how open to be about their sexuality? Workers can tell us about the workplace, but they can also give us important information about the creative process.

employees. This kind of open stance about issues of sexual politics is relatively rare. Even conservative organizations that have supported antigay causes have tried to keep those activities relatively secret.

VIEWER DISCRETION

Little is known about how sexuality shapes the experiences of receiving and interpreting films. As with television, there is a long history of queer readings of film, but such readings have lent themselves more to the kind of episodic character development found in TV. Cultural studies scholars have presented their own queer readings of some films. James R. Keller's *Queer (Un)Friendly Film and Television* (2002) offers queer readings of *Gladiator* and *The Usual Suspects*, among others. Although we know that some queer audiences may become invested in queer readings and may be actively involved in constructing queer meanings for seemingly hetero films, we do not actually know that straight people are not just as interested in "discovering" queerness in straight films. Moreover, many gay audiences reject the notion that sexuality is the primary lens through which they choose and consume culture. After all, gays and lesbians are also people who are identified by their race, class, gender, and disability status. They are individuals and are also part of the collective social fabric.

We still have much to learn about how sexuality shapes audiences. Most of the attention paid to this issue has focused on queer interpretations of shows that seem to feature straight narratives. These are discussed in one segment of the excellent documentary *Off the Straight and Narrow*, which examines lesbian, gay, and bisexual images on television. Some queer interpretations involve reading into certain ambiguities about character relationships. Along these lines, Batman and Robin, Captain Kirk and Mister Spock, and Cagney and Lacey have all been read as secret queer couples. Other queer readings lean into the campiness of characters like Dominique Devereaux from *Dynasty*, described by a commentator in the documentary *Off the Straight and Narrow* as "TV's first black bitch!"

If queer readings offer a window into queer interpretations of straight story lines, then shows like *Will and Grace* offer an opportunity to understand how straight audiences comprehend gay story lines (see Image 5.3). Sociologist Evan Cooper (2003) has offered such an analysis, examining how his straight college students engage with the very different gay images presented by the characters Will and Jack, as well as the straight image of Grace and the widowed-but-somewhat-queer image of Karen. Cooper found, for example, that men are most likely to identify Grace as their favorite character, whereas women divide somewhat evenly among the characters, leaning somewhat more in favor of Jack. Yet both men and women identify Jack as the funniest

Image 5.3. The characters on *Will and Grace* provided many Americans with their first gay "friends" (SOURCE: EVERETT COLLECTION).

character. This indicates some level of discomfort among men with identify-ing a gay male as their favorite. Only 13.3 percent of men thought Grace was the funniest, whereas 44.2 percent said she was their favorite. Although 48.9 percent of men said Jack was the funniest, only 20.9 percent identified him as their favorite. Clearly, gender shapes the ways that men and women are able to engage with queerness on television.

Another sociologist, Thomas Linneman (2008), offers even further audi-ence analysis using the show *Will and Grace*. Linneman focuses on a very particular rhetorical element in the show—moments in which gay male characters are feminized linguistically using feminine pronouns and names. Linneman produced a thirteen-minute tape containing twenty-five clips of these sorts of references. He showed the tape to six focus groups: one drawn from a gay and lesbian youth group, one group of straight high school stu-dents, a group of gay and lesbian college students, a group of straight college students, a group of gay and lesbian adults, and a group of straight adults. He found three key responses to the feminizing moments presented in the clips. The first response was obliviousness, which he found in both straight and queer groups, but more often in the straight respondents. The second response was anger. This was also found in all groups, but seemed more pro-nounced in the gay and lesbian adults. The third response was acceptance. Gay, lesbian, *and straight* respondents indicated that gay men frequently fem-inize each other in everyday life and therefore felt that this plot element was a necessary reflection of the social world.

Sexuality, it seems, is one of many influences on the ways that we interpret the culture we consume. Business professor Gillian Oakenfull has studied the influence of gay identity on reactions to advertising. In a study published in 2007, she compared gay and lesbian responses to print advertisements that target gay consumers. Her research design allowed her to compare the expe-riences of gay men to lesbian women in a world that tends to privilege the gay male experience as *the* LGBT experience. She also examined what she calls "degrees of gayness," using Vanable and colleagues' "Identification and In-volvement with the Gay Community" scale (Vanable, McKirnan, and Stokes 1994), but modified in a way that accounted better for lesbian participation. Ranking her respondents on this scale, she then used the median scores to designate "high gay identity" and "low gay identity" gay men and lesbians. Categorizing her respondents in this way allowed her to compare within gay and lesbian groups to find additional audience differences.

Oakenfull showed respondents from all four of her groups (low and high gay identity men; low and high gay identity women) a set of three advertisements, all for alcoholic products. One of the ads relied on implicit imagery, using recognizable gay symbols (rainbow flag, pink triangle) and language (coming out) to signify the gay character of the ad and, by extension, of the target audience. One of the ads used explicit placement of lesbian women to signify gayness, while the third ad relied on explicit placement of gay men. Oakenfull hypothesized that the association of visual stimuli with male sexuality would lead gay men to prefer the ads featuring explicit imagery, and that the association of lesbian identity with gender politics would lead lesbian women to prefer implicit imagery. But the introduction of high and low gay identity made the study more complex. Oakenfull found that women of low gay identity generally preferred images with explicit lesbian imagery, whereas their high gay identity counterparts preferred images with implicit imagery. Men with low gay identity generally preferred images with implicit imagery, whereas their high gay identity counterparts preferred images with explicit gay imagery. The influence of level of gayness pointed in opposite directions for men and women.

Another study that examined the intersections of gender and sexuality is Mimi Schippers's (2000) ethnography of the world of alternative rock music. She studied the gendered and sexual interactions within the community of "active participants" in the alternative rock scene of Chicago. What makes this scene so interesting is that the participants have internalized a lot of messages from feminist and queer politics. Schippers notes that men avoid making overt comments about women and women's sexuality, and that there is a subculture norm of taking great offense to homophobia. Women, on the other hand, are much more comfortable making overt sexual statements, often about other women. Although none of the men or women in her study identified as gay, lesbian, or bisexual, Schippers identifies the women as queer because of the ways they sexualize each other as well as the ways they sexualize the music. Schippers provides a model for extending queer analysis to people other than gays, lesbians, and bisexuals.

Online, the construction of sexual identities becomes very complicated and very interesting. Sociologists Margaret Cooper and Kristina Dzara (2010) used participant observation to explore the ways that Facebook mediates the identity process for LGBT users, focusing on three key issues: identity construction, identity management and negotiation, and collective identity. They conclude that Facebook offers new possibilities for identity construction, especially for young people. Every aspect of a Facebook profile, from the initial "about" information to the ongoing status updates, is a form of identity construction. For LGBT users, this form of public identity construction also raises issues of sexual identity disclosure. A young person who wishes to be very open about sexual identity has a number of tools for making that identity very clear, from posting pictures to liking organizations, to using status updates to focus on gay-themed issues. But a young person wanting to limit sexual identity disclosure has to struggle with these same tools. He may be tagged unwittingly in a photograph that suggests his sexuality. He may have to think carefully about whose friend requests he accepts. He may have to delete comments from friends who are not sensitive to his disclosure concerns. This raises a host of issues for identity management. Cooper and Dzara list some hypothetical scenarios:

- Rob is "out" to friends in real life. He is not out on Facebook, however, because not all of his family members know. He plans a secret trip with his new boyfriend, who posts that he can't wait for their romantic European vacation.
- Sarah is also "out" in everyday life, but has not posted this, or any indicator of this, on Facebook, because she may face discrimination at work. Several coworkers have added her to their friends list. She states in a status update that she can't wait to go to a movie on Saturday night. One real-life friend posts, "Can't wait to meet your new lover!" Another friend posts, "You guys will like her! She's really nice!"
- Cary is out to friends and family, yet some of his family members are conservative and uncomfortable with public displays of affection between Cary and a partner. A friend of Cary's posts pics of him and his boyfriend in an embrace at a party. Another pic posted shows Cary's boyfriend in drag at a fund-raiser. (2010, 104–105)

Some readers may be wondering why Rob, Sarah, and Cary do not just update their privacy settings. But longtime Facebook users know that privacy settings have evolved over several years and have occasionally reset without warning to users. That means that LGBT Facebook users, like all kinds of teens in various ways, have to be very careful about disclosure even as they use social

Methodology Moment
AUDIENCE INTERVIEWS

Interviews provide an exciting way to probe deeply into the process by which audiences of consumer culture make meaning out of that culture, then act on that meaning in the social world. A social researcher wishing to use interviews needs to begin by formulating a clear research question that can be clearly answered by interviews. Let's consider a few possible questions:

Question 1: Are gay television characters placed in more prestigious roles than straight television characters?

This is a good research question, but it is best answered through examination of content, not audiences.

Question 2: Do gay audiences look more favorably than straight audiences on shows featuring major characters who are gay?

This is also a good research question, and it is best answered through a focus on audiences. However, this is not a question that needs to be answered through interviews. The researcher answering this question could devise a simple survey question and deploy the survey to a wide range of audience members. There is no need to answer this question by speaking face-to-face with one person at a time.

Question 3: How do straight audiences compare to queer audiences in terms of the kinds of television that they watch, the ways they make sense of television, and the ways they act on television?

This is an excellent research question for using interview methods. This would be very difficult to reduce to a set of survey questions. Even if a survey could be devised, the researcher would lose the opportunity to ask follow-up questions and probe respondents in depth.

Let's imagine creating a research proposal to answer this question. Note that the question, as phrased here, does not presume gay-themed television or even a particular genre of television. We are leaving it to the audience members to tell us about the kind of television they consume. Because we are interested in comparing gay and straight audiences, we are going to need to recruit respondents by their sexual identity. If we decide that we want equal numbers of gay men and lesbian women, then we will

continues

also want to recruit equal numbers of straight men and straight women. That will allow us to investigate the intervening role of gender.

How many people from each group do we need to recruit? Obviously just one or two from each group is far too few. How can we make claims about gay male TV watchers based on just two gay male respondents? Even a pool as large as twenty will give us limited capacity to make claims about the much larger population, but it lets us make *much* safer claims than a pool of just two. If we decide that twenty in each category is a good number, that actually means recruiting eighty respondents. If our interviews are an hour each, that is going to mean eighty hours of interview time, and those interviews have to be transcribed. When I first began conducting interviews in graduate school, I learned that each hour of interviews would be followed by six to eight hours of transcribing. At that time (I completed my PhD in 2004, so we are not talking about ancient history), transcription meant listening to the playback of an audio recording and pausing frequently to type up whatever was heard, then reviewing the document for errors. Now, thanks to much improved dictation and transcription software, the transcription process for an hour of interviews can take an hour or less. Still, eighty hours of interviews plus transcription time will add up very quickly. That level of work seems appropriate for a collaborative project among a few researchers or for a graduate student dissertation or a faculty member's ongoing project. But eighty interviews is probably too many for a smaller project by a single scholar. We may need to reduce the number of people in each category to fifteen or ten. For now, we will work with fifteen. We can illustrate our desired respondent pools with Table 5.1.

TABLE 5.1. Sample Respondent Pool			
	Male	Female	Total
Gay	15	15	30
Straight	15	15	30
Total	30	30	60

continues

Methodology Moment: AUDIENCE INTERVIEWS *(continued)*

As a shorthand, sociologists often talk about the number of people they need for each "cell" of their research, referring to the cells in a table like this one. Now, how do we find these people? Because straight people significantly outnumber gay people, we cannot simply dial random telephone numbers and hope to get a good balance of gay and straight. We may need to reach out to a gay organization to see if its e-mail listserv can be used to recruit additional gay respondents, or we could post requests for participants in gay and straight coffee shops. It is important not to rely on personal networks to find respondents. We are studying the larger social world, not just our own microcosm within that world.

Before we sit down with our participants, we need to devise a list of interview questions that are directly connected to the research question. It can be tempting to make a long list of questions that we want to ask, but if we want respondents to answer our questions in depth, assuming we have limited time with them, we have to limit ourselves to a few broad questions. Our main research question divides neatly into three sets of questions: (1) about television consumption, (2) about television interpretation (meaning-making), and (3) about social action. So our interview questions might look like these:

Question 1: Please list the television shows that you watch and how often you watch them.
  Prompt: Any other genres of shows that you like?
  Prompt: Are there other shows that you watch during the off-season?
  Prompt: What about morning or daytime shows?

Question 2: For you, what makes a TV show "good"?
  Prompt: What about the characters?
  Prompt: What about the themes?
  Prompt: What about the genre?

Question 3: Can you think of a time when something you saw on TV helped you decide how to act on an issue in real life?
  Prompt: Has TV ever influenced the way you act at work?
  Prompt: Has TV ever influenced the way you act in a relationship?
  Prompt: Has TV ever influenced the way you think about social or political issues?

continues

Methodology Moment: AUDIENCE INTERVIEWS (*continued*)

If we were to carry out this interview, I suspect that these three questions, with three prompts apiece, would actually generate a lot of information from each respondent. Once the interviews were complete, we would analyze the transcripts looking for key differences between demographics (gay/straight, male/female), as well as interesting similarities. We should also look for important differences within our demographic categories.

media to practice with identity construction and the presentation of self. Finally, Cooper and Dzara point out that many LGBT young people use causes and likes and other formats on Facebook to align with LGBT activism, finding collective identity in addition to creating individual identity. This can be particularly powerful for young people who are isolated from such activity by geography.

WRAP-UP

Jamey Rodemeyer did not live his life in the closet. The world of popular culture—from Lady Gaga's music to the It Gets Better campaign on You-Tube—gave Jamey the tools to leave the closet behind at a very young age. But the world of popular culture also provided Jamey's tormentors with the tools they needed to keep rebuilding that closet, if not around Jamey, then around their own notions of sexuality. Even with a growing emergence of gay characters in film and television, gay popular culture is still pressed into a closet in many ways. Gay visibility is allowed only to a few, who are often white, male, and economically privileged. Gay musicians continue to turn away from mainstream music to find accepting and eager audiences. Gay Facebook users find that the Internet provides as many tools for coming out as it does for "staying in." The metaphor of the closet continues to haunt gay, lesbian, and bisexual representations in popular culture. It continues to be a very real and powerful force for gay, lesbian, and bisexual workers in the culture industries. The closet still matters for audiences, too, but they at least are reminding us that there are many far more interesting metaphors for gay life that popular culture needs to draw from. Gay audiences, through the act of queer readings, are taking the raw materials of Hollywood, New York, Nashville, and our other cultural production centers around the world and twisting these resources into new imaginings, not only of the gay experience, but also of the human experience.

RESOURCES

Resources for Examining Sexuality in the Social World

- The Trevor Project: http://www.thetrevorproject.org.
- It Gets Better: http://www.itgetsbetter.org.
- Films: *Before Stonewall* (1984) and *After Stonewall* (1999), from First Run Features.

Resources for Examining Sexuality in Popular Culture

- No Homophobes, a website that tracks homophobic language on Twitter: http://www.nohomophobes.com/#!/today.
- AfterElton, a website of gossip and media posts about gay representations in popular culture: http://www.afterelton.com.
- AfterElton's Top 50 Gay Men in Music: http://www.afterelton.com/people /2011/02/top-50-gay-musicians.
- AfterEllen, a website of gossip and media posts about lesbian representations in popular culture: http://www.afterellen.com.
- GLAAD, the Gay and Lesbian Alliance Against Defamation, posts a variety of media resources on its website. Perhaps the most useful is the annual Network Responsibility Index. http://www.glaad.org.
- Video: *Off the Straight and Narrow: Lesbians, Gays, Bisexuals and Television, 1967–1998*, from the Media Education Foundation.
- Video: *Further Off the Straight and Narrow: New Gay Visibility on Television, 1998–2006*, from the Media Education Foundation.
- Video: *The Celluloid Closet*, from Sony Pictures.
- Video: *Fabulous!: The Story of Queer Cinema*, from IFC.

6

Image 6.1. Tod Browning's 1932 film *Freaks* featured many characters who would now be considered disabled (Source: Everett Collection).

WE ACCEPT HER, ONE OF US

Pinhead. According to the *Online Slang Dictionary*, it means "an unintelligent person."* Know any pinheads?

Arguably the most famous pinhead in contemporary American culture is Zippy the Pinhead, from a comic strip that first appeared in the 1970s and has been a syndicated staple of the comic page since the 1980s (see Image

---

* http://onlineslangdictionary.com/meaning-definition-of/pinhead.

Image 6.2. The comic strip *Zippy* featured a pinhead clown who made cunning pop culture commentary (Source: King Features Syndicate).

6.2). Zippy is known for his heavy consumption of popular culture and for the cultural commentary he delivers through non sequiturs, usually in conversation with his friend Griffy, a sort of stand-in for the cartoonist, Bill Griffith.* Zippy wears clown shoes and a polka-dotted muumuu and has a striking head shape and size characteristic of people with microcephaly. *Microcephaly*, also known as microencephaly, is a developmental disorder that is characterized by reduced head and brain circumference. Beyond his appearance, Zippy is known for making hilarious commentary that is nevertheless illogical or senseless. Zippy is "an unintelligent person" who sees right through the fog of contemporary popular culture. His pinhead wit is written for the very intelligent reader.

Zippy the Pinhead's character is based, at least in part, on a man named Schlitze Surtees, a circus sideshow performer who also worked in films. Schlitze, as he is commonly known—his birth name is uncertain and he only took the surname Surtees in his thirties when a chimpanzee trainer adopted him—was a person with microcephaly who is believed to have been born in 1901. He began his work in circuses as a child and moved from one to the next throughout his life. He was billed as a missing link and as the "Last of the Aztecs." He was often dressed in a muumuu and presented as a woman.

Schlitze's most famous role was as himself in the 1932 film *Freaks*, directed by Tod Browning (see Image 6.3). *Freaks* takes viewers into the social world

---

* http://www.zippythepinhead.com.

Image 6.3. Schlitze (left) with Rose Dione and Daisy Earles in a scene from *Freaks* (1932) (Source: Everett Collection).

of circus performers, secretive and fiercely protective of each other against the harsh judgment of the outside world. Circus performers, as people who travel constantly and always perform in other people's communities, are perpetual strangers in the truest sense of Georg Simmel's essay. But within this secretive social world, according to the film, there is also a divide between the sideshow freaks and the normals who perform in other ways—such as the strong man or the trapeze artists. The freaks must be even more guarded than everyone else and must carefully guard the boundaries of their social world. They do not let others in easily or casually.

The story in *Freaks* is that a beautiful trapeze artist named Cleopatra discovers that a dwarf performer named Hans has a sizeable inheritance and decides that she wants to get her hands on it. Hans is in love with Frieda, another dwarf performer, but he is soon won over by the attentions of Cleopatra and leaves Frieda to marry Cleopatra. At the wedding feast, the circus freaks—Schlitze among them—perform a ceremony to welcome Cleopatra into their world, singing, "We accept her, one of us, we accept her, one of us, gooble gobble, gooble gobble, one of us, one of us," while passing around a "loving cup," from which Cleopatra will drink last to solidify her new place in this world. But Cleopatra is horrified at the thought of becoming a freak and instead throws the wine back at them and yells "Freaks!" This begins the undoing of Cleopatra's secret plan to seize Hans's money, and together the freaks begin to plan their revenge.

The freaks in the film were professional circus performers. Tod Browning made a bold decision to hire actual sideshow performers rather than cast Hollywood actors in freakish makeup. That allowed these circus performers to play a role in how their own story was told. Today many of these freaks would be identified as disabled. In the world of the Americans with Disabilities Act (ADA), passed in 1990, such people are unlikely to work as circus performers and are much more likely to participate in the educational and occupational institutions of American society.

Freaks tells a story about disability from before there was such a thing as "disability." The concept has not been around forever. It is a socially constructed idea that is really quite arbitrary. This aspect of disability is discussed more below.

What does *Freaks* teach us about these people who live and work in the freak show? We learn that they live complex and multidimensional lives. They work, love, marry, and raise children. They have an intricate social world that reveals how well they understand the larger social world around them. But as the story unfolds, we also learn that they are vengeful and sinister and can be the stuff of horror movie nightmares.

Freaks has been the inspiration for much more than *Zippy the Pinhead*. In 1977 the punk rock band the Ramones released the album *Leave Home*, which included the song "Pinhead." Videos of their performances of "Pinhead" can be found on YouTube. The lyrics are simple and catchy. With its very title, the song makes a reference to the pinheads of Freaks, of which Schlitze was the most prominent, and it also draws in the key line of indoctrination from the wedding feast in the first line: "Gabba gabba we accept you, we accept you one of us."

The song's message is confusing, because it is explicitly accepting, as this first line indicates, yet includes lines about not wanting to be a pinhead, "I don't want to be a pinhead no more," and the phrase "D-U-M-B, / Everyone's accusing me." But it is a song that is perhaps best experienced rather than closely parsed. As sociologist Donna Gaines explains in *A Misfit's Manifesto* (2003), the Ramones offered a message of acceptance to anyone who felt like a freak and a misfit. She has discovered a host of fans from many generations who say that the Ramones saved their lives. Anyone who identifies with Schlitze or the other freaks might turn to the music of the Ramones for solace, acceptance, friendship, and the right to celebrate that "Life's a Gas"—the title of one of their songs.

Another incarnation of *Freaks* is found in the television show *American Horror Story: Asylum*, the second installment in the *AHS* franchise. The character Pepper, a patient and resident at Briarcliff Mental Institution, is deliberately crafted after Schlitze. The actress Naomi Grossman methodically transformed her appearance for each episode, giving herself the appearance of a person with microcephaly. Her performance has received rave reviews. The comparison between Schlitze and Pepper must be noted. Schlitze the actor was a microcephalic person who played the role of a microcephalic person, giving the role a strong dose of reality. Naomi Grossman is a person who is not disabled who uses makeup and performance to play the role of a microcephalic person.

Should people who are not disabled play disabled roles? This is very much an open and controversial question. The craft of acting implies that humans can perform roles that are very different from their own lives. But do actors who are disabled bring more depth to a disabled role than those who are not? If nondisabled actors play these roles, does that take away work for disabled actors? Do actors who are disabled have the opportunity to play nondisabled roles?

Schlitze died in 1971 at the age of seventy. He continued performing until the very end of his life.*

THE SOCIAL MODEL OF DISABILITY

Schlitze's performance and his life are part of the web of meaning that American culture has sewn around the concept of disability. These representations tell stories with both explicit and implicit conclusions about people who have disabilities, their lives, and their place in American culture. Max Weber, though not a theorist of disability, is the classical sociologist who gave us the most

---

* http://thehumanmarvels.com/130/schlitzie-the-pinhead/pinhead.

direct methodological discussion of the issue of meaning. In much of social science, meaning is treated as a subjective value system that should be set aside during moments of sociological analysis. But the opening sections of Weber's two-volume work *Economy and Society* insist that we must take meaning seriously and that our scientific assessment of the social world requires an account of the systems of meaning through which we engage the world: "[I]t is the task of the sociologist to be aware of this motivational situation and to describe and analyze it, even though it has not actually been concretely part of the conscious intention of the actor; possibly not at all, at least not fully" (Weber 1978, 10). As humans, we live and act within complex meaning systems, which include religion, politics, economic systems, and even popular culture.

Weber would be the first to teach us not to take the word *disability* at its face value. We cannot simply say that it refers to a specific list of physical conditions. Instead, it is loaded with meanings that need to be analyzed, historicized, and disentangled. **Interpretive sociology**, which is a paradigm developed by Weber and is continued today within the subfield of cultural sociology, focuses on taking meaning seriously and examining how meanings shape social dynamics. The interpretive approach to disability focuses on where and how the word is deployed and the kinds of meanings that are carried in that deployment. Popular culture is certainly one of the places where the meaning of disability is constructed.

Sociologists think about disability in a unique way that is very different from how it is often understood, especially in the media and public discussions. The usual understanding of disability is that it refers to a physical or intellectual impairment that causes suffering and merits medical treatment. This is called the **medical model of disability**, because it views disability primarily through a medical framework. The medical model does not ignore the negative social experiences associated with disability, but it does treat them as consequences of physical and intellectual conditions.*

Those sociologists who study disability often examine the issue through a lens known as the **social model of disability**. This model treats disability as a consequence of social inequalities and understands the concept of disability as a form of **social construction**. Put simply, this approach claims that the meaning of social life is not inherent to our experiences, but rather

---

* This paragraph and the remainder of this section are revised from a chapter I contributed to another book (Kidd 2012).

is constructed in ways that are fluid, often ambiguous, and usually quite powerful. So what it means for someone to be disabled depends on how society constructs and approaches the idea of disability and how society selects which kinds of physical experiences determine who is disabled. The problem that sometimes occurs with the social model is that it can ignore physical conditions and even ignore the body altogether. However, sociologists like Carol Thomas, the director of the Centre for Disability Research at Lancaster University in the United Kingdom, are working to transform the social model so that it is capable of acknowledging physical conditions. Thomas defines disability in a way that focuses on the social condition of people with impairments: "[O]nce the term 'disability' is ring-fenced to mean forms of oppressive social reaction visited upon people with impairments, there is no need to deny that impairments and illness cause some restrictions of activity—in whole or in part" (2004, 579).

Peter Conrad, one of the major sociologists who studies the history and meanings of medicine, defines *medicalization* as "defining a problem in medical terms, using medical language to describe a problem, adopting a medical framework to understand a problem, or using a medical intervention to 'treat' it" (1992, 211). Some of the most striking work in this field focuses on ailments that are initially not viewed in medical terms but come to be understood through a medical framework at specific points in history. Attention deficit disorder (ADD), for example, refers to behavior that presumably occurred among children for most of human history but only came to be "medicalized" when (1) the social life of children conflicted with that behavior, and (2) the medical field was able to understand and treat the behavior.

One of the key issues is understanding the medical field itself. Although health practitioners can be found in many societies and throughout history—including healers, witch doctors, and modern surgeons—only in the modern era are those practitioners part of a distinctly medical field. In earlier times these healers were often part of the religious system, and no medical system was present. Having a medical field has required the development of medical education, the credentialization of doctors, and the creation of a profession through organizations like the American Medical Association (AMA).

To bring Weber and Conrad together, we can say that although the meaning of disability is not fixed in place, it is nevertheless socially situated. It is not individuals who determine what disability is—neither individual disabled people nor individual doctors—it is rather social institutions that do this meaning-making work. Physical conditions may be experienced by the individual and often in private settings, but the meanings of disability are social and public. We work together, consciously and unconsciously, to construct these meanings. Like all forms of culture, the meanings of disability are passed from one generation to the next through specific mechanisms of cultural transmission. Popular culture has become the strongest mechanism of cultural transmission in the contemporary era because of its sheer ubiquity. What are the stories of disability that we tell ourselves through the commercial culture of this age?

DISABILITY IN THE SOCIAL WORLD

What kind of word is *disability*? Is that an odd question? We often think of disability as a medical term. The logic goes like this: particular medical conditions, generally of a chronic or permanent character, place some individuals within the category of disabled. That seems right. Right?

But of course we do not really imagine a doctor saying, "My diagnosis is that you are disabled." Doctors do not diagnose disability; they diagnose specific ailments and conditions. So why are some ailments and conditions, and not others, assigned the label *disabled*? Perhaps it is a matter of duration. Short-term illnesses and injuries are exempt, but long-term conditions are disabling. But that explanation does not hold water. I have had asthma all of my life, and no one has ever suggested that I am disabled.

It becomes tempting to think of disability as a cultural term, with a level of arbitrariness in its definition. Shifting social boundaries move certain types of bodies into or out of a social category called "disabled," a word that seems to refer to one's physical means of achieving the cultural goals of the society. I am referring again to Robert Merton's ideas in "Social Structure and Anomie" (1938). If our bodies make it harder, or impossible, to attain the American dream, then that would seem to make us disabled. If the cultural goals shift in a way that our bodies are no longer an impediment, then perhaps we are no longer disabled. Under this cultural approach, defining disability would seem to be a matter of making a list of those conditions that have been socially labeled as disabled. A short version of the list could include blindness, deafness, paralysis of one or more limbs, loss of one or more limbs, and certain cognitive disorders. These physical circumstances have almost nothing in common, yet they are lumped together as a category of human identity. Seems like an odd cultural practice.

If disability is cultural, and not medical, how do we count the number of people who have disabilities? We can ask doctors about medical categories, but whom do we ask about cultural categories? This is where disability becomes especially interesting and especially complicated. The reality is that disability is a political and bureaucratic category. The government needs a count of who might qualify for disability benefits and what kinds of health resources are needed in particular communities. So our demographic information on disability comes from the US Census Bureau. Although the decennial census asked about disability through the year 2000, the 2010 census did not include disability. However, the American Community Survey, also conducted by the Census Bureau, does ask about disability. According to the disability report from 2010, disability is defined by the census using the broad definitions listed in Table 6.1. The ACS identifies both disabilities and severe disabilities. For example, difficulty reading is a disability; blindness is a severe disability.

TABLE 6.I. Overview of Disability Types as Categorized in the 2010 American Community Survey	
People who have disability in the communicative domain reported one or more of the following.	1. Were blind or had difficulty seeing. 2. Were deaf or had difficulty hearing. 3. Had difficulty having their speech understood.
People who have disability in the mental domain reported one or more of the following.	1. Had a learning disability; an intellectual disability; developmental disability; or Alzheimer's disease, senility, or dementia. 2. Had some other mental or emotional condition that seriously interfered with everyday activities.
People who have disability in the physical domain reported one or more of the following.	1. Used a wheelchair, cane, crutches, or walker. 2. Had difficulty walking a quarter of a mile, climbing a flight of stairs, lifting something as heavy as a 10-pound bag of groceries, grasping objects, or getting in or out of bed. 3. Listed arthritis or rheumatism, back or spine problem, broken bone or fracture, cancer, cerebral palsy, diabetes, epilepsy, head or spinal cord injury, heart trouble or atherosclerosis, hernia or rupture, high blood pressure, kidney problems, lung or respiratory problem, missing limbs, paralysis, stiffness or deformity of limbs, stomach/digestive problems, stroke, thyroid problem, or tumor/cyst/growth as a condition contributing to a reported activity limitation.

(SOURCE: BRAULT 2012.)

According to the 2010 ACS, 18.7 percent of Americans identify as having a disability, and 12.6 percent identify as having a severe disability. *Nearly one-fifth of Americans are disabled! Over one-tenth are severely disabled!*

Here we see the divide between a cultural definition and a political definition. Culturally, disability is treated as unusual or extreme. A disabled person is treated as anything but normal. The political and bureaucratic approach to disability used by the Census Bureau shows that disability is in fact very normal. This chapter explores how the disjuncture between the cultural perceptions and the political realities of disability has shaped the production, content, and audience of popular culture.

THE VISIBILITY OF DISABILITY

Isolation is the word most frequently used to explain how characters with disabilities are represented in popular culture. The most prominent use of the term is in the title of Martin Norden's historical account of disability in film, *The Cinema of Isolation* (1994). The isolation imposed on disabled characters takes many forms. In some cases the character is presented as so inhuman that he simply cannot be part of human social life. In others the character is seen as having or being a virus that can taint the rest of the population, and therefore she must be quarantined from the social world. A third version is self-imposed isolation. The disability is presented as having psychic consequences, regardless of the nature of the disability itself, and this psychosis leads the disabled character into a life of solitude. This solitude is sometimes treated as an act of kindness toward the world and sometimes as a critique and rejection of the world.

As Norden points out in the introduction to *The Cinema of Isolation*, the "typical moviemaker use of disability" is "to suggest some element of a person's character" (1994, 5). The literary term for this is *physiognomy*: the notion that we wear our internal selves on our external bodies in some way, such that a scar, a mole, or a limp is emblematic of a regret, an anxiety, or a weakness of character.

While Norden offers a thorough and critical analysis of filmic mis/representations of disability, I find Fiona Whittington-Walsh's (2002) study to be particularly useful for grouping these representations into a set of sociological codes. Whittington-Walsh draws from existing studies, including Norden's, as well as her own close examination of *Freaks*. Whereas *Freaks* has been critiqued by Norden and others as yet another terrible misrepresentation of persons with disabilities, Whittington-Walsh takes a very different view: "I argue what truly offends, shocks audiences and critics alike, and the reason for the film's continued banishment is not only the visibility of the actors with disabilities, but also the fact that Browning and his actors found no shame in showcasing their diversity" (696). For Whittington-Walsh, *Freaks* is an exemplar of an ideal "mode of representation" that she holds up against more common modes. The mode in *Freaks* provides a multidimensional representation of the social world of the person with a disability. *Freaks* highlights the intensely protective social world of the disabled performers themselves, even as it also shows the many ways that they participate in, construct, and are rejected by the broader social fabric. Although *Freaks* demonstrates that a discriminatory society pushes disabled people toward isolation, the film also shows that such isolation is never fully realized. The "freaks" are at least not isolated from one another.

Whittington-Walsh contrasts the *Freaks* mode of representation with five other styles: savants, isolation and pathology, self-sacrifice, asexual and dependent, and violent. The trope of the savant emphasizes the special talents that a person with a disability may have. Although it seems positive to characterize any person as talented, there is a particular aspect of this kind of talent that taints the representation. The talent of the savant is presented as abnormal, paranormal, or even supernormal—freakish indeed—which makes it very clear that the person in question is absolutely not "normal." In film, savant talents have ranged from the mathematical prowess of Dustin Hoffmann's character in *Rain Man* to Quasimodo's beautiful bell-ringing in *The Hunchback of Notre Dame*.

The trope of isolation and pathology draws on the same basic concepts as those highlighted by Norden's work—the idea that people with disabilities are withdrawn and are not socialized into society and that the root cause of their difference is biological, which means that they have a fundamentally different kind of body from nondisabled persons. Isolation and pathology may seem like two distinct issues, but they are inextricably linked, because "normal," nondisabled humans are presented as inherently social creatures, and the antisocial isolationism of the disabled is portrayed as a consequence of pathological difference. Whittington-Walsh gives the example of Karl in the film *Sling Blade*, who moves between living in various garages and confinement in mental institutions, never living fully with others in a family home.

The trope of self-sacrifice may initially seem positive. Sacrificing oneself for others is considered a virtue in Western society, though we also often speak of self-made martyrs in a negative way. In the case of the filmic trope of the self-sacrificing disabled person, the implication is that this person only becomes virtuous and socially worthy precisely in that moment when she sacrifices herself for someone else, sometimes even dying. As Whittington-Walsh points out, these characters are only allowed to sacrifice for the benefit of others, not "for their own emancipation" (2002, 702). That message highlights the second-tier status accorded to disabled characters in many films.

The trope of asexuality and dependence highlights the fact that those with disabilities are not presented as capable of full maturity, sexual or otherwise. They are often presented as childlike and perpetually dependent upon their families for care. Whittington-Walsh says that the asexuality of disabled characters is partly a function of the fact that most disabled representations are male, and the sexual objectification of women seen in film does extend to disabled women.

Finally, the trope of violence in disabled representations provides a lens for thinking of those who are disabled as essentially untrustworthy. In much the same way that we often say a wild animal cannot be tamed, many filmic portrayals of disability convey the notion that disabled people simply cannot be fully socialized into the human world, despite whatever strength of character they may achieve through their self-sacrifices and special talents.

Sharon Snyder and David Mitchell (2010) shift the comparison from different modes of representation to different genres. They compare comedy, horror, and melodramatic films as different types of "body genres," arguing that in comedies, the disabled representation often comes through a "faked impairment," whereas disability in horror is a matter of "inborn monstrosity," and in melodrama it focuses on "maimed capacity" (188). Although Snyder and Mitchell are largely critical of filmic representations of disability, they do identify two genres that offer some alternative notions. First, they celebrate the fact that many science fiction/comic book films "dramatize a canny awareness about a social model of disability" (192). Though such films maintain a strong boundary between disabled/superhero and nondisabled/nonhero, the boundary is more clearly social, and its consequences are manipulated by the politics of the setting. Second, Snyder and Mitchell praise disability documentary cinema, not only for giving greater voice to disabled perspectives but also for shedding light on the "meaningful influence that disability has upon one's subjectivity and even cinematic technique itself" (194). Snyder and Mitchell take an important step further than many other scholars of filmic portrayals of disability, because they go beyond the reflection question of how disabled people appear in the mirror of film into the realm of production itself and the possibilities of disabled cinema.

Disability is relatively invisible on television. One study by Dennis Ganahl and Mark Arbuckle (2001) focused on the appearance of persons with visible impairments in prime time advertising. Analyzing two years of advertising, they found that only 0.5 percent of commercials showed persons with disabilities.

In my analysis of prime time programming for 2010–2011, I found that 4.7 percent of roles represented persons with disabilities. This is far more than the 0.5 percent found in ads, but is far less than the 18.7 percent of Americans who claim disabilities in the 2010 ACS. Disabled characters are primarily white and almost all straight.

Finding disability on television is actually quite difficult. Disability is a nebulous concept off-screen and becomes trickier on-screen. The question of what kinds of bodies count as disabled has never been settled. From a medical perspective, disability is an empty concept, because physicians treat specific conditions, not "disability." No one is ever diagnosed with disability; we are diagnosed with conditions or impairments, and it is left to nonmedical authorities to determine which count as disabilities. The primary authority that identifies disability is the government, which has created broad categories. These impairments become meaningful politically when they limit access to important social interactions and the capacity to work.

On television, it is difficult to tell when those conditions are met. Some characters are quickly identified as disabled when they use wheelchairs, when they are blind or deaf, or when we are told that they have a cognitive disability such as Down syndrome. But many physical representations on television are not so easy to label. I was hesitant to think of overweight people as disabled, but the participants in NBC's *The Biggest Loser* tell a different tale. Their discussions of their lives at home and work, and their interactions with the show's doctor, reveal that their weight has significantly limited their movement, interactions, and work potential. In fact, obesity accounts for most of the disabled representations on television.

It is no surprise then that 13.8 percent of reality show roles are held by disabled persons, given the high number of participants on *The Biggest Loser*. By comparison, 2.1 percent of characters on sitcoms are disabled, and 3.2 percent of characters on dramas are disabled. On dramas, people with disabilities are typically either patients in medical dramas or criminals in crime dramas. Crime dramas often present narratives of disabled people who are driven to criminality by their impairments. In animation, 8.6 percent of characters are disabled. They are a mix of one-off characters who may be the brunt of jokes and regular characters who are treated more sympathetically. (See "Disability Demographics by TV Genre.")

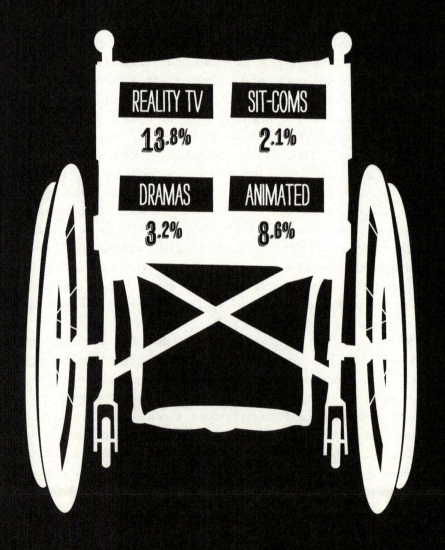

Disability provides some of the major tropes for the genre of science fiction, which appears in various formats, including books, comics, film, and television. Lydia Fecteau (2004) points out that the mutant, a transformed biological entity, appears throughout science fiction. As she explains, the relationship between science and warfare in the twentieth century gave rise to new imaginings of transformed humanity. Nuclear war, in particular, influenced the creation of many mutants in science fiction. Examples include *Omega Man, Night of the Living Dead*, and *28 Days Later*. The characters in the *X-Men* series represent the most direct and deliberate treatment of mutants as a new class of humans.

Another science fiction character that seems to map onto the issue of disability is the cyborg. Cyborgs are blends of humans and machines. They are robots with intelligence and feelings. Any disabled person using assistive technology, including new advanced forms of prostheses, might be seen as a cyborg of some sort. Consider the famous track athletes who compete on blades, such as (now infamous) Oscar Pistorius. In *Star Trek: The Next Generation*, the character Geordie LaForge represents a type of cyborg. The character Data, by comparison, is an android who is human-like but entirely nonhuman. Cyborgs and mutants are generally presented as strong positive characters who expand our understanding of the human experience. For this reason, science fiction has often been seen as a positive genre for representations of disability.

In music, we find that much in music theory and performance intertwines with issues of disability. Musicologist Joseph N. Straus (2006) examines the basic elements of classical music theory and finds that notions of musical form are deeply connected to ideas about the body:

> There are two persistent strains in studies of musical form, reaching back to the end of the eighteenth century and becoming increasingly pronounced over the course of the nineteenth. The first is the conception of musical form as a CONTAINER, an arrangement of bounded spaces that contain musical content (themes and/or harmonies). FORM IS A CONTAINER is an embodied image schema. Through it we understand that musical form can speak to us of human bodies, and that musical forms, like human bodies, may be well-formed or deformed. The possibility of formal deformation links this conception of musical form to the history of disability.
>
> A second strain in form studies is the sense that form is a norm, a normative or conventional arrangement of musical elements. In this sense, forms may be normal or abnormal. FORM IS A NORM is not an embodied

image schema, but the possibility of formal abnormality links this conception also to the history of disability. (126–127)

Both musical history and the evolving conception of disability reveal a cultural fascination with idealized forms and notions of deformity.

Shifting from classical to popular music, we should note the centrality of "freaks" in rock music and rock's younger cousins, such as punk and postpunk. David Church (2006) explores this through a study of Ian Curtis, the lead singer of Joy Division. Before he became a music star, Curtis held a bureaucratic job assisting people with disabilities in the United Kingdom. He was diagnosed with epilepsy right as Joy Division was developing its first album. His onstage performances increasingly became performances of seizures. As his condition worsened, he was known to have actual seizures on stage. Church refers to this as the "freakery" of rock, a deliberate appropriation of the freak show as a model of rock 'n' roll rebelliousness. Incorporating the seizure into the performance added a level of authenticity—or at least perceived authenticity. Sociologist Gary Alan Fine (2004) argues that the quest for authenticity is behind the success of "outsider art"—art that is made by self-taught artists. Curtis was diagnosed with epilepsy in 1978. Joy Division released its first album in 1979. Curtis committed suicide by hanging in May 1980, just two months before the release of Joy Division's second album. Church's final assessment of Curtis's life and death is that Ian Curtis was ultimately exploited by the nondisabled music industry and audience in much the same way that sideshow performers were exploited by the circuses and their visitors. An alternative perspective is that Curtis embraced his disability to remain a freak within an otherwise homogenizing culture machine.

Methodology Moment
THICK DESCRIPTION

The direct inheritor of Max Weber's interpretive sociology is, surprisingly, an anthropologist. Clifford Geertz's *The Interpretation of Cultures* (1973) expands on Weber's introduction to interpretive sociology to generate a more fully developed interpretive method. He calls this method **thick description**, because it involves capturing meaningful detail and

continues

preserving as many layers of detail as possible. Geertz's thick description has four components:

1. Thick description is interpretive. Its focus is on layers of meaning that must be understood. We cannot simply describe what we see at the surface level. Instead, we must capture how we feel and trust our gut when it tells us that something we see may actually mean something much deeper or more complex.

2. Thick description focuses on social discourse. Literary criticism, history, and other forms of the humanities have a lot in common with thick description in their focus on interpretation, but the key difference is that for the cultural scholar who is following the interpretive paradigm, the *text* that is being examined is society itself. A social scientist engaging in thick description may be very interested in cultural objects like books or television shows or films, but the focus is not strictly on the content of the cultural object. Instead, the analysis of that content is always used as a way of interpreting the larger social world. Interpretive scholars watch television not to understand the internal poetics of television as a genre, but rather to make sense of the role that television plays in constructing wider meaning systems.

3. Thick description captures and preserves detail that would otherwise disappear as a moment passes. The institutions that preserve meaning are not just large formal ones like religion and education. Many of the most important components of culture are formed through everyday norms, or what we might call informal institutions. These rules are never written down, but they are tremendously important just the same. The method of thick description pushes the ethnographic observer to record these moments and the rules that they imply. This recording and preserving of such ephemeral details makes them available for scholarly analysis.

4. Thick description is microscopic. Or rather, it begins from the microscopic and uses these microlevel events to make sense of the macro: social structure, economic order, history, and so forth. In the case of popular culture, this means watching individual episodes and films, listening to individual tracks, reading individual novels, or participating in individual online forums to understand how these fleeting

continues

Methodology Moment: THICK DESCRIPTION *(continued)*

cultural moments contribute to the construction of a larger cultural system. Meaning is not constructed in any single powerful moment; it is constructed through millions of passing cultural moments: a look on a character's face when something is said, a joke expressed in five words, a line in a song right before the bass kicks in.

The job of the interpretive social scientist—whether a sociologist like Weber or an anthropologist like Geertz—is to capture these everyday moments in rich detail and describe their larger significance through a thorough understanding of their social context.

DISABLING PRODUCTION

People with disabilities are heavily underrepresented in the labor force for popular culture, although we have very limited data on the subject. According to the Bureau of Labor Statistics, only 20.7 percent of disabled adults are working full or part time (in any industry), compared to 68.7 percent of adults without disabilities, based on data from March 2013.* That contrast is stark, but it is important to bear in mind that disability is primarily a political category used to determine who qualifies for particular government benefits, and that political category is heavily intertwined with employment status.

Although there are no data specific to the film or television industries, the BLS does indicate that 1.6 percent of workers with disabilities are employed in "arts, design, entertainment, sports, and media occupations," of which film and television are a part. By comparison, 2 percent of workers without disabilities are in this field. So when we look only at the population of workers, disabled people seem marginally underrepresented, but we also need to account for their massive absence from the workforce. While 18 percent of Americans have some form of disability, the Screen Actors Guild (SAG) estimates that 2 percent of all TV roles are for disabled characters. Although our measures are imprecise, it is nevertheless clear that those with disabilities are underrepresented in the film industry.

The Screen Actors Guild has conducted surveys of its disabled members to learn more about their employment experiences (Raynor and Hayward 2005).

---

* http://www.bls.gov/news.release/empsit.t06.htm.

But those data are not presented with a comparison to nondisabled SAG members, nor do they identify what percentage of SAG members are disabled. Over a quarter of respondents have an unspecified disability, while another quarter have a mobility impairment, and nearly a quarter have a hearing impairment. Some 11.9 percent have an emotional or intellectual disability, and another 10.9 percent have a learning disability. Nearly a third of disabled SAG members made no income from work on SAG-contracted projects, and most rely on outside sources for a significant portion of their income. So being disabled in the film or television industries not only means having limited roles, it also means having limited income.

Laura Kissel (2009), a documentary filmmaker, does not identify as disabled, but her work largely focuses on the politics of disability in the United States. Growing up with a brother with cerebral palsy, she frequently observed firsthand the isolation that the world imposes on persons with disabilities, often forcing them out of full participation in social life. To her this is an issue of citizenship, which is why she titled one of her films *Campaign for Full Citizenship*. She explains the goal of the disability documentary in her essay "Disability Is Us":

> My primary goal is to make the invisible history of disability visible. This is a political objective and a guiding metaphor for the film. Many people with disabilities are segregated from society in institutions and nursing homes; just as the visual record of disability is hidden from view, so too are many lives. Opening the archive and releasing images of disability can establish the context for a scene of collective and politicized remembrance. (21)

Although she does not use the term *isolation*, Kissel is clearly drawing on the concept. Society isolates people with disabilities both physically and symbolically, by locking them away and by erasing them from the visual storytelling of our culture. So Kissel's purpose as a disability documentarian is to render these stories visible.

ABLE AUDIENCES

Disability raises intriguing and complex questions when it comes to audience reception. Film and television are sensory experiences that are received by the eyes and ears. Music is an auditory experience that is also a tactile experience—we can *feel* the beat. The assumed mode of reception for

Methodology Moment
ORGANIZATIONAL REPORTS

Professional associations frequently collect data and issue reports about their members. These reports provide valuable information for the sociologist who is interested in studying the labor force of a particular industry. Although the research may follow different protocols than those that a sociologist might use, the information gathered can be very helpful to a scholar who has little direct access to that labor force.

These associations may take the form of guilds, academies, or trade unions (see Table 6.2), and their websites include useful information about their members as well as access to research reports.

They provide a window into the organized and professional lives of employees in the culture industries. Their missions and activities highlight the interests of their members. Their research reports provide valuable data about the production process and the labor force experience.

TABLE 6.2. Trade Unions and Professional Associations in the Culture Industries

Major Professional Associations for Television and Film	Academy of Television Arts and Sciences Academy of Motion Picture Arts and Sciences Actor's Equity American Federation of Television and Radio Artists (AFTRA) American Film Institute Directors Guild of America International Alliance of Theatrical Stage Employees, Moving Picture Technicians, Artists, and Allied Crafts (IATSE) Motion Picture Editors Guild Moving Picture Machine Operators National Association of Broadcasters Producers Guild of America Screen Actors Guild Writers Guild of America

continues

Methodology Moment: ORGANIZATIONAL REPORTS *(continued)*

Major Professional Associations for Music	American Federation of Musicians American Composers Alliance American Society of Composers, Authors, and Publishers (ASCAP) Association of Music Professionals Country Music Association Experience Music Project National Association of Record Industry Professionals (NARIP) Recording Industry Association of America World Folk Music Association
Major Professional Associations for Publishing	American Society of Magazine Editors Association of American Publishers Association of American University Presses Association of Learned and Professional Society Publishers International Publishers Association Magazine Publishers of America Small Publishers, Artists, and Writers Network
Major Professional Associations for Digital Culture	Association of Information Technology Professionals Digital Media Association (DiMA) International Association of Internet Professionals Internet Association Internet Marketing Association

published work and for the Internet is to *view* it and read it. Although we know that there are assistive technologies for all types of media formats, we might still wonder how sensory-related and other types of disabilities change or influence the way that we receive culture.

Beyond sensory differences, which are not relevant for many disabilities, we have to ask whether being disabled makes a person more inclined toward some types of culture than others, and whether people with disabilities interpret the culture they consume in ways that differ from how people without disabilities do. Again, we do not currently have any studies on this, so we do not know. We do know that many people with disabilities are using the Internet and other media to share their perspectives on disabled representations.

When the film *Tropic Thunder* hit screens in 2008, disabled groups took a stance against the film's casual use of the word "retard" and the portrayal of a character named Simple Jack. In the film, Ben Stiller plays an actor whose previous roles included playing Simple Jack. So even in this fictional film, the character is abstracted as a fictional representation—which actually supports Snyder and Mitchell's claim that comedic films rely on "faked impairment." *Tropic Thunder* includes a faux trailer for Simple Jack that draws on the worst extremes of all the tropes listed by Whittington-Walsh (2002). Jill Egle, a woman with developmental disabilities who had once been labeled retarded, made a video plea to Ben Stiller on YouTube titled "Can We Talk, Ben Stiller?" Egle was at that time the coexecutive director of the Arc of Northern Virginia, an organization that advocates for the rights of people with intellectual and developmental disabilities, and she has since become an active public speaker.

In her YouTube video, Egle leans into the stereotypes portrayed by Stiller and explains them by discussing the economic, medical, and other social realities of people with developmental disabilities. She also explains the important role that film plays in the lives of people with developmental disabilities and points out that they may be major consumers of film, in part because of their exclusion from the workforce and other aspects of social life. She ends the video by asking and answering an important question: "Why does this hurt so much? Because you made us feel unwanted."*

How are people with disabilities faring in the Internet age? Does the Internet provide new means for overcoming the limitations created by some disabilities? Or do technological advancements create deeper inequalities between the disabled and nondisabled? Kerry Dobransky and Eszter Hargittai (2006) investigate these questions using nationally representative data. They find that people with disabilities do use the Internet at lower rates than people without disabilities, but much of this is due to economic factors. When the researchers control for income, they still find somewhat lower rates of Internet use among people with disabilities. However, this effect depends on the type of disability. They find that people with disabilities related to hearing or to walking show no difference in Internet use compared to nondisabled people of the same socioeconomic status. People with disabilities that impact seeing or typing do have lower rates of use than their peers at the same income level.

---

* http://www.youtube.com/watch?v=7eOBOAlQH54.

Methodology Moment
AUTOETHNOGRAPHY

Sociologists are expected to be value free, which means that we do not impose our own ethics and opinions on the social situations that we observe. In the case of popular culture, this means that I cannot simply defend the culture that I love and tear down the culture that I disdain. Instead, I need to pay attention to how these cultural objects work within the larger social world and how they interact with their audiences.

But many sociologists have insisted that being value free does not mean that the scholar disappears altogether. Every scholar who studies the world does so from a particular position within that world. Standpoint theorists tell us that our perspective on the world is shaped by how we are situated within the world, and this is no less true for the scholar than it is for anyone else. Autoethnography provides a method by which we can examine the social world while paying attention to the uniqueness of our own vantage point on that world. These are the basic features of an autoethnography:

1. First-person narrative.
2. Reflexive analysis: The author determinedly reflects upon his own role within the larger social world that is at work.
3. Acknowledgment of alternative perspectives: By acknowledging her particular position, the researcher can also consider the alternative perspectives of people operating from a different vantage point.

The subject of disability in popular culture provides some interesting autoethnographical possibilities. First, it provides an opportunity for scholars with disabilities to provide their perspectives on how they engage popular culture, from going to concerts and films to consuming music and television. Consider the following narrative from Anne Finger's "Blinded by the Light, Or: Where's the Rest of Me?":

> Now Irma is stepping up to the box office and saying, "One disabled, for *Mata Hari*." Through the invocation of this magic word, "disabled," she pays six dollars for her ticket, instead of nine, and gains admission to this Sunday afternoon movie, part of a series this multiplex is running in one of its mini-theaters, Classics of the Hollywood Cinema. (2010, 210)

continues

Methodology Moment: **AUTOETHNOGRAPHY** *(continued)*

Full disclosure: this is a short story, not an autoethnography. But it reveals the kind of insight that can also come through in a self-reflexive autoethnographic analysis.

Second, scholars without disabilities can use autoethnography to study and explore their experiences with disabled characters and performers in popular culture, from watching characters like Arty or Becky on *Glee* to listening to music by Ray Charles or Stevie Wonder.

Third, and finally, any scholar can use autoethnography to explore the relationship between popular culture and embodiment, from how we engage the bodies we see in film and television to the ways our own bodies respond to the rhythm of music or the feel of the pages of an old book. Disability is ultimately a way of thinking about types of embodiment and the relationship between our bodies and society.

WRAP-UP

Disability is both clearly present and ambiguous in American society. Americans with disabilities are no longer physically isolated from their neighbors in special schools and hospitals. The Americans with Disabilities Act of 1990 dramatically increased educational, occupational, and leisure opportunities for disabled Americans. The ADA effectively transformed disability from a cultural category into a political and bureaucratic one. That change allows us to quantify the number of Americans with disabilities and to recognize that 18.7 percent of Americans are disabled.

There is a significant gap between the demographics of disability in the American social world and the demographics of disability in popular culture. Although disabled Americans are no longer physically isolated, they are nevertheless symbolically isolated by being largely excluded from the content of popular culture.

One of Lady Gaga's popular songs, "Paparazzi," is promoted by a video in which she plays a famous woman living in a mansion who is thrown over a balcony by her lover, played by the actor Alexander Skarsgård from the *True Blood* series. She survives and returns to her home in a newly disabled form, appearing both in a wheelchair and walking with arm braces. The assistive devices become incorporated into the sexuality of the video. Gaga is seen in metallic gold lingerie and black high heels while dancing in her arm braces. The disability that is represented in the video is just as artificial as Lady Gaga's striking outfits. It is fetishized and eroticized, and then it is abandoned. A suddenly healed Gaga loses the braces and the wheelchair, poisons her lover, and uses the media attention to regain her fame.

Such is the relationship between disability and popular culture. For the most part, disability is missing in popular culture. But a few films, episodes, videos, books, and so forth latch onto an idea of disability to milk it for a quick plot arc, then drop the issue just as quickly. When the film ends, the audience goes home, and the freaks return to the sideshow.

RESOURCES

Resources for Examining Disability in the Social World

- Video: *Disability Culture Rap*, parts 1 and 2. Available on YouTube.
- Video: *The Rupture Sometimes*. Available on YouTube.
- Video: *(Sex)abled: Disability Uncensored*. Available on Vimeo.
- Video: *Sound and Fury*. Documentary about cochlear implants and their impact on deaf culture. Available on YouTube. More information is available at http://www.pbs.org/wnet/soundandfury.
- Blog: Don't Hide It, Flaunt It: http://www.megzucker.com.

Resources for Examining Disability in Popular Culture

- Blog: Media Dis and Dat: http://media-dis-n-dat.blogspot.com.
- Website: Disaboom's entertainment pages: http://www.disaboom.com /entertainment.

7

Translating Harry Potter
GLOBAL PERSPECTIVES

Image 7.1. Fleur Delacour, a French student from Beauxbatons who competed in the Triwizard Tournament in *Harry Potter and the Goblet of Fire* (SOURCE: EVERETT COLLECTION).

INTERNATIONAL FRIENDSHIP
AND THE OPPRESSION OF HOUSE-ELVES

Magic knows no national boundaries. We learn this from the novels and films of the world of Harry Potter. The magic that young Harry possesses, and learns to hone during his studies at Hogwarts Academy of Witchcraft and Wizardry, would seem at first glance to be particularly British, drawing on the lore of the Celts and other tribes who shaped the history of the British Isles. But in the fourth novel of the series, *Harry Potter and the Goblet of Fire* (Rowling 2000), we get our best taste of the international wizarding world, when the school is visited by students from Beauxbatons Academy of Magic in France and the Durmstrang Institute, located somewhere in northern Europe (possibly Norway) (see Image 7.1). These students have come to participate in the Triwizard Tournament, a competition among Europe's three largest schools for magic: Hogwarts, Beauxbatons, and Durmstrang. We also learn in the same novel of an unnamed school in Brazil and of the Salem Witches' Institute. The online Pottermore, an interactive space in which users can further explore the world of Harry Potter, tells us of a school in Japan called Mahoutokoro.* So the secret world of magic is an international one to be sure.

An intriguing aspect of *Harry Potter and the Goblet of Fire* is that it blends the story of the Triwizard Tournament with the story of the Society for the Promotion of Elfish Welfare (S.P.E.W.), the brainchild of Hermione Granger, known to some as the brightest witch of her age. S.P.E.W. offers Hermione the opportunity to argue for the rights of house-elves, a species of magical creatures who were enslaved to magical families. In the earlier novel *Harry Potter and the Chamber of Secrets*, Harry frees a house-elf named Dobby from his cruel master, Lucious Malfoy, by tricking Malfoy into handing Dobby a sock (Rowling 1999). The only way to free a house-elf is to give him or her an item of clothing. Harry earned a loyal friend thanks to his success at freeing Dobby. But Dobby is not the only house-elf in the magical world, and Hermione's creation of S.P.E.W. allows her to petition for the freedom of house-elves everywhere, beginning with those working in the kitchens of Hogwarts. She chastises Harry and Ron for their ignorance of the plight of house-elves: "You do realize that your sheets are changed, your fires lit, your classrooms cleaned, and your food cooked by a group of magical creatures who are unpaid and enslaved?" (Rowling 2000, 239).

The oppression of house-elves is just part of the matrix of domination and oppression—to borrow the phrase from Patricia Hill Collins—that structures the wizarding world. In the wizarding world, species-ism and other intersecting magical oppressions supersede, but never fully replace, the Muggle matrix of race, class, and gender.† The most privileged of the magical world are wizard-born wizards (pure bloods) with strong magical abilities. By

---

* http://www.pottermore.com. Visitors must become members to explore the site. Information revealed on Pottermore is summarized on the Harry Potter Wiki, including the information about Mahoutokoro: http://harrypotter.wikia.com/wiki/Mahoutokoro.

† In the Harry Potter novels, the term *Muggles* refers to nonmagical people.

comparison, Muggle-born wizards and witches, half-bloods (those with one magical parent and one Muggle parent, often derisively called mudbloods), and squibs (those who have magical families but lack the gift themselves) experience less social power and greater stigma. But identity and inequality along lines of race, class, and gender are also still present. The Weasley family, for example, is mocked for its shabby home, particularly by the wealthy Malfoys.

One important lesson of *Harry Potter and the Goblet of Fire*, presented through both the story of the Triwizard Tournament and the story of S.P.E.W., is that although identity-based inequalities are universal, their dimensions and character do vary from one cultural setting to another. The goal of this chapter is to extend our sociological analysis of the relationship between popular culture and identity to the global level. The key issues vary in any given setting we might turn to, because both the meaning of identity and the structure of the culture industries vary across societies. So the task ahead is enormous. We will not look at every national setting or every variation of identity. This chapter simply provides a series of snapshots taken from a sociological tour of popular culture destinations around the globe. How will we manage such treacherous terrain? Headmaster Albus Dumbledore says it well when he bids farewell to the students of Beauxbatons and Durmstrang: "Differences of habit and language are nothing at all if our aims are identical and our hearts are open" (Rowling 2000, 723). So throughout this chapter, as I examine popular culture in contexts that may seem quite unfamiliar, I keep my eye on my central research questions even as I remain open to variations by culture and context.

THEORIZING THE GLOBAL LOCAL

Before we begin to think about the *differences* in popular culture around the world, it may be useful to think about *common* human experiences of identity that can help us better understand those differences. I turn here to the most micrological set of theories within sociology, *symbolic interactionism*, which is a theoretical paradigm that examines the way meaning shapes the behavior of individuals toward the objects and persons in the world around them. Symbolic interactionism is similar to interpretive sociology in its emphasis on meaning as a shaper of human life. But in symbolic interactionism, the focus is on the power of meaning to shape individual behavior, whereas in interpretive theory the focus is on the power of meaning to shape institutions and groups. Symbolic interactionism is most associated with George Herbert Mead, who developed its central tenets while teaching at the University of

Chicago between 1894 and 1931. Mead's work was significantly influenced by his early teachers, Charles Horton Cooley and John Dewey. Mead, who never completed his dissertation, influenced many young sociologists who later became important in the field, but he never wrote a full treatise on symbolic interactionism. Several of Mead's students worked together to publish many of his lectures and collected writings after his death. One of his students, Herbert Blumer, elaborates on Mead's work in *Symbolic Interactionism: Perspectives and Methods* (1969).

In symbolic interactionism, the most basic unit of human behavior is the act, and acts that are social in nature—involving two or more persons—are gestures. The most sociologically significant gestures are what Mead calls *significant symbols*, which are layered in shared meanings. The person making the gesture and the person receiving the gesture both understand its meaning. Extending a hand is a significant symbol so long as both parties understand that a handshake is being invited, and that this handshake constitutes friendship, connection, and trust.

It may seem as though I am drawing on some very different ideas in this chapter: Harry Potter, global comparisons of popular culture, significant symbols. . . . "Where is he going with this?" you ask.

Popular culture is one of the greatest producers of shared meanings, that is, significant symbols. Through popular culture, microexchanges between creator and audience, mediated by cultural objects, become mass phenomena. Within a given social unit, such as American society, the likelihood that the creator and the audience will recognize the same meanings in the gesture of the cultural object is quite high. But as we move across social units, and as culture moves across political boundaries, the risk of misinterpretation increases significantly. So the global trade in cultural objects is much more than just an economic process. It is very much a cultural process, in which meanings are repackaged and repurposed as they are bought and sold around the world. The globalization of culture must be understood as an act of symbolic interactionism. When a work enters a new context and finds a new audience, what kinds of meanings are shared, and what new meanings emerge?

To understand this process, we must examine the dynamics of international cultural exchange, which is a form of globalization. Globalization is often discussed primarily in economic terms, with a focus on massive global conglomerations that have become so powerful they appear to supersede state powers. But globalization also has political and cultural dimensions that overlap with economic factors. One of the foremost scholars of these intertwining globalizations is the sociologist George Ritzer, whose work provides a modern extension of the theories of Max Weber. Ritzer is perhaps best known for developing the concept of **McDonaldization**, a way of thinking about contemporary forms of capitalist production (Ritzer 1993). According to Ritzer's theory, processes of production and consumption have taken on four major characteristics:

Efficiency: Products are produced and made available to consumers in the most efficient manner possible. Novels like *Harry Potter* are printed in mass quantities and distributed primarily through major booksellers like Barnes and Noble or Amazon.com. The option to download the e-book version makes the process even more efficient.

Calculability: Producers use a range of quantitative methods to assess the market for various products, track sales, and predict the success of future goods. The rise of *Harry Potter* from a small English novel to a worldwide multimedia blockbuster is the story of very careful market research and development, a story that is told in detail in Susan Gunelius's book *Harry Potter: The Story of a Global Business Phenomenon* (2008). She points out that 64 publishers around the world have been involved in the printing and distribution of the books. From an original printing of 500 hardback copies the book really has reached all corners of the earth, thanks to a massive marketing strategy.

Predictability: Consumers can anticipate the quality and content of the products they are buying because the production process has been standardized. I know that I can find the Harry Potter books when I walk into the bookstore. I knew, back when each book was first being released, that they would be prominently featured at the front of the store. I know now that I can find them in the young adult section, even though many of the readers do not fit into that category. The system is routinized so that consumers and sellers know exactly what to expect.

Control through Nonhuman Technology and Deskilling of the Labor Force: The corporations that produce the goods we consume are getting more and more powerful and the role of the labor force is rapidly declining. With books, for instance, we talk about the publishing companies, most of which are part of larger global media conglomerates, but we rarely talk about the printing process and the people who make it happen. In college, I briefly worked for a printing company that mostly produced self-help books for a particular publisher. I worked there briefly because the work was grueling and felt fairly mindless. An order would come in for a particular number of copies of a particular book. Copies of the sheets of pages had already been produced at another location and sent to us. My job was to go to each stack of sheets and count the number that had been ordered, lay them on a belt in just the right order, and pull a lever that sent them into a machine to be collated, cut, and bound. I remember going to bed every night unable to stop the endless counting. We talk about *Harry Potter* as a major success for Bloomsbury, the original English publisher, and for Arthur A. Levine, the division of Scholastic that bought the US rights to the series, but we do not discuss the printing companies like RR Donnelly and Sons that made the actual books because the control of the process is very much held by the corporations and not by the labor force that makes these cultural goods (Martin 2007).

McDonaldization is not a theory of globalization per se, but rather of economic production; it is useful for thinking about, and describes a process that certainly contributes to, globalization. In addition to the McDonaldization of production, Ritzer is also interested in changes to processes of consuming. He describes these changes as the **new means of consumption**, a range of consumption spaces like megamalls and online stores that allow us to consume at a frenetic pace (Ritzer 1999). What makes these means of consumption so new is their focus on making the process of consumption so central to daily life, rather than a secondary process that supports other aspects of our lives such as family and career.

Both McDonaldization and the new means of consumption are cultural-economic forces that are being exported around the globe (Ritzer and Malone 2000). I use the term *cultural-economic* because the two dimensions are inseparable in these processes. Economic drives are present in both processes, but both also change the way we make meaning in the world, deciding what and how to value.

Popular culture, like many other industries, has been McDonaldized, and its consumption does happen within the new means that Ritzer discusses. Just today I downloaded a television show through my Amazon Prime membership, read a comic book on my iPad after purchasing it from iTunes, and played several video games on my phone. The processes of exporting American popular culture globally and of importing culture from around the world are characterized by both McDonaldization and the new means of consumption.

GLOBAL IDENTITIES

In principle, we might presume the ratio of men to women in the world to be 1:1. A number of variables affect this ratio, including the genetic predisposition to have girls or boys, as well as changes in the timing of childbirth in the life course, which can also impact the sex of the children produced. These variables tend to offset one another across generations, keeping the ratio at roughly 1:1. However, a number of patterns across the globe are currently trending against the likelihood of female births, including a variety of cultural patterns that lead to preferences for males and the increased availability of contraception and abortion. The current sex ratio worldwide is 102 males for every 100 females,* based on population estimates from 2010. Despite being almost half the world's population, women's life chances are limited by social norms that powerfully favor men. These social norms begin with birthrates and extend to every facet of human life.

Estimating the global population of racial categories is especially problematic. The racial categories used most often in the United States reflect particular histories of difference that cannot be safely extended to the entire world. We may say, for example, that colonialism is a product of the West, rooted in white European culture. But only some cultures in Europe participated in the project of colonizing the world. The notion that all traditional European cultures are white is a kind of retroactive application of a modern conception of race that ignores the complex, diverse groups that have populated the European continent. Measuring the black population of the world would require that we specify which African countries are racially constituted as black and then add to that the number of black-identified individuals who now live on the other continents of the world. This is an impossible task. There are popular infographics floating around the Internet that claim to accomplish just such a thing, but they are endlessly disputed, and their data sources are questionable. An attempt to racially categorize all persons currently living on the continent of Asia would similarly constitute a misuse of a largely American notion of racial categories while also ignoring the migration patterns that bring people to Asia from other parts of the world. The fact remains that all kinds of people live in all kinds of places on the six populated continents of the earth. Nevertheless, racial *and ethnic* hierarchies do exist. But what those hierarchies are, what categories they embody, and what they *mean* culturally vary greatly.

---

* http://www.geohive.com/earth/pop_gender.aspx.

Similarly, class inequalities are found around the globe, but there are no salient worldwide class groups. The economic power of political or financial leaders is very different from one country to the next. What we do know about class is that the level of global inequality is tremendous. The vast majority of the world's wealth is held by a tiny fraction of the world's richest people. Some level of inequality exists in every country, as measured by a tool called the Gini score, but this is a variable. Some countries are more unequal than others. Gini scores can be found online for comparison purposes.* The lowest Gini scores (the least amount of inequality) are found in European societies.

Disability is yet another concept that is not universal, nor do those cultures that acknowledge it agree on what it means or how it is defined. On the one hand, we know that more economically developed countries have better health care and greater access to health insurance, which might lead us to expect that disability would be less prevalent in those countries. But it is precisely in these economically developed countries that the bureaucratic order requires a rigid system for determining who counts as disabled, so that state benefits can be appropriately disbursed. The development of a system for labeling—and subsequently stigmatizing—disability goes hand in hand with economic development. Furthermore, advanced technologies of industrial production, transportation, and military warfare have broadened the nature and scope of the disabilities that may be acquired during the course of a lifetime.

Finally, sexual identity is also difficult to quantify across societies. I think we can safely say that every society has had men who have sex with men and women who have sex with women. But the meaning of that sexual behavior can vary widely. *Gay* and *lesbian* are terms that describe much more than just particular sexual behaviors. They also tacitly describe the social position of the people who engage in those behaviors, the culture associated with this social position, and the biases embodied by the larger culture. If American gay commentary increasingly wonders about the "post-gay" possibilities of a world in which gay marriage may be federally recognized across the United States (ignoring other sexual inequalities like LGBT homelessness, suicide, job discrimination, etc.), in many other societies the appropriate term might be "pre-gay"—not because same-sex sexual experiences are absent from them, but because their cultures have not determined fully what those experiences mean and how they will be incorporated into the larger social structure.

---

* http://data.worldbank.org/indicator/SI.POV.GINI.

I am saying that it is nearly impossible to make global claims about sexuality, disability, class, race, and gender. This fact in no way diminishes the importance of these systems of inequality, both internationally (in every national setting) and globally (looking across nations). From an intersectional perspective, globalization is a long historical process in which one matrix of inequality encounters another (or several others), and a series of negotiations occur about what new system of inequality will emerge. From a global perspective, intersectionality begins with hierarchies of state power that allot varying levels of privilege to some states and varying levels of oppression to others on an international stage. In this sense, globalization and intersectionality are both lenses through which we can understand the process of symbolic interaction at the level of groups and states.

POSTCARD: THE WIZARDING WORLD OF HARRY POTTER

Harry Potter is at once both an inspirational boy hero and "the centerpiece of a global corporate strategy" (Goff 2006, 34). Consider the level of cross-promotion that has occurred with Harry Potter, made possible in large part by the complex horizontal and vertical integration manifest in Time Warner:

1. The seven novels
2. The associated books like *Fantastic Beasts and Where to Find Them*, *Quidditch Through the Ages*, and *The Tales of Beedle the Bard*
3. The eight films (the last novel was split into two films)
4. The Wizarding World of Harry Potter theme park at Universal Orlando
5. The soundtracks from the films
6. The countless toys and figures associated with Harry Potter, including several Lego sets
7. The video game series made by EA, including one for each film, plus *Lego Creator: Harry Potter* and *Harry Potter: Quidditch World Cup*
8. A range of associated websites, including
   - http://www.jkrowling.com
   - http://www.pottermore.com
   - http://harrypotter.scholastica.com
   - http://www.mugglenet.com
9. The Whimsic Alley Wizard Cruise, run by Princess Cruise Line along the California coast
10. The hundreds of books about the Harry Potter phenomenon

And there is much, much more. Harry Potter has reached a level of cross-promotion never seen before, and it is now the model for other cultural goods. This global corporate strategy is a profit generator in countries all around the world. Harry Potter, we might say, is not only a global force; he is even a globalizing force, because his popularity as a product has helped to open new cultural markets.

In her analysis of Harry Potter from an international relations perspective, Patricia M. Goff offers an excellent analysis of the role of international governments in supporting the production of and building the market for popular culture, both at home and abroad: "[T]he globalization of culture . . . is not solely the result of impersonal market forces or technological advances, which governments cannot control. Rather, government action can influence the pace and direction of some key aspects of cultural globalization" (2006, 27). She explains that cultural production is a growing component of international trade relations, including the North American Free Trade Agreement (NAFTA), the General Agreement on Tariffs and Trade (GATT), and the World Trade Organization (WTO).

But what is the meaning of Harry Potter, and how does this meaning vary around the world? What are the lessons of these novels? What do the fictional characters tell us about what it means to be a boy or girl, a woman or man, in the "real" Muggle world? A common perception about meaning in works of art or culture is that the creator decides on the meaning, instills it into the object, and then sends the meaning on its way, wrapped in the container (book, CD, performance, episode, etc.) that delivers it to the audience. Once the container is opened, the meaning is delivered. As I have stated at various points throughout this book, that model overlooks the many ways that meaning is created and transformed by a variety of agents throughout the processes of production and reception.

When we think about the creation and distribution of meaning in a global context, the role of audiences becomes even more complex. The concept of globalization tends to elicit images of a massive globalizing force homogenizing the world. Scholars of globalization balance that notion of a universalizing force with increasing attention to the local and particular dynamics of consumption. The concept that has emerged from this work is called *glocalization*. Glocalization provides a way to pay special attention to what happens when an object produced in one cultural context and distributed in a global marketplace is consumed in a variety of unique local settings.

Patrick Thaddeus Jackson and Peter Mandaville, scholars of international relations and government, respectively, use the idea of translation to study the forces of glocalization: "Translation might be thought of as the effort to take something that is meaningful in one context and reproduce it so that it is meaningful in another context" (2006, 46). As they explain, there are two ideal types of translation: literal and free. Literal translations focus on maintaining the form of the original as closely as possible, whereas free translations focus on the essence. Take the Bible as an example. Many modern translations have focused on approximating a literal translation—as closely as possible given that the original languages either are no longer extant or have changed dramatically—and differ only because they look to different scholars and scholarship for the best literal equivalent of the meaning of the original. The New International Version (NIV) is a widely used literal translation of the Bible (Holy Bible 2011). In stark contrast to the NIV is *The Message*, by Eugene H. Peterson (2002). This is an idiomatic, free translation that claims to capture the spirit of the text. The implication of the title is that literal translations lose the overall message—the forest—amid the minute, detailed meanings of each individual word—the trees.

Popular culture faces similar issues when it is translated across cultures. Translations take many forms. Adding subtitles to a film is a kind of translation that raises questions about whether the subtitles selected are literal or free translations. Dubbing a film in a new language using voice-overs is another kind of filmic translation. Both subtitles and dubs can be distracting, in different ways. But dubbing tends to incite the most criticism, because the performance embodied in the original actor's voice is lost.

Another way to translate a film is to remake it entirely. When a film is remade, it can be recast entirely, rescripted, and rebranded in the image of the culture receiving it. One of my favorite films is the 2006 Martin Scorsese drama *The Departed*. I have seen this film several times and always thought it was a great American, and distinctly Bostonian, epic. But as it turns out, it is a translation, a remake of the 2002 Hong Kong film *Infernal Affairs*. Obviously a remake is a free translation, rather than a literal one, at least in this case. The essence of the film was translated into the idioms of American and Boston culture.

The act of translation is both deeply problematic and incredibly ordinary. It is problematic because something is always lost in a translation, regardless of whether it is free or literal. But it is ordinary in that it happens all the time, in ways we rarely even recognize. When we read a novel that was written in an earlier time period, an act of translation occurs, even if that novel is part of our own cultural history. Translation is an element of both the production and reception processes, and it highlights how impossible it is to pin down meaning, even though meaning is incredibly powerful.

Using this broader conception of translation, we could say that the *Harry Potter* novels are among the most translated cultural objects in contemporary global society. According to the *New York Times*, the books have been translated into at least seventy languages.* *Harry Potter* book sales have surpassed the 450 million mark. Worldwide box office sales for the eight films is nearly $8 billion. The total production budget for the films is $1.2 billion.† The eight films are all among the Top 40 worldwide highest grossing films of all time, holding positions 4, 16, 18, 20, 21, 26, 30, and 40.‡

Perhaps most surprising is that these English-language books had to be translated for American audiences. In England the title of the first book is *Harry Potter and the Philosopher's Stone*. In English mythology, philosophy is associated with the practice of alchemy, the quest to turn ordinary objects into gold or into stones than can extend youth and preserve life. In America, philosophy is associated with abstract and esoteric college professors—nothing magical about them at all. So when the novel was sold to Americans, the title was changed to *Harry Potter and the Sorcerer's Stone*, because sorcery has that magical connotation that the author wanted to achieve. The title was not the only thing that was changed. Throughout the novel, terms that were deemed too English were Americanized. Sellotape became Scotch tape, car park became parking lot, biscuits became cookies, and so forth. These are minor changes in some ways, but they are still an act of translation. American readers still understand that the story is set in Britain, but they read this British tale through a lens of Americanized English.

Harry Potter can be understood as a migrant, moving from the Muggle world to the magical world at regular intervals across the course of a year. This way of thinking about Harry is pointed out by educators Catherine L.

---

* http://topics.nytimes.com/top/reference/timestopics/complete_coverage/harry_potter/index.html.

† http://www.the-numbers.com/movies/franchise/Harry-Potter.

‡ http://www.the-numbers.com/movies/records/worldwide.php.

Belcher and Becky Herr Stephenson in *Teaching Harry Potter* (2011). In one chapter they focus on reading and teaching *Harry Potter* in bilingual classrooms along the border of the United States and Mexico. The novels, available to kids in either English or Spanish, are quite popular, even though the educational system set up for nonnative English speakers—particularly for Hispanic students—is based on a presumption that these students are not interested in reading and not even especially interested in education. The authors find, from talking to these students and their teachers, that the kids are very interested in good stories. One teacher describes bribing her students to study hard for the California Standardized Test by promising that they could spend their afternoons reading *Harry Potter* if they had productive mornings of test preparation. In this way, the experience with the novels helped to mitigate the frustrating focus on teaching as preparation for standardized tests. But the experience of reading *Harry Potter* collectively, as a class, mostly with the teacher reading it to them in Spanish, was much more than just an escape from test preparation. The teacher explains:

> A lot of time went into reading the book; we had to talk about it a lot. I read it in Spanish, but felt *Harry Potter* gave the students a chance to connect with this "other" English culture they were living in because they could connect with the kids and school in the book. Potter provided a way to connect with a friendly English environment. The bilingual class is a bubble, and many were going to transition to English the next year, which can be scary. Our class was also safe because I speak Spanish, and no one was going to tell them "you have to speak English!" They needed to make a connection to the English-speaking world, though, and I thought this book could help them. (Belcher and Stephenson 2011, 41)

In this border town classroom, Harry Potter becomes a model of the immigrant experience as well as a welcoming face in an English-speaking world, presented to the students through a Spanish translation.

Suman Gupta (2009) explores Harry Potter's reception around the world in the second edition of *Re-Reading Harry Potter*. In one chapter he explains the seemingly peculiar "Bulgarian connection" to Harry Potter. The connection hinges on Viktor Krum and the Bulgarian National Quidditch Team as they appear in *Harry Potter and the Goblet of Fire*. The summer before he comes to Hogwarts for the Triwizard Tournament, Viktor Krum competes in the Quidditch World Cup finals for his native Bulgaria.* In terms of the Harry Potter chronology, the Quidditch World Cup would have been held in 1994, the same year that Bulgaria reached fourth place in the FIFA World Cup, drawing attention to the country from around the globe. According to Gupta, Bulgarian readers recognized Viktor Krum's surname as a reference to Khan Krum, an early-ninth-century Bulgarian ruler who expanded the kingdom and introduced Bulgaria's first legal code. Khan Krum is recognized as a major heroic figure in Bulgarian culture. A Bulgarian-born (English-raised) child actor named Boris Mitkov was cast as one of the students in Gryffindor in the film version of *Harry Potter and the Sorcerer's Stone*, although his role is small enough that he is not credited. And another Bulgarian-born actor, Stanislav Ianevski, was cast as Viktor Krum in *Harry Potter and the Goblet of Fire*. To Bulgarian audiences, Rowling seemed to be giving their country an enormous plug at a historical moment when Bulgaria was actively rebranding itself on the international stage to gain entry into the European Union. This is a level of meaning that Bulgarian readers drew from the books that was not relevant to English or American readers, and it is a reminder that the meaning of the books and of the Harry Potter phenomenon is not fixed in place by the author, but is instead created anew as fresh audiences receive the works.

POSTCARD: SOUTH KOREA

The journalist Mark James Russell offers an excellent overview of South Korean (hereafter Korean) popular culture in *Pop Goes Korea* (2008), covering the growth of film, television, music, and comic books. Although all of these industries have lengthy histories in Korea—popular films were screened at least as early as the 1920s—the culture industries of Korea saw a particular boom in the 1990s. As with American culture industries, the trend is toward a very small number of massive conglomerates that control production *and* distribution in a number of media formats.

The story of Korean film is particularly interesting. As in many smaller countries, the tendency in South Korea for the past several decades has been

---

* The fact that Viktor Krum is from Bulgaria should not be taken as evidence that Durmstrang is located there. Durmstrang appears to have accepted students from across Europe, and the details that we know of Durmstrang indicate that is located too far north to be in Bulgaria.

protectionist, which means that the government instituted policies to prevent Korean culture from being overrun by external influences. In film, the Motion Picture Law of 1962 allowed distributors to import just one foreign film for every three domestic films made. This helped to encourage domestic film production, as long as the law was enforced. Excitement about showing particular foreign films meant that film distributors had good reason to invest in making or distributing South Korean films to earn the right to bring in the foreign ones.

The Motion Picture Law was revised in 1985. The new rule required movie theaters to screen Korean films for 40 percent of the year. This was reduced to 20 percent in 2006. So over time the protectionist inclination has diminished, though not without pushback from Korean cultural defenders. Even as the requirements have relaxed, Korean cultural production has increased, with perhaps as much as 60 percent of films shown in South Korea being domestically produced. That cultural boom had not yet begun in the early 1990s. Russell says of that period:

> The movie industry was, to be polite, disorganized. At times, to be less polite, it bordered on organized crime and impending anarchy. Instead of competing to make the best movies and getting as many people as possible to watch them, the movie business was focused on protecting itself from risk—keeping costs down and competition weak. (2008, 8)

He looks at particular industry leaders to help explain the dramatic comeback of South Korean popular culture.

One of the most important leaders of the film industry is a company called CJ Entertainment, founded by Jay-hyun and Miky Lee, a brother and sister who are the grandchildren of Samsung's founder, Lee Byung Chull. CJ Entertainment is a subsidiary of CJ Corp., a former member of the Samsung family of companies that split off in 1993 and was placed under the leadership of Jay-hyun Lee. Lee wanted to build a strong entertainment portfolio for CJ Corp. and began by making a surprising and dramatic investment of $300 million in Dreamworks SKG—an investment that allowed both Dreamworks and CJ Entertainment to come into existence. The deal gave CJ Entertainment most of the Asian distribution rights for Dreamworks productions as well as a significant level of prestige as it entered competition for Korean audiences against older and more established South Korean entertainment companies.

The economic crisis of the late 1990s was tough on CJ Entertainment and nearly destroyed it, but the company survived while other similar ones disappeared. CJ Entertainment emerged from the crisis as one of the most powerful entertainment companies in Korea. It split from CJ Corp. in 2000 and quickly began acquiring additional holdings beyond film, including the following:

- Multiplex chain CJ CGV
- Music channel M.Net
- Cable channel division CJ Media
- Cable service provider CJ Cablenet
- Online gaming service CJ Internet
- Music publishing service M-Net Media
- Xbox distributor CJ Joycube

CJ Entertainment even bought one of its rivals, Cinema Services. This left CJ Entertainment one of just three major media companies in South Korea, along with Orion and Lotte Cinema. CJ Entertainment has since returned to the family of CJ Corp. and remains closely connected to Samsung.

Throughout the late 1990s and into the 2000s, South Korean film production increased dramatically. Russell identifies the first Korean blockbuster as *Shiri*, which opened in February 1999. It made $36 million and sold 6.2 million tickets. This placed it well ahead of *Titanic*, which was out in Korea at the same time and sold 4.5 million tickets. *Shiri* was expected to succeed, but that level of blockbuster success was unprecedented. The word *shiri* was suddenly appropriated for everything from clothes to household items and restaurants. It was a Korean phenomenon. *Shiri*'s success was followed just over a year later by another blockbuster, *JSA: Joint Security Area* (2000). These two films, like many successful Korean films, focused on tensions and relationships between North Korea and South Korea. That focus sets these films apart from both early Korean films and those that have found the most success in the global market. For the most part, it has been Korean horror films like *Host* (2006)—also now the biggest blockbuster success in South Korea—that have had the largest market worldwide. However, at least at the time Russell wrote his book, the most successful Korean film to hit Western markets was the quiet, meditative drama *Spring, Summer, Fall, Winter . . . and Spring* (2003).

The organization of South Korea's cultural industries is increasingly similar to that of the United States, and both follow a model that may become the global standard. But the content of South Korean popular culture reflects the unique character of Korean society and the particular anxieties and aspirations found there.

POSTCARD: ARGENTINA

Why are so many young women apparently captivated by sexist music? I was asked once to visit a sorority to give a talk about representations of women in music. Before introducing me, the organizer played a series of clips from songs that she thought were particularly troubling, in the hopes that I might address some of them. One of the songs was "Ho" by Ludacris, which opens with the lines:

> *Hooooooooo (Ho)*
> *Youza Hooooo (Ho)*
> *Youza Hooooo (Ho)*
> *I said that youza hooooo (Ho)* (Ludacris 2000)

As these opening lines played, the women in the room starting pointing at each other and singing or lip-synching the lyrics, while I watched in horror. The talk I gave did not directly address the song "Ho," but I used the question and answer period to turn the tables on the students and ask them what that moment was about. I can only paraphrase their answers, but they basically played it off and said that it was a fun song, and that they point at each other during the opening lines as a kind of humorous bonding moment. In other words, they definitely did not believe that they were calling their sisters slutty just by pointing at them and saying "youza ho."

I wasn't buying it. But perhaps surprisingly, an analysis by a team of scholars studying popular music in Argentina has given me new ways to think about how young women respond to sexist lyrics. This research is summarized in *Troubling Gender*, by Pablo Vila and Pablo Seman (2011). These scholars were focused on a particular subgenre of Argentine popular music called *cumbia villera*. The larger genre of cumbia has its roots in nineteenth-century Colombia and blends African, Amerindian, and European musical elements. The cumbia villera style became popular in Argentina in the 1990s and is musically distinctive for its incorporation of synthesizers and drum machines. But what really sets cumbia villera apart from other musical styles is the sexual content of the lyrics. Consider these two songs, translated into English: "Your specialty is oral sex / you do it quite well / Don't pretend to be classy / Because they saw you sucking dick in a truck."* Or "And I see you with my friend, handing over your ass. / Is this the way you love me? Fucking my friend. / Is this the way you love me? Fucking my friend. / Fuck you! Fuck you!"†

It seems obvious that these lyrics are sexist. They reduce women's lives to their sexual relationships with men and suggest that women are endlessly seeking sex. But is the meaning of the lyrics the same as the meaning of the music? Where is meaning actually located?

Vila and Seman argue that we must look for meaning in the context of musical performance and reception, not simply in the lyrics. Although cumbia villera can be enjoyed at home, the genre is really associated with dance halls and is either performed live by the bands or played by DJs. To understand the meaning of the music in this context, Vila and Seman conducted a number of interviews with audience members to compare what males and females had to say. They found that many men reproduced sexist notions of women as they made sense of the song lyrics, particularly by suggesting that the songs simply portray women as they really are. Some men offered more nuanced views of the lyrics or suggested that the lyrics do not apply to all women. Some men expressed frustration with the repeated messages about women and sex. But what the men did not do, as compared with the female respondents, is turn the meaning of the lyrics around.

The female fans of cumbia villera demonstrated a range of strategies for interpreting the songs they listen to. At stake for these women is that this musical style is important to their social worlds and provides many of their social experiences. Many were able to see that the lyrics present a distorted view that is really harmful to women overall. Some women expressed feelings of shame with regard to the *lyrics*, but stressed that this music is about *dancing*, and the lyrics are really secondary to the experience. Some women interpreted the lyrics as a joke, simply refusing to believe that anything so over the top should be a cause for concern. The interviews with women also highlighted the fact that many women go to these performances to dance alone and with each other, rather than dancing with men. This fact diminishes the role of the songs as mediators of a sexual or romantic encounter between a woman and her male

---

* From the song "Que Peteas" by La Base Musical. Quoted in Vila and Seman (2011, 55).

† From the song "Entregadora del Marron" by Flor de Piedra. Quoted in Vila and Seman (2011, 59).

dance partner, instead suggesting that the songs mediate friendships and re-lationships among women. Women may even feel empowered by these lyrics as signs that their sexuality is real and powerful and need not be protected or patronized. Vila and Seman refer to what they call the "activation of women," which is the increased agency that women possess and the increased role they play as aggressors and sexual beings. They conclude:

> What may look like girls' becoming accomplices of the enthusiastic recep-tion of their own objectification, celebrating themselves from the point of view of a sexist male gaze, can have a completely different meaning from the perspective of young women whose character decodes the lyrics and the behaviors in the baile [dancehall] from a very different standpoint. (Vila and Seman 2011, 158)

Vila and Seman make an important claim about the ways that we study cultural reception. It is very tempting to think of our trained academic eyes as authorities that will discover what audiences are doing and report their behaviors back to them if they happen to take our classes. But if these scholars had tried to make sense of cumbia villera simply by reading lyrics written on a page, they never would have captured the incredible dynamics of what the au-diences are actually doing, especially the female audience members. We have to take our cues not from the books and articles we have read, but rather from the people whose social worlds we are trying to understand. Any attempt to make sense of cultural reception needs to begin by asking very open-ended questions of the audience members themselves.

POSTCARD: INDIA

The Indian commercial music industry began in 1902, right after the advent of commercial recording in the world. The Gramophone Company of India (GCI) was one of several early recording companies, but it became dominant early on. This story, and the larger story of Indian popular culture, is told in Asha Kasbekar's *Pop Culture India!* (2006). Despite being British owned, GCI gained dominance in 1908 by opening a record press in Calcutta—the first on the subcontinent. GCI, with its label HMV (His Master's Voice), was pur-chased by the international conglomerate EMI in 1931. HMV continued to hold the lion's share of the Indian music market until the entrance of Polydor in 1961. Even then, HMV remained the major label in India, with 60 percent

TABLE 7.1. Distribution of the Indian Music Market	
Film Music: 66%	Nonfilm Music: 34%
Hindi: 61% Regional: 5%	Devotional: 10% International: 8% Pop Music: 8% Other: 8%

(SOURCE: CITED IN KASBEKAR 2006.)

of the market. The two companies managed to stave off other competitors for several decades. A "cassette revolution" in the 1980s brought a level of democratization, letting more people become creators and distributors of music with their own simple recording devices. This allowed for a new flourishing of regional and religious devotional music. Nevertheless, the Indian music industry maintains a close relationship to the film industry. The arrival of satellite television in the 1990s allowed pop music to gain a larger share of the market thanks to music television (including MTV and the India-based Channel V) and music-focused competition shows. Kasbekar cites a 2003 industry report indicating that 61 percent of the Indian music market consists of film songs recorded in Hindi, as shown in Table 7.1.

According to Kasbekar, India is the third largest book market in the world, the third largest producer of English-language books, and the seventh largest producer of all books. India has eleven thousand publishers and produces seventy thousand books per year, making it a billion dollar industry. After the country gained independence from Britain in 1947, the major dilemma facing the Indian publishing industry was whether to publish in English. Hindi was declared the national language, but English was well established as a major language for publishing. Initially the industry preference was for Hindi, but Salman Rushdie's 1981 publication of *Midnight's Children* helped to solidify the return of English. Now English is used for everything from the pulp fiction novels of Shobhaa De to the comic books of Anant Pai, both of which are discussed in Kasbekar's work.

The Indian television industry began in 1959, experiencing its most significant growth in the 1980s and 1990s. Kasbekar counts 224 channels by the year 2003, making it a sizeable pop culture outlet. Soap operas are the most popular form of entertainment television and are modeled on the Latin American telenovela more than the American soap opera. But American soap operas like *The Bold and the Beautiful* have also been popular with Indian audiences. There are a growing number of regional, national, and international news channels. India exports its television programming to Indian audiences around the world—an estimated twenty million people living outside of India. One of the major functions of Indian TV has been to produce a level of national consciousness in a very diverse nation comprising many languages, ethnicities, and religions. This televisual consciousness tends to reflect the values of northern India, the Hindi language, and the Hindu culture more than the values and cultures of the rest of the nation.

The popular culture format that India is perhaps best known for is film, thanks to the global popularity of Bollywood. Bollywood refers both to the important role that Mumbai (formerly Bombay, the Hollywood of India) plays as a center for film production and to a particular genre of Indian film that features spectacular music and dance numbers combined with epic stories. As Kasbekar explains, film is the largest and most important component of Indian commercial culture. India is the largest producer of films in the world, averaging eight hundred to a thousand films per year. Although Bollywood films dominate the market, India has several regional film centers, and Indian films are made in all eighteen national languages. Chennai and Hyderabad are two of the biggest film centers outside of Mumbai. Exportation of Indian film poses a major challenge to Hollywood's hold on the global film market.

George Ritzer would probably argue that Indian commercial culture has been McDonaldized. Although the survey of Indian culture provided by Kasbekar reveals a tremendous amount of diversity, it is not reflective of the massive complexity of Indian cultures. Over time each of these industries has narrowed its usual processes to make the practice of producing film, television, books, and music more efficient and more predictable. The question remains whether this McDonaldizing process hampers creativity by homogenizing the culture or fosters it by making the creative industries economically viable.

POSTCARD: NIGERIA

Africa is a continent comprising forty-five countries (including adjacent island nations), yet we have little scholarship in English about the commercial culture they produce and consume. As scholars like Karin Barber have pointed out, this is because of an odd and unfortunate binary in scholarship about African culture that tends to divide African cultures into two categories: traditional (defined as tribal and premodern) and elite (defined as Western and high) (Barber

1997). But there is a tremendous amount of popular culture in African countries that fits neither of these categories. African countries *are* modern, and they
are continuously engaged in new forms of cultural production:

> What this binary paradigm has obscured is the cultural activities, pro-
> cedures, and products of the majority of people in present-day Africa.
> There is a vast domain of cultural production which cannot be classified
> as either "traditional" or "elite," as "oral" or "literate," as "indigenous" or
> "Western" in inspiration, because it straddles and dissolves these distinc-
> tions. In recent years, Ghanaian concert parties have toured thousands
> of towns; Yoruba popular theatres have broken into film, television and
> video; young men and women in Nairobi have read *Mbatha and Rabeke*;
> Tanzanian writers have published hundreds of detective novels in Swa-
> hili; cartoonists in Cameroon have celebrated the egregious antics of polit-
> ical thugs; Basotho migrant workers have sung about their experiences in
> South African mines; and men and women have composed Chimurenga
> songs to help them mobilize against the Rhodesian Front. These genres
> are not repositories of some archaic "authenticity": on the contrary, they
> make use of all available contemporary materials to speak of contempo-
> rary struggles. . . . They are the work of local cultural producers speaking
> to local audiences about pressing concerns, experiences and struggles that
> they share. (Barber 1997, 1–2)

I quote Barber at length here both because she provides an amazing tour
through some of the popular cultures of Africa and because Barber is so elo-
quent about the need to disrupt the traditional/elite binary and the myth that
anything contemporary in African culture is merely a result of Western influence. African cultures are active players in the contemporary world. They are
producers of a tremendous range of cultural forms, and they are *audiences* to a
wide spectrum of contemporary media.

Wikipedia maintains a "List of Television Stations in Africa"* that includes about three hundred stations spread across the forty-five African nations, ranging from just one in several countries to a few dozen in Nigeria.
As Bisi Adeleye-Fayemi (1997) explains in her analysis of Nigerian dramas,
Nigerian television began in 1959. The dramas that frequently appear on Nigerian television are a continuation of those created by the Nigerian culture

---

* http://en.wikipedia.org/wiki/List_of_television_stations_in_Africa.

of traveling theater that developed in the 1940s. To understand the content of these dramas, we have to understand the roots of the theater movement that both predates television and continues to this day. These theatrical and televised dramas are almost entirely authored by men and place women in what Adeleye-Fayemi refers to as the "either/or" position. "If a woman is portrayed as a powerful priestess, it is to show society that women have the power to give and destroy life, and if they are shown as good time girls, in a didactic sense, it is supposed to teach other young women a lesson and to ask men to beware of them" (128). Throughout Nigerian dramas, Adeleye-Fayemi finds women who are represented as either holy or wholly corrupt, whereas men seem to linger in a vast middle ground between these polar positions. As theater, these dramas were presented by and to lower economic groups. Moving them onto television allowed them to reach a more middle-class audience without changing the class of the characters, which means these dramas tell a powerful story about both class and gender to a privileged middle-class audience.

POSTCARD: AL JAZEERA

Al Jazeera is an excellent example of a transnational cultural format that is swiftly globalizing and not rooted in the American culture industry. It is a media outlet, known best for its television news. Al Jazeera was created in 1996 in Qatar, after the closing of BBC's Arabic-language station, thanks to a large investment by the Emir of Qatar (Miles 2005). According to Allied Media, Al Jazeera has an Arab audience of about forty million.* The viewers skew young, male, urban, and low income. Al Jazeera English launched in 2006, offering Web- and satellite-based programming in English to an audience that is estimated by the network at 250 million households in 130 countries. Its programs can be streamed online, and the network also maintains an active YouTube channel. Al Jazeera began its US launch in 2013.

American political leaders and American audiences have a complicated relationship with Al Jazeera. In the late 1990s Al Jazeera was praised as an independent news source that could escape the censorship and propaganda of the various state television networks in the Arab world. But the association of Al Jazeera with the Arab world made it a target after the attacks of September 11, 2001. When it aired tapes made by Osama bin Laden, it was accused of supporting terrorism. Journalist Hugh Miles is quick to point out that there

---

* http://www.allied-media.com/aljazeera/al_jazeera_viewers_demographics.html.

is an important difference between airing the voice of terrorists and actually supporting them:

> The network has never supported violence against the United States. Not once have its correspondents praised attacks on coalition forces in Iraq. The network has never captured an attack on the coalition "live," and there's no evidence Al Jazeera has known about any attack beforehand. Despite claims to the contrary, the network has never aired footage of a beheading. . . . Allegations of supporting terrorism remain just that— allegations. (Miles 2006, 20)

The network's format is known for presenting extreme points of view, not unlike American cable news programming. Al Jazeera may take strong stances against the United States at times, but it also takes strong stances against Arab state leaders. Despite being demonized by Western political leaders in the early years of the twenty-first century, Al Jazeera is again being seen as a legitimate news outlet, particularly as it continues to win major journalism awards. In recent years Al Jazeera has won the Columbia University Journalism Award, the Huffington Post Ultimate Media Gamechanger Award, the George Foster Peabody Award, the Robert F. Kennedy Journalism Award, and many others. Al Jazeera, like the Bollywood films of India, offers an important reminder that the globalization of popular culture is not limited to the globalization of *American* culture.

WRAP-UP

As this short list of postcards indicates, it is difficult to maintain a strong grasp on popular culture practices around the world. But making comparisons across nations is important for at least three reasons. First, when we examine a system of popular culture that is different from our own, we see that another way is possible. It is by no means a given that we must make our popular culture in the style that we do now. Second, when we find similarities in popular cultures across the world, we begin to understand the truly global power of the massive transnational cultural conglomerates. Although it is possible that international economic and political forces may one day break up these massive corporate forces, the trend is still moving in the opposite direction. Global cultural conglomerates are becoming bigger in size and fewer in number. Third, globalizing forces like immigration, mass religion (Islam, evangelical Christianity, Catholicism), international academic exchange, global politics, and global economies are making it increasingly important to understand popular culture at the global level. If popular culture is indeed one of the primary sources, if not the main one, of meanings about identity and everyday life, then it is imperative that we understand each other at least partly through the lens of popular culture.

RESOURCES

Resources for Examining Global Identities

- The Global Identity Project: http://www.global-identity.org.
- Gender Across Borders: http://www.genderacrossborders.com.
- Pew Analysis of Gay Marriage Around the World: http://www.pewforum .org/Gay-Marriage-and-Homosexuality/Gay-Marriage-Around-the -World-2013.aspx.
- Washington Group on Global Disability Statistics, a United Nations initiative: http://www.cdc.gov/nchs/washington_group.htm.
- World Population Data Sheet: Available as a download at http://www .prb.org/ (Click on "Doing Research" > "Data Sheets").
- UC Atlas of Global Inequality: http://ucatlas.ucsc.edu.

Resources for Examining Global Popular Culture

- Darcy Paquet's site on Korean Film: http://koreanfilm.org.
- WWiTV, World Wide Internet Television: http://ucatlas.ucsc.edu. Live streams of television from around the world.
    Includes a page on Nigerian television at http://wwitv.com/tv_channels /b6475-Channels-TV.htm.
- Al Jazeera: http://www.aljazeera.com.
- National Geographic's World Music Site: http://worldmusic.national geographic.com.
    Includes a page on Argentine music: http://worldmusic.national geographic.com/view/page.basic/country/content.countryargentina_13.
- Translating *Harry Potter*, an Internet resource: http://bytelevel.com /global/translating_harry_potter.html.
- Bollywood Hungama: http://www.bollywoodhungama.com.

8

Freaks in the Matrix
A CONCLUSION AND AN INVITATION

Image 8.1. An image of the digitized matrix from the film *The Matrix* offers a metaphor for the culture industry (SOURCE: EVERETT COLLECTION).

WHAT IS THE MATRIX?

In the 1999 film *The Matrix*, we meet Thomas Anderson—a young, socially awkward software company employee who lives a secret life as a computer hacker named Neo. Neo deals in computer secrets the way that others might deal in drugs. In one scene we see him lured into an underground hard rock club, following the white rabbit tattoo of a woman named Dujour. Following the white rabbit, a cultural reference to *Alice's Adventures in Wonderland*, marks the beginning of Neo's adventures in and out of the matrix. (See Image 8.1.)

Neo is a freak. He refuses to live out the script that has been written for his life. His boss explains this contradiction to him:

> You have a problem with authority, Mr. Anderson. You believe that you are special, that somehow the rules do not apply to you. Obviously you are mistaken. This company is one of the top software companies in the world because every single employee understands that they are part of a whole. Thus, if an employee has a problem, the company has a problem. The time has come to make a choice, Mr. Anderson. Either you choose to be at your desk, on time, from this day forward, or you choose to find yourself another job. (Wachowski and Wachowski 1999)

Neo understands himself as more than just "part of a whole." Not only that, he believes that his unique computer capabilities and the freedom of his mind give him the potential to undermine the larger whole, but he does not fully understand how or why. He is a freak because he refuses to conform to the constraints of social demands. He may look like a regular guy wearing a suit and going to work, but his ideas make him a stranger in his own world.

In the film Neo ultimately chooses not to be at his desk, and that choice takes him down a bizarre and compelling path. He meets Trinity, who helps him realize that he is driven by a question: What is the matrix? He discovers that the matrix is a vast illusion that we are all living in. We think we have day-to-day, ordinary lives, but in reality our bodies are lying dormant, being used as batteries for a massive system of artificial intelligence. Neo leaves the matrix with the help of Morpheus, a leader with a vision to bring it down. Morpheus is driven by a prophecy that "the one"—the hero who can destroy the matrix and save us all—is out there. He believes that Neo is that one. Neo joins a team of people who have unplugged from the matrix and begun to rescue others. One member of this team is Cypher, who is acting as a double agent in hopes of returning to a "normal" life within the matrix.

The Matrix can be viewed as a metaphor for the mass media matrix and more broadly the corporate matrix that spans the globe. Humanity has created a race of nonhumans that has now seized control. This race is composed not of robots or computers, but of corporations. We created them, gave them life, and then named them persons. The Fourteenth Amendment to the US Constitution, which was passed to guarantee equal protection to blacks after the end of slavery, has been used since the late 1880s to provide equal protection to corporations as recognized persons. Today some of these corporate persons really have to be seen as super-persons. They encompass hundreds of companies, sit on massive holdings and assets that span a slew of industries, and reside across many national boundaries. These entities can be fined, but those fines are a drop in the bucket of the massive profits they make when they break the law. They cannot be jailed or executed. They are sometimes deemed "too big to fail." These are diabolical and seemingly unstoppable villains. They shift speedily from side to side, dodging whatever punches or bullets we throw their way. Disappearing at the first sign of danger, they reappear out of the mists months, years, even decades later. They have endless aliases. Although they bear the strength of human intelligence and creativity, they lack the grounding of human morality. They are at war with us, and they want greater control.

The corporate matrix is hungry for power, and it has found the greatest source imaginable: not oil, or wind, or the sun—us. The mass media matrix is the power division of the corporate matrix. It is the mechanism by which we are plugged in and harnessed for power. The power we provide has at least two components. The first is money. Our purchases keep capital streaming into these corporations. The second component is our own distraction. By not paying attention to the massive size and frequent crimes of major corporations, we give them the political breathing room to continue their quest.

To harness these powers from us, the mass media matrix needs us to be plugged in. We need to watch television, go to the movies, read magazines and newspapers and novels and comic books, play video games, listen to music, and otherwise fill our lives with the ideas and stories of popular culture. We need not engage all of these outlets; one or two will suffice. Once we are plugged in we can be persuaded however the mass media matrix needs us to be. Our consent to the survival and dominance of the mass media matrix can be manufactured within us through the stories that we are told (Herman and Chomsky 1988). Once we are plugged in, we are told a very powerful story about our identities and our bodies: that we are deeply flawed, yet our flaws can be overcome through the thorough and frequent application of the balm of consumption. We may buy creams and lotions, cars and homes, clothes and personal trainers. They will always make us better, but only slightly and only for a short time. We will always need to buy more in order to become less of a stranger in our own lives and communities. This problem of the self becomes the great problem of our lives, distracting us from wars, genocides, and the destruction of the earth.

Some people plug themselves in willingly. They want to taste the flavors that the mass media matrix provides and to do so without any feelings of guilt.

These folks are the *Cyphers* of the mass media matrix, named for the character who chooses to get plugged back into the system. They watch television on cable every night, while surfing the net on their laptops. They love pop music, go to the movies on the weekend, read all the best sellers on their Kindle readers, and own all the latest gadgets and games. To them, the consumption of popular culture is the good life, and it symbolizes human triumph: the capacity to surround ourselves with stories that entertain and excite us.

At the opposite extreme from the Cyphers are the *Locks*, a reference to Commander Lock in the film, who prioritizes defending the rebel outpost of Zion over fighting the matrix and rescuing more humans from its grasp. They attempt to avoid popular culture entirely. They do not have cable television, and perhaps they do not even own a television set. They do not go to the movies or listen to the radio. They generally prefer local culture, and they listen to local bands who perform in locally owned coffee shops and bars. The Locks are practicing a kind of defensive resistance, locking themselves away from commercial culture but not actively doing much to change the system. They are so small in number and so powerless to recruit others that the mass media matrix need not worry about their loss. Besides, even the Locks read books and use computers, so the matrix still has some hold on them.

In between the Cyphers and the Locks is a range of characters with varying relationships to the mass media matrix. There are the *Trinities*, who live both inside and outside the matrix. They are hopeful that commercial culture has its weaknesses and is not an all-powerful, unstoppable force. The Trinities often undermine the mass media matrix, taking its tools and twisting them around, using them against the matrix itself. They only watch certain shows, only visit the movies occasionally. They read intellectual books, including a great deal of nonfiction. But they also appreciate local culture, travel, history, and politics. They are able to wage a limited fight against the mass media matrix because they understand it from within. Despite their hope, Trinities do not actually have a plan for destroying the matrix. They have grown accustomed to living part time in the world of the matrix, and they take some pleasure in time spent with media culture.

Some of us take a stronger stance and are even more hopeful than the Trinities. But we know that we are not the ones who are going to bring down the mass media matrix. We are the *Morpheuses*, the college professors and high school teachers and mentors who believe we may one day help some student see a new path and then make that path happen. We rely on our wit and wisdom, our books and research, to persuade the students we teach, and then we wonder who among them may prove to be the *Neos* who will change everything. Perhaps the young woman in the front of the room will become a media executive who will pay more attention to representations of women. Perhaps the older male student at the back will become a politician who will pass laws challenging the personhood of corporations. Perhaps the boy in the wheelchair will become a television writer who will create more interesting characters reflecting the true diversity of the world. Perhaps the first generation college student from North Philadelphia will create a media literacy program for the kids in her neighborhood. The revolutionary power of the *Neos* will be measured not in firefights and explosions, but rather in participatory creation (production), revolutionary stories (content), changed lives (audience), and transformed communities (social world) (see "The Cultural Diamond: Beyond the Mass Media Matrix").

DIRTY SLIMY FREAKS

Perhaps the greatest filmic window into the world of circus freaks is Tod Browning's 1932 film *Freaks*. Browning takes his audience behind the curtains of the circus tent to see the social world of circus performers. We discover two very different social circles there. One is a world of "normals"—people who seemingly have every access to the larger social world in which the circus operates. These people are tall and white, with bodies that never encourage a lingering stare, unless it is to enjoy the beauty of an elegant trapeze artist like Cleopatra or the broad muscles of a strong man like Hercules. For these performers, the circus is largely spectacle and artifice. They could conceivably walk away and take jobs in any other industry, leaving the circus lifestyle behind.

The other social world is that of the freaks, the assemblage of dwarves, pinheads, quadriplegics, bearded ladies, and human skeletons for whom many of the doors of society have been shut because of the way they look, think, or act. These freaks lack the social access and the options available to the normals. Although their jobs bring them together and make them mutually dependent, the freaks and the normals do not fully mix. The freaks distrust the normals because they see in them every person who has ridiculed them. The normals distrust the freaks because they refuse to see them as fully human. To the normals, the ways of the freaks are exotic and unfathomable. The normals need the freaks to exist so they can define themselves against them. As long as *those people* are freaks, then *we* are normal.

CULTURAL DIAMOND

BEYOND THE MASS MEDIA MATRIX

TRANSFORMED COMMUNITIES

PARTICI-
PATORY
CREATION

CHANGED
LIVES

REVOLUTIONARY STORIES

The freaks maintain the social boundaries of their community very care-fully, as an act of self-preservation. But the boundaries need some degree of porousness to allow the community to grow. So would-be newcomers to the community must enter through a ritualistic process. Cleopatra experienced this when she decided to marry Hans. She was welcomed into the fold of freaks as part of the marriage ceremony. "We'll make her one of us. A lov-ing cup! A loving cup! We accept her—one of us—gooble, gobble—we accept her—one of us—one of us." The freaks sang a song in unison that announced her transformation into one of them. The words "gooble gobble" affirmed the freakishness of her new identity. Her terrified response—"Slimy . . . dirty . . . freaks!"—revealed that the marriage was a sham and that she was only after Hans's money.

Freaks can be seen as a metaphor for the matrix of privilege and oppression that includes the intersections of race, gender, class, disability status, and sex-uality, among other forms of identity and inequality. The matrix of privilege and oppression creates what appears to be a rigid boundary between the nor-mals and the freaks. Normals are not normal in the usual sense of the word; their behavior is no more commonplace than that of freaks. What makes them so normal is that their identities are privileged and given a taken-for-granted status. This privilege is invisible to them; they do not have to think about it. It is there before they open their eyes in the morning, so they never actually see it come into being. It is built into the structures of society.

Freaks are not necessarily numerical minorities, and even when they are, it is not their number that matters. It is their access to social power, which is determined by their position within the matrix of privilege and oppression. The system makes it seem as if everyone is either a normal or a freak. But the reality is that we can be privileged in some ways and oppressed in others. This system privileges men, whites, heterosexuals, the middle class, and those without disabilities. A person may be privileged by her class position, but op-pressed because of her gender. A person may be privileged by his race, but oppressed because of his disability.

The categories can seem sharply drawn and impermeable, but there are pores. A genealogical history may change how you think about your race, if you discover that you have a racially different ancestor whom you did not an-ticipate. The racial identity of your family may change as you and other family members take romantic partners, conceive children, or adopt children who are racially different from you. Growing numbers of people are changing their gender every year. Many gay, lesbian, and bisexual people come out to their families and friends, and themselves, after puberty, which means the social understanding of their sexualities has to change. A person without disabilities may become disabled through disease or accident at any point in the life cycle. New technologies may allow people who identify as disabled to find themselves no longer disabled. Class position can change as people experience mobility, both up and down. But people do not move across identities casually or easily. The notion of the coming out story is perhaps the most salient indicator that identity transformation is difficult and requires some level of ritual to mark the change.

The matrix of privilege and oppression makes many people feel like freaks within their own society and strangers within their own communities. For some, this freak status is inscribed on their bodies and easily visible to all. These are the *Schlitzes* of the freak show, who play themselves in the movies. They wear the freak badge proudly, but they have never had much access to privilege. For other freaks, the thing that makes them a freak is not so visible, but they choose to make it known to the world. These are the *Josephine Josephs*. Josephine Joseph claimed to be a hermaphrodite. This word really describes whole species that have no sex division. In humans, it is associated with a few conditions that can be related to chromosomes, genes, hormones, and secondary sex characteristics. But none of those conditions results in a line down the center of the body separating a male side from a female side. That line was drawn by Josephine Joseph to be a visible manifestation of her freak side.

Some people become freaks because they want to escape the oppressiveness of the normal and privileged world. These are the *Bird Girls*, who have no disability but perform as freaks anyway because doing so provides a community in which they feel at home. Finally there are *Venuses*, who are unable to deconstruct their own privilege but nevertheless choose to ally with the freaks. They see the inequality caused by the matrix of privilege and oppression, and they work to remedy as much oppression as they can.

On the privilege end of the spectrum, we have *Cleopatras* and *Phrosos*. Cleopatras manipulate the system of inequality and actively seek to benefit from it. Phrosos are good people, like Phroso the clown in *Freaks*, who simply do not see their own privilege. It truly is invisible to them. They are nice to oppressed groups, befriending them and joking with them, but they do nothing to actually undermine the system of inequality. Every person with privilege has some capacity to identify with and even become a freak. The question is: *What kind of freak are you?*

FREAKS LIKE US

Freaks are unsettling by definition. Any person whose appearance or behavior unsettles us is likely to be labeled a freak, whether we say it out loud or not. As Simmel says, "The stranger is an element of the group itself . . . an element whose membership within the group involves being both outside it and confronting it" (2010, 303). Neo is a stranger and a freak in the humdrum work world of the opening to *The Matrix*, because his participation in the secret underworld of computer hacking takes him outside the group, even as his rebelliousness places him in confrontation with that group. The group is all those corporate drones who show up on time and do as they are told, never questioning the world around them. Hans and the other circus freaks are strangers, not to each other, but to the larger social world in which they move and operate. The circus transforms these freaks into wanderers, and the touring of the circus delivers them into the lives of people who otherwise might never see anyone like them.

In Simmel's essay, the true stranger is not the wanderer who appears today and leaves tomorrow, but rather the one who appears today and stays around. That stranger becomes an ongoing presence in our lives, reminding us of his strangeness, but also reminding us that we might be the strange ones in the larger world. Following Simmel's logic, circus freaks are not true strangers in the towns they travel through, but they are true strangers to the normals in the circus who play no role in the freak show. The normals are confronted daily with the strangeness of the freaks, and the guarded social boundaries that the freaks maintain also serve to perpetuate their strangeness. But as Simmel points out, strangers are an element of the group. They are not exterior to the group, but rather deliver "outsiderness" into the group boundaries. They force the group to define itself in relationship to a *perception* of what is beyond the social boundaries. The normal is a normal, because she is not a freak. This begs the question, do normals decide who the freaks are, or do freaks decide who the normals are?

This brings me to a more recent theorist, Judith Butler. Butler's writings about gender and performance use the notion of drag to reveal that gender is always a kind of performance. The fact that men can theatrically present themselves to the world as women reveals that women are also theatrically performing *womanness* or femininity and that their behaviors are not intrinsic to their physical being as women. Similarly, men are not inherently or a priori masculine. *Maleness* is a performance that is equally delivered by masculine and feminine men. Butler's point extends beyond the bounds of gender. Any aspect of our identity for which we have constituted a normal/freak divide is in actuality a set of "theatrically produced effects that *posture* as grounds, origins, the normative measure of the real" (Butler 1991, 103).

When you peel back the layers of normal society, you discover a lot of freaks. The question shifts from "what makes some people freaks?" to "what makes some people normal?" In a society that privileges men, all women are freaks regardless of whether they adhere to defined scripts for women's lives. In a society that privileges whites, all nonwhite people are freaks, whose cultures are exoticized and whose bodies are fetishized. In a society that privileges heterosexuality, all gays, lesbians, and bisexual people are freaks, whose private sexual desires are politicized and publicly debated. In a society that privileges fixed identities and trusts doctors to determine those identities, all trans people are freaks for daring to define their gender from within their own hearts, minds, and bodies. In a society that privileges the middle class, all poor people are freaks, with bad grammar, values, and taste. Even rich people are treated as freaks in this matrix, as evidenced by the ridiculous behavior of "real" housewives on TV and the fascination with the "lifestyles of the rich and famous." In a society that privileges very specific kinds of bodies, disabled people are freaks, fat people are freaks, old people are freaks—even "average" people are freaks! In a society that privileges church attendance, but not *too* much church attendance, both atheists and zealots are freaks, whose irrationality is crippling public discourse.

At the end of the day, we do not have many real normals left. We may all feel a little normal, because we all experience at least a little privilege, but how many are truly normal? All the cheerleaders and football players have joined the glee club.

What I am suggesting here is that we are all freaks within the massive matrix of popular culture. We become freaks first when we are told we are by the external machinery of commercial culture. If we are lucky, we become freaks again when we embrace our inner freak. Invitations to embrace our inner freak permeate the very culture that uses the label *freak* as a way to marginalize us and persuade us to buy its goods and services:

On the television show *Heroes*, a character named Zach—an outcast in his high school who is frequently ridiculed for his presumed sexuality—helps his friend Claire accept that she is gifted with the superpower to heal herself: "You've gotta embrace your inner freak. Because the only thing you'll regret is denying who you really are" (Kring 2006).

A lyric from a song by P!nk: "So raise your glass if you are wrong, in all the right ways, all my underdogs. We will never be, never be anything but loud and nitty gritty, dirty little freaks!" (P!nk 2010).

In February 2013 AMC premiered a new reality show called *Freakshow*, which follows the lives of the performers in the Venice Beach Freakshow. In episode 1 former music producer Todd Ray tries to build his freak show business by recruiting a giant and a bearded lady. The giant is George Bell, who at seven foot eight was declared the tallest man in the United States by the *Guinness Book of World Records* in 2007. Bell has spent his life trying to be normal and expresses some discomfort with joining a freak show. Ray explains to him that the freak show is about reclaiming the word "freak" and making something positive out of it.

In 1967 The Jimi Hendrix Experience recorded the song "If 6 Was 9," about a world turned upside down—a world in which he would still be true to his unique self: "White-collar conservatives flashing down the street / Pointing their plastic finger at me. / They're hoping soon my kind will drop and die, / But I'm gonna wave my freak flag high . . . HIGH!"

The 1970 Crosby, Stills, Nash & Young song "Almost Cut My Hair Today" tells the story of a man choosing not to cut his hair in order to avoid being normal: It was gettin' kinda long, / I could-a said it was in my way, / But I didn't and I wonder why. / I want to let my freak flag fly.

The 2010 song "Take It Off" by Ke$ha (what kind of a freak has a dollar sign in her name?) describes a special hangout for freaky people that seems to be a mixture of dance floor and sex club (the video is set in a waterless motel pool): "There's a place downtown, / Where the freaks all come around. / It's a hole in the wall. / It's a dirty free for all" (Ke$ha 2010b). This song is meant to be an anthem for those who feel marginalized by mainstream culture, even as Ke$ha's music is a product of that mainstream.

From pinheads to nerds; from rednecks to losers; from cyborgs to guerrilla girls: freaks are storming in from the margins. The question of how identity influences popular culture is open to ongoing analysis and subject to new answers as audiences find new ways of making meaning and press for new forms of participatory culture.

Reader, let your freak flags fly!

APPENDIX I
A Brief History of Printing and Publishing

The ability to mass produce printed materials is often attributed to Johannes Gutenberg's invention of movable type in the mid-fifteenth century in Germany. In fact, similar technology had been invented in China four hundred years earlier by Bi Sheng, according to the records of a Song dynasty scholar named Shen Kuo. Sheng's system used characters carved into clay. Later developments in China used wood and bronze. In Europe Gutenberg's press is credited with helping to spur the Renaissance by allowing the mass reproduction and spread of ideas, while also encouraging a higher level of literacy. Gutenberg is best known for printing copies of his famous *Gutenberg Bible* on the press, but he also used it for a variety of commercial and church purposes. According to one source, about twenty-five hundred cities and towns in Europe had printing presses by the end of the fifteenth century.

The printing press facilitated the mass production of books, but it was a laborious process. However, the press also made it possible for much shorter tracts, often political or religious, to be produced and distributed cheaply. Some of these tracts should be seen as the origins of the modern newspaper, because they allowed for dissemination of information about recent events combined with an editorial perspective that told readers how to feel about the events of the time.

Newspapers, in various forms, began to appear in England in the 1600s, beginning with *The Weekly Newes* in 1622 and culminating with *The London Gazette*. *The London Gazette* was published by the court of Charles II and is still published today. Newspapers began to appear in North America in 1690 with the founding of *Publick Occurrences* in Boston.

The invention of both steam paper mills and the steam printing press in the early 1800s meant that paper could be produced quickly and cheaply, in mass quantities, and books could be printed with far less labor than before. As Wilson and Lucyk (2012) explain, the development of the modern book industry was a result of mechanization and industrialization, oriented toward the new notion of a mass market, with large regional, national, and international audiences.

The "paperback revolution" began transforming the book industry in 1935, with the introduction of the Penguin line in the United Kingdom. By 1960 paperback sales had surpassed those of hardbacks.* Since 1960 the field of publishing has been characterized by the same process as other media sectors: conglomeration. Publishing houses have mostly been bought up by larger corporations, including the major media conglomerates:

> Publishers could increase a parent corporation's profits in their own right, but also through books could speak to other media products such as movie novelizations and tie-ins, published transcripts of radio plays, biographies of celebrities, etc. Beyond the financial attraction, publishing houses still retained enough cultural prestige to appeal to conglomerates, as an intangible, but valuable added benefit. Media conglomerates could tout their publishing subsidiaries as cultural and intellectual ventures, rather than as sheer entertainment factories. (Wilson and Lucyk 2012)

Although publishing is much older than our other cultural industries, it is no less a part of the commercial culture system. There can be a tendency to leave publishing out of discussions of popular culture, focusing instead on music, film, and television. But that is a mistake, for several reasons. First, publishing is organizationally located within the culture industries as part of the consolidated media system. Second, it is subject to the same market forces as the other cultural industries, including both the quest for the blockbuster and what one scholar refers to as the FUD factor—fear, uncertainty, and doubt (Keh 1998). The agents who search for the next big authors are little different from the agents who search for the next big pop star. Third, and finally, publishing is less intellectually driven than it gets credit for, while the other cultural industries are more intellectual than they get credit for. Publishing has maintained a strong sense of intellectual integrity because of its connections to academia. Most academics make their careers by publishing articles and books. By comparison, very few academics make films or recorded music, and even fewer make television programming. The standard college course requires a trip to the bookstore to buy books, not CDs or DVDs (though admittedly these are being assigned in higher numbers today than in years past).

In the 1990s the book industry was transformed by the development of big box bookstores like Borders and Barnes & Noble, and then by the growth of online book sales thanks to Barnes & Noble and Amazon. Both of these changes

---

* http://www.crcstudio.org/paperbacks.

had a major impact on the local bookstore, and many have closed their doors. This is not just an economic change but also a social one. Historically, bookstores have been places of collective action where people came together to share ideas. They were known as places where someone could post a notice about a meeting or event, or where poetry readings and political events actually took place. Feminist, black, and queer political organizing in particular have been linked to local bookstores.

The latest technological impact on the book industry is the digitization of books, magazines, and newspapers. Amazon developed the Kindle, and Barnes and Noble developed the Nook, to meet the new demands of the digital era. But other e-readers are readily available as well. Some magazines and newspapers have developed their own applications to facilitate digital distribution. The digital era has been more positive for the book industry than for newspapers and magazines, many of which have folded as consumers increasingly demand free access to news and editorial content.

The corporations that dominate the publishing industry have been referred to in recent years as the "Big Six," a name that no longer fits because two of them merged on July 1, 2013. That is when the Penguin Group, owned by UK-based Pearson, merged with Random House, which was owned by Germany's Bertelsmann. The new venture is called Penguin Random House; Bertelsmann holds a 53 percent interest and Pearson holds the remaining 47 percent. The other four major publishing houses are Simon and Schuster, which is owned by CBS; HarperCollins, which is owned by News Corp.; Macmillan, which is owned by the German company Holtzbrinck; and Hatchette Book Group, which was formerly owned by Time Warner but is now owned by the French company Lagardere.

APPENDIX 2
A Brief History of the Music Industry

Music as a cultural form is timeless. Humans are singing creatures, much like birds. Music is found among all societies and across time. So a history of music is beyond the scope of this appendix. Instead, I present a history of the music industry as a modern organization of the musical field.

The technology for recording music dates to Thomas Edison's invention of the phonograph in 1877. Many inventors and scientists were studying sound and looking for ways to record it. Edison's work built on the accomplishments of others, including the 1857 invention of the phonautograph, which recorded the shapes of sound waves to make it easier to study it. Edison's phonograph recorded sound by etching grooves into a cylinder. Ten years later, in 1887, Emile Berliner invented the gramophone (or phonograph), which etched the grooves into a flat disc. This disc was easier to produce and reproduce, which proved to be an advantage in the commercial development of recording.

Radio technology also played a major role in the development of the music industry. That technology dates back to the work of Nikola Tesla and Guglielmo Marconi in the late 1800s. Wireless broadcasts of entertainment programming began in 1920 by a number of broadcasters across the United States and in other parts of the world. The FM technology, which reduces static, was patented in 1933. The Federal Radio Commission was founded in 1926 to handle the licensing process in the United States; it was replaced by the Federal Communications Commission in 1934.

Richard A. Peterson, an important sociologist of culture broadly and music specifically, describes the musical terrain in the early twentieth century in his analysis of the origins of country music:

In 1923 the commercial music industry in America was dominated by a few large New York–based music publishing houses. They produced sheet music for public performance halls, the vaudeville performance circuit, restaurants,

233

and home pianos. All would-be country music composers were effectively barred from this market by the working of the one major performance rights organization of the day, the American Society of Composers, Authors, and Publishers (ASCAP). It had recently been formed to ensure the payment of royalties to all member publishers and composers. Virtually all country music, jazz, and blues composers were systematically excluded from the benefits of ASCAP membership, and their virtual exclusion continued into the 1940s.

The other major component of the commercial music industry in 1923 had to do with providing live music for dances, musical theater, other enter-tainment, and public occasions. The American Federation of Musicians had contracts with all the large venues in the major cities stipulating that only its member musicians could be hired to perform. (Peterson 1997, 13)

Radio and recording both expanded rapidly throughout the 1920s. NBC and then CBS were the major radio broadcasters, joined in the 1930s by ABC. The audio programming offered by radio stations transitioned rather easily into television programming later. As pop music gained prominence in the 1950s and 1960s, the record became a central component of American culture.

The eight-track tape, or Stereo 8, challenged the prominence of records in the 1970s, but was then replaced by the cassette tape. Cassettes were also introduced in the 1970s, but gained a greater hold on the industry in the 1980s with the in-troduction of portable listening devices like boom boxes and the Walkman. Com-pact discs swept the market in the 1990s and held sway until the introduction of the digital format in the late 1990s. Services like Napster, which allowed users to "pirate" digital copies of music, posed a challenge to the music industry in 1999 and 2000, until a series of lawsuits shut it down (although its assets have been bought and sold since, and the name is still considered synonymous with the new era of online music). Services such as iTunes and Amazon have mastered the sale of digital formats, and online ventures such as Rhapsody and Spotify have created accounts-based services for providing musical content to audiences.

Thanks to the power of ASCAP, writing songs and selling sheet music has remained a powerful commercial element of the music industry. But recording music is also commercially valuable and has a stronger hold on the public percep-tion of the music industry. Most major music labels are tied to music publishers, which reduces the licensing costs of recording music.

Today the largest music corporation is Universal Music Group, which is owned by Vivendi. Universal acquired most of the holdings of EMI in 2011, strengthen-ing its hold on the industry. Universal is one of the music industry Big Three, the three corporations that control most of the industry. The other two are Warner Music Group and Sony Music Entertainment.

APPENDIX 3
A Brief History of Film

The American film industry emerged in the last years of the nineteenth and early years of the twentieth centuries. Creating the world of cinema necessitated several social and technological changes that could not occur simultaneously. Technologically, it required the discovery of the right kind of film, the right kind of machine for capturing images on this film, and the right kind of projection system for displaying those images. In terms of the market, it required the emergence of a business model for producing films, the generation of interest among would-be audiences, and a cinema system that could deliver films to those audiences.

Cinema's prehistory includes peep shows, magic lanterns, and camera obscura—various forms of entertainment that played on the use of moving images, often a combination of peep holes, slides, shadows, mirrors, and light. The transition from these early models into motion pictures required the development of both celluloid film and the motion picture camera. Celluloid was the first film that could effectively capture images of moving objects. The motion picture camera allowed succeeding images of a moving object to be captured on the same reel. This technology was strictly visual and did not allow for the inclusion of audio. Work on the kinetoscope by Thomas Edison and his employee, William Kennedy Laurie Dickson, in the late 1880s led to the earliest commercial film endeavors. Edison's kinetoscope debuted in 1893. His earliest films were created by his studio, The Black Maria. Kinetoscope films could only be viewed individually, by looking through a viewing glass on a large cabinet. The next key piece of film technology that was needed was the projector. That technology was developed in France by Louis Lumiere, whose father, Claude-Antoine, had seen Edison's kinetoscope a year earlier. Thanks to the development of Louis Lumiere's cinematographe, created with the help of his brother Auguste, cinemas opened in Europe and the United States in 1896.

Edison attempted to control the American film industry through control of film-related patents, but he ultimately lost when the US Supreme Court found him in violation of antitrust laws in 1915. Film scholar Paul Monaco (2010) suggests that early movie studios located to Los Angeles to escape both the industrial control of Thomas Edison and the cultural hegemony of the East Coast. Hollywood was a six-year-old village within Los Angeles when William Selig moved his company, Polyscope, there from Chicago in 1909.

Paramount Pictures and Universal Pictures were both founded in Hollywood in 1912. Several other major studios opened soon thereafter, many of which still exist. Fox Film Corporation opened in 1915 and became Twentieth Century Fox in 1935. Warner Bros. opened in 1918. Columbia Pictures and United Artists both opened in 1919. Metro-Goldwyn-Mayer (MGM) was formed in 1924 from three studios that were all founded in 1915 or 1916. Radio-Keith-Orpheum (RKO) was created in 1928 by RCA. The business model of the American film industry today is attributable largely to the practices of Paramount and other studios in the opening years of the medium.

However, as Monaco (2010) asserts, the format of American film follows D. W. Griffith's 1915 *The Birth of a Nation*, which was made prior to the full establishment of the studio system. Monaco says that *The Birth of a Nation* was the first embodiment of the combination of sentiment and spectacle that has come to dominate the storytelling form of film. Charlie Chaplin's silent film *The Gold Rush*, made by United Artists (UA), appeared in 1925. UA was formed by Chaplin, Griffith, Douglas Fairbanks, and Mary Pickford. These two films, *The Birth of a Nation* and *The Gold Rush*, provide bookends for Hollywood's silent era.

The year 1927 marks the divide between the silent era and the modern movie industry. Warner Brothers released the first commercially successful film with synchronous sound, *The Jazz Singer*, in 1927. The film starred Al Jolson in a part that featured both dialogue and singing. "Talkies" were the standard within a year.

The other key technology needed for the transition to modern films was color. Color technology developed in fits and starts. The earliest film in two-color Technicolor dates to 1917. Other color films appeared in the 1920s, but the technology was still expensive and difficult. In the early 1930s color was primarily used in animated shorts, such as Walt Disney's *Silly Symphony* series. Color films made greater strides in the late 1930s and throughout the 1940s, including *The Wizard of Oz* (1939). But color was not fully embraced until the 1950s.

The Academy of Motion Picture Arts and Sciences, often called simply the Academy, was formed in 1927 through the leadership of MGM's Louis Mayer. The Academy was intended to bolster the image of the film industry and to provide a third party to mediate labor disputes. Its members are actors, directors, producers, writers, and technicians. Douglas Fairbanks Sr. was elected the first president; one of his first actions was to create the Academy Awards. The awards, later dubbed the Oscars, were first bestowed in 1928.

In 1933, just a few years after the creation of the Academy, the Screen Actors Guild was formed as a labor union to represent the growing body of actors performing in

Hollywood films. To this day, new actors may play only a limited number of roles before they have to join SAG in order to continue acting in SAG productions.

In 1947 movies became tangled up in politics when the House Un-American Activities Committee launched hearings to investigate communist influences on the film industry. Eleven Hollywood professionals—writers, directors, and producers—were called to testify as suspected communists. Eventually six were jailed, not for communist activity but rather for contempt of Congress, because they had refused to answer questions and challenged the legitimacy of the hearings.

In 1948 the Supreme Court heard a case brought by the Justice Department against five vertically integrated Hollywood studios: Paramount, Twentieth Century Fox, Warner Brothers, MGM, and RKO. The Court mandated that the studios sell off their exhibition divisions, meaning that they could no longer own the theaters that showed their films. The Court also ended the practices of *block booking*—renting films to theaters in sets so that a theater had to rent several titles just to have access to a popular one—and *blind booking*—renting sets of films without revealing all of the titles. All of these changes reduced the capacity of the studios to expand the profit margins on their films.

By 1950 Hollywood studios were forced to regard television as a real threat to their audiences and to integrate television production into their work: "Even as major Hollywood studios were publicly proclaiming that movies were better than ever, resources and investment [were] being shifted to production for television after 1955" (Monaco 2010, 159).

The acquisition of many film studios by larger corporate conglomerates began in the late 1960s. Today, although there are many film studios, only six parent corporations control the majority of film production: Time Warner, Disney, Sony, News Corp., Viacom, and Comcast/GE. Comcast and GE are separate corporations, but their co-ownership of NBC also gives them shared control of Universal Pictures.

The development of videotape, particularly the video home system (VHS), transformed the film industry in the 1980s. The videocassette recorder (VCR) was developed in the 1970s and provided the opportunity for home recording on videotape. In the 1980s, as the market for VCRs grew despite a format war between VHS and Betamax, the video rental industry burgeoned. Blockbuster Video opened as a video rental chain in 1985. After a brief flirtation with other formats such as the laserdisc, the industry embraced the DVD format in the late 1990s. Since 2006 the DVD format has competed with both HD-DVD and the blu-ray disc formats. Digital downloads are increasingly challenging these other forms of film sales and rental.

From VHS to digital download, these new formats mean that audiences increasingly consume film at home, which is opening up new possibilities for revenue while also challenging the cinema industry. Although Hollywood blockbusters are doing well, smaller films often struggle to reach an audience at the movie theater, which in turn can limit their success in other formats.

Another recent challenge to the established Hollywood film industry has been the rise of the indie, or independent, film. The term *indie film* refers to those movies made outside the major Hollywood studios. It can refer to films made in other parts of the country (outside Hollywood or LA), films made by directors not associated with a studio, films made by small studios, and even films made by art house studios that are part of the holdings of a much larger corporation. All of the major corporate owners of the film industry include an indie or art house studio among their holdings. For example, Warner Bros. owns Castle Rock Entertainment, and Disney owns Miramax Studios. Although truly independent small studios still produce a tremendous number of films, the major corporations play a surprisingly large role in the indie film conversation in the United States.

Although the term *indie* dates to the 1990s, there has been independent—small studio and nonstudio—filmmaking throughout the history of the medium. Indie film today, and its associated film festivals, continues to be a major source of innovation within the industry.

APPENDIX 4
A Brief History of Television

Television owes its origins to both the telephone and the radio. *Television* and *telephone* are similar words, but their uses over the last few decades have been so different that we forget the original technology had so much in common. Of course today many of us watch television on our phones, so the devices are coming together again.

The first television demonstration occurred in England in January 1926. Scottish inventor John Logie Baird used a wireless transmitter to send images of human faces as a demonstration for members of the British Royal Institution. This television, like those that followed over the next few years, is referred to as a *mechanical television*, in contrast to the *electronic television* that we have known since 1935. Mechanical television broadcasts utilized the AM radio band.

Mechanical television technology was developed in the United States a year later by the Bell Telephone Laboratories, a research and development lab that was co-owned by Western Electric and American Telephone & Telegraph (AT&T). The *Indianapolis Star* covered the news:

> Television, a scientific dream ever since the telephone was perfected, has at last been realized, according to dispatches from New York describing the latest modern miracle. Secretary Hoover delivered a short address over telephone at Washington and he was seen as well as heard at Bell telephone laboratories at the metropolis.*

The televisions of this time had very small screens, 2 x 3 inches, which provided the best picture clarity.

---

* Scan of the newspaper story can be found at http://tvhistory.tv/pre-1935.htm.

As these televisions entered the market, at between $40 and $80, a handful of radio stations began to broadcast portions of their programming on television. The first station to experiment with television was W2XB in Schenectady, New York.

Electronic television was first developed in 1927 by Philo Farnsworth. The difference between mechanical and electronic television lies in how the image is captured and reproduced. For the mechanical television, images are captured when light is beamed through a scanning disk with a series of holes that spiral out from the center to the edge. This allows the camera to capture a series of images that the brain interprets as continuous. The electronic television replaces the light method with a beam of electrons, which greatly increases the potential resolution of the image.

A patent battle between Farnsworth and RCA prevented the electronic television from hitting the market until 1935, when Farnsworth won the battle and prevented RCA from claiming full patent control. Although the mechanical television remained dominant in the late 1920s and early 1930s, after the patent dispute was settled, the electronic television, with its vastly improved resolution, quickly took hold of the market. Mechanical television broadcasts effectively ended in 1939.

The years before 1939 might be called television's prehistory, a period when television sales and television broadcasts happened in fits and starts. The development of a television industry is surprising when we think of what had to be accomplished to pull it off. Why invest in complicated studio broadcasts if no one had television sets yet? By the same token, why purchase a television if there was nothing to watch on it? This is similar to the struggles faced by the radio industry just a few years earlier, but in radio it was possible to have two-way communication at much cheaper costs. People were more willing to buy radios even if there was no radio broadcast in their areas. As radio developed into a broadcast industry, it became a one-way medium, but even today individuals can purchase affordable radio systems that allow them to broadcast themselves. By contrast, television has never been a two-way medium.

Another key event in television's history in the 1930s was the establishment of the Federal Communications Commission (FCC) through the Communications Act of 1934. This act created the FCC as a body of commissioners charged with regulating the use of the radio spectrum and wire communications, interstate communications, and international communications that originate in the United States. The FCC was intended "to make available, so far as possible, to all the people of the United States, without discrimination on the basis of race, color, religion, national origin, or sex, a rapid, efficient, Nation-wide, and world-wide wire and radio communication service with adequate facilities at reasonable charges." The radio waves were essentially defined as a public good, but with a role to play in national defense. One of the FCC's major duties was, and still is, to issue licenses to stations to establish their right to use a very particular segment of the radio spectrum. The FCC is funded entirely by license, application, and other regulatory fees. Today the

FCC continues to regulate television, radio, and other communications that use wire and broadcast, but it is also charged with regulating satellite and cable communications. The FCC's regulatory role is diverse, but its public discussions generally focus either on its regulation of markets, under the banner of consolidation, or on its authority over certain content boundaries such as foul language or nudity.

The era of broadcast television was solidified in 1939 at the World's Fair in New York City, when David Sarnoff, the president of RCA, debuted the regular broadcasting of his new network, the National Broadcasting Company (NBC). Franklin D. Roosevelt, appearing at the opening ceremonies of the fair, was the first president to be on television. RCA began selling new televisions immediately and developed its broadcast schedule. Other networks developed in the following two years. Then America's entry into the Second World War in 1941 halted the production of television equipment and significantly reduced broadcasts.

Television production resumed in 1946, which also initiated the race for color. Inventors had dabbled with the possibility of color since at least the late 1920s, and a German television inventor had filed for a patent on color television as early as 1904, but that technology had yet to move into commercial production. As soon as the war ended, CBS began developing color technology for a mechanical television system. RCA fought to maintain the dominance of the black and white standard, with the goal of buying itself more time to prevail in the color market.

The FCC intervened on RCA's behalf in 1947, ruling that the mechanical color system developed by CBS was not ready for commercial distribution. RCA continued development of its electronic color system and completed it in 1950, the same year that CBS received FCC approval for its mechanical color television. CBS debuted color broadcasts of *The Ed Sullivan Show* in 1951, just as RCA was unveiling its version of the color TV. But later that year color TV production halted in response to the Korean War, which ended in 1953. Even before production stopped, the major problem faced by CBS was that its color broadcasts were not compatible with existing black and white televisions, and sales of the new color sets were very low. While production was halted, the National Television System Committee (NTSC) worked with RCA to develop a color broadcast that was compatible with black and white sets, meaning that a black and white TV would still be able to receive a program that was broadcast in color. The NTSC was an independent committee formed in 1940 by the FCC. RCA's development of an electronic system that was compatible with existing black and white TVs allowed it to take control of the market by 1954. The role of the NTSC was so pivotal that RCA's color system was called NTSC color.

But the cost of the new color TVs was high, $1,000, and initial sales were so slow that a couple of years later *Time* magazine called the color TV "the most resounding industrial flop of 1956."* RCA continued to push the development of

---

* As cited in "Television History: The First 75 Years," http://www.tvhistory.tv.

the color TV industry by broadcasting increasing portions of NBC's schedule in color. But the growth was slowed by the resistance of other networks to broadcast in color, which in turn slowed consumer interest in buying color TVs. NBC moved the game forward in 1965 by broadcasting most of its prime time schedule in color. When the other networks increased their prime time color offerings in order to hold audiences, sales of color TVs finally took off. Color TV sales finally exceeded black and white sales in 1972. In the years that followed the technology for TVs did not change much except for the increasing size of screens.

Cable television began transforming television content in the 1970s. The technology was used prior to that period, primarily to deliver broadcast television to places that signals could not reach, but in 1972 FCC deregulation allowed cable to become a source of original programming. Ted Turner was the first to invest in cable as a method for delivering new content, with his WTBS cable network, now known simply as TBS. Turner, and those who followed him, used satellite technology to deliver programming to their cable networks. Pat Robertson came close on Turner's heels with the Christian Broadcasting Network (CBN), which is now known as ABC Family after its purchase by Disney. CBN continues to produce Christian shows such as *The 700 Club*.

Premium, or pay cable, developed alongside basic cable. Home Box Office (HBO) first appeared on the national market in 1975, after starting as a local service in Wilkes-Barre, Pennsylvania. HBO's premier cablecast was the famous boxing match between Muhammad Ali and Joe Frazier. Cable TV is able to focus less on drawing advertising revenues than broadcast TV, which allows it to cater to smaller audiences. Although the FCC regulates cable, those regulations do not include content restrictions. The continued use of advertising on most nonpremium stations nevertheless functions to limit content, because advertisers are very careful about what their brands are associated with.

Cable service spread across the country throughout the 1980s and 1990s. According to the research firm SNL Kagan, 57.1 percent of households with televisions now have at least basic cable. Over 75 percent of cable revenues come from residential subscription services, with the remainder generated largely by advertising.

The most recent shift in television technology has been the conversion to digital television delivery, a process that was largely complete by 2009. Digital television relies on digital rather than analog signals. The difference is fairly technical, but the conversion allows for higher resolution images to be delivered across the airwaves using a much smaller portion of the radio spectrum. The conversion has freed up segments of the broadcast spectrum for other purposes, while also allowing many broadcasters to beam multiple signals. Many local affiliates use these extra signals to broadcast traffic information, news, or local programming. This conversion was mandated by the US Congress. The transition forced many viewers to obtain conversion boxes and high definition (HD) antennae, but much of the technology is now built into new televisions.

The other major technology that is reshaping the television industry is the Internet, which now provides a host of ways for viewers to watch television on their computers or to stream Internet content onto their televisions. Most networks provide some or all of their content on their own websites and also allow access to their content through services like Hulu. Content may also be purchased through providers such as iTunes and Amazon. Older content is increasingly available through Netflix, although restructuring of that company may limit that access again. And of course content can be pirated on the Internet as well. Initial fears that Internet piracy might cripple the industry have been alleviated as new innovations have allowed broadcasters to reach audiences on their own terms, without compromising revenues. However, as the Internet is used increasingly as a content source, it remains to be seen what relationship television content will have with the original model of network affiliates broadcasting programs to actual television sets.

APPENDIX 5
A Brief History of the Internet

Internet refers to a network of connected computers and is a much broader concept than the more recent "World Wide Web." The concept of the Internet dates back to the 1960s, when the Advanced Research Projects Agency (ARPA)—part of the US Department of Defense, now known as the Defense Advanced Research Projects Agency (DARPA)—began funding initiatives to create a network of computers that could allow scientists working on defense projects to collaborate with one another. The original network was called ARPANET.

When I was in graduate school, I made extra money teaching basic HTML courses. HTML—Hypertext Markup Language—is the basic language for programming Web pages. I was told to include as part of the course a brief overview of the Internet as it was summarized in the course materials. That overview claimed that the Internet was designed as a military tool to connect defense stations, with the goal that if one military site were destroyed by a nuclear bomb, the other sites would remain in contact with each other. That assertion appears in a variety of discussions of Internet history, but it has been debunked. ARPANET was really a way for scientists to communicate.

The first message was sent through ARPANET on October 29, 1969, and the first network of four computers was established on December 5, 1969. ARPANET played an important role in fostering computer science in the 1970s and 1980s, but was decommissioned in 1991, because many other networks had gained prominence in the growing Internet system. Leiner and colleagues explain how the development of e-mail turned out to be one of the most important contributions of ARPANET:

> While file transfer and remote login (Telnet) were very important applications, electronic mail has probably had the most significant impact of the innovations from that era. Email provided a new model of how people could communicate

245

with each other, and changed the nature of collaboration, first in the building of the Internet itself and later for much of society. (2009, 25)

My first experience with e-mail occurred in 1993, in my last year of high school, when my biology teacher let us choose some questions to ask of a college professor that she knew. She used the one networked computer in the school to e-mail the questions to him, and he responded about a week later.

In 1995 Sandra Bullock starred in *The Net*, a fearful exploration of a seemingly new world in which people conducted their lives online. Bullock played a software engineer who worked entirely from home through the Internet, which allowed a rival to delete her identity, give it to someone else, and frame her as a criminal. The film is a cautionary tale about the new online world order.

The World Wide Web is a specific application within the Internet. It was invented by a British scientist named Tim Berners-Lee while he was working at CERN, the European particle physics laboratory in Switzerland. He began working with hypertext as early as 1980, but did not have all of the components needed for the Web until 1990. Those components included the markup language HTML, the information protocol system HTTP (hypertext transfer protocol), and the basic Web browser. Berners-Lee had designed a system for CERN that was easy to expand to a much larger audience. The Stanford Linear Accelerator Center (SLAC) brought the technology to North America in 1991. Mosaic, one of the first major browsers, was introduced in 1993 and was the result of Al Gore's High Performance Computing and Communication Act of 1991 (the reason Gore has claimed to have invented the Internet). Mosaic later changed its name to Netscape Navigator.

In the late 1990s most companies were creating their first promotional websites, while scholars and libraries were learning to upload and exchange information on the Web. The website archive.org allows visitors to tour through various stages of the World Wide Web and includes a feature called the Wayback Machine that lets you enter a Web address to view archive snapshots of that site across several years.

The later years of the 1990s are referred to as the dot com boom, whereas the first three years of the twenty-first century are described as the dot com bust. Despite the bursting of the bubble, the World Wide Web became ubiquitous, thanks in part to the development of both the smartphone and social media. Since 2005 social media have dominated the landscape of interconnected computing and information sharing.

Years of Debut for Major Applications of the World Wide Web and Social Media

AOL 1991	Craigslist 1995
Yahoo 1994	Amazon 1995
eBay 1995	Ask 1996

Netflix 1997

Google 1998

Blogger 1999

Wikipedia 2001

Friendster 2002

WordPress 2003

MySpace 2003

LinkedIn 2003

Facebook 2004

YouTube 2005

Twitter 2006

Hulu 2007

Tumblr 2007

Instagram 2010

Pinterest 2010

REFERENCES

Abercrombie, Nicholas, Stephen Hill, and Bryan S. Turner. 1980. *The Dominant Ideology Thesis*. London: George Allen and Unwin.

Adeleye-Fayemi, Bisi. 1997. "Either One or the Other: Images of Women in Nigerian Television." Pp. 125–131 in *Readings in African Popular Culture*, edited by Karin Barber. Bloomington: Indiana University Press.

Altheide, David L., and Christopher J. Schneider. 2013. *Qualitative Media Analysis*. 2nd ed. Los Angeles: Sage.

Barber, Karin. 1997. "Introduction." Pp. 1–12 in *Readings in African Popular Culture*, edited by Karin Barber. Bloomington: Indiana University Press.

Barnett, Lisa A., and Michael Patrick Allen. 2000. "Social Class, Cultural Repertoires, and Popular Culture: The Case of Film." *Sociological Forum* 15: 145–163.

Barss, Patchen. 2010. *The Erotic Engine: How Pornography Has Powered Mass Communication, from Gutenberg to Google*. Toronto: Doubleday Canada.

Bechdel, Alison. 1986. *Dykes to Watch Out For*. Ann Arbor, MI: Firebrand Books.

Belcher, Catherine L., and Becky Herr Stephenson. 2011. *Teaching Harry Potter: The Power of Imagination in Multicultural Classrooms*. New York: Palgrave Macmillan.

Benjamin, Walter. 1968. "The Work of Art in the Age of Mechanical Reproduction." Pp. 217–251 in *Illuminations: Walter Benjamin, Essays and Reflections*, edited by Hannah Arendt. New York: Schocken Books.

Bielby, Denise D., and William T. Bielby. 1996. "Women and Men in Film: Gender Inequality Among Writers in a Culture Industry." *Gender and Society* 10: 248–270.

Billboard. 2010. "2010 Hot 100." http://www.billboard.com/charts/year-end/2010/hot-100-songs.

Binder, Amy. 1993. "Constructing Racial Rhetoric: Media Depictions of Harm in Heavy Metal and Rap Music." *American Sociological Review* 58:753–767.

Birleffi, Bobbie, and Beverly Kopf, dirs. 2011. *Chely Wright: Wish Me Away* [documentary film]. First Run Features.

B.o.B. 2010. "Airplanes." Track 4 on *B.o.B. Presents: The Adventures of Bobby Ray*. Grand Hustle.

Bordo, Susan. 1999. *The Male Body: A New Look at Men in Public and in Private*. New York: Farrar, Straus and Giroux.

Boucher, Cindy. 2008. "Newly Imagined Audiences: Folkways' Gay and Lesbian Records." *Journal of Popular Music Studies* 20:129–149.

Bourdieu, Pierre. 1977. *Outline of a Theory of Practice*. Cambridge: Cambridge University Press.

———. 1990. *The Logic of Practice*. London: Polity Press.

Bourdieu, Pierre, and Jean-Claude Passeron. 1977. *Reproduction in Education, Society and Culture*. Translated by Richard Nice. Beverly Hills, CA: Sage.

Bradley, Christopher. 2009. "'I Saw You Naked': 'Hard' Acting in 'Gay' Movies." Pp. 41–54 in *Filming Difference: Actors, Directors, Producers, and Writers on Gender, Race, and Sexuality in Film*, edited by Daniel Bernardi. Austin: University of Texas Press.

Brault, Matthew W. 2012. *Americans with Disabilities: 2010. Current Population Reports*. Household Economic Studies. Washington, DC: US Census Bureau.

Brennan, Ian, Brad Falchuk, and Ryan Murphy. 2009a. "Pilot." *Glee* [TV show]. Season 1: Episode 1. Fox.

———. 2009b. "Showdown." *Glee* [TV Show]. Season 1: Episode 7. Fox.

———. 2009c. "Mash-Up." *Glee* [TV Show] Season 1: Episode 8. Fox.

Browning, Tod. 1932. *Freaks* [film]. MGM.

Butler, Judith. 1991. "Imitation and Gender Insubordination." Pp. 13–31 in *Inside/Out: Lesbian Theories, Gay Theories*, edited by Diane Fuss. New York: Routledge.

Capsuto, Steven. 2000. *Alternate Channels: The Uncensored Story of Gay and Lesbian Images on Radio and Television, 1930s to the Present*. New York: Ballantine.

Cash, Johnny, with Patrick Carr. 1997. *Cash*. New York: Harper One.

Cazwell. 2006. "All Over Your Face." Track 4 on *Get Into It*. West End Records.

———. 2010. "Ice Cream Truck." Nonalbum single. Peace Bisquit/West End Records.

Church, David. 2006. "'Welcome to the Atrocity Exhibition': Ian Curtis, Rock Death, and Disability." *Disability Studies Quarterly* 26. http://dsq-sds.org/article/view/804/979.

Cohen, Michael. 1973. *What Did You Expect? . . . Songs about the Experiences of Being Gay*. Folkways.

Collins, Patricia Hill. 1990. *Black Feminist Thought: Knowledge, Consciousness, and the Politics of Empowerment*. New York: Routledge.

Conrad, Peter. 1992. "Medicalization and Social Control." *Annual Review of Sociology* 18:209–232.

Cooper, Evan. 2003. "Decoding 'Will and Grace': Mass Audience Reception of a Popular Network Situation Comedy." *Sociological Perspectives* 46:513–533.

Cooper, Margaret, and Kristina Dzara. 2010. "The Facebook Revolution: LGBT Identity and Activism." Pp. 100–112 of *LGBT Identity and Online New Media*, edited by Christopher Pullen and Margaret Cooper. New York: Routledge.

Corse, Sarah M., and Saundra Davis Westervelt. 2002. "Gender and Literary Valorization: The Awakening of a Canonical Novel." *Sociological Perspectives* 45:139–161.

Crenshaw, Kimberle. 1989. "Demarginalizing the Intersection of Race and Sex: A Black Feminist Critique of Antidiscrimination Doctrine, Feminist Theory and Antiracist Politics." *University of Chicago Legal Forum* 1989:139–167.

Crosby, Stills, Nash, and Young. 1970. "Almost Cut My Hair Today." Track 3 on *Déjà vu*. Atlantic.

Cruz, Taio. 2009a. "Dynamite." Track 1 on *Rokstarr*. Island.

———. 2009b. "Break Your Heart." Track 2 on *Rokstarr*. Island.

DeNavas-Walt, Carmen, Bernadette D. Proctor, and Jessica C. Smith. 2012. "Income, Poverty, and Health Insurance Coverage in the United States: 2011." US Census Bureau.

Dobransky, Kerry, and Eszter Hargittai. 2006. "The Disability Divide in Internet Access and Use." *Information, Communication and Society* 9:313–334.

Du Bois, W. E. B. 1903. *The Souls of Black Folk: Essays and Sketches*. Chicago: A.C. McClurg.

———. 1926. "Criteria of Negro Art." *The Crisis* 32:290–297.

———. 1995 [1899]. *The Philadelphia Negro: A Social Study*. Philadelphia: University of Pennsylvania Press.

Dubin, Steven C. 1987. "Symbolic Slavery: Black Representations in Popular Culture." *Social Problems* 34:122–140.

Durkheim, Émile. 1938. *The Rules of Sociological Method*. Translated by S. A. Solovay and J. H. Mueller. Chicago: University of Chicago Press.

———. 1951. *Suicide: A Study in Sociology*. Translated by John A. Spaulding and George Simpson. Glencoe, IL: Free Press of Glencoe.

Elliot, Missy. 2002. "Work It." Track 14 on *Under Construction*. Goldmine/Elektra.

Emerson, Rana A. 2002. "'Where My Girls At?': Negotiating Black Womanhood in Music Videos." *Gender and Society* 16:115–135.

Eminem. 2010. "Love the Way You Lie." Track 15 on *Recovery*. Aftermath.

Fecteau, Lydia. 2004. "Mutant and Cyborg Images of the Disabled Body in the Landscape of Science Fiction." Unpublished paper, obtained from the author.

Fine, Gary Alan. 2004. *Everyday Genius: Self-Taught Art and the Culture of Authenticity*. Chicago: University of Chicago Press.

Finger, Anne. 2010. "Blinded by the Light, Or: Where's the Rest of Me?" Pp. 207–216 in *The Problem Body: Projecting Disability on Film*, edited by Sally Chivers and Nicole Markotic. Columbus: Ohio State University Press.

Fire, Kathy. 1979. *Songs of Fire: Songs of a Lesbian Anarchist*. Folkways.

Fiske, John. 1992. "Audiencing: A Cultural Studies Approach to Watching Television." *Poetics* 21:345–359.

Foucault, Michel. 1990 [1976]. *The History of Sexuality, Volume 1: An Introduction*. New York: Vintage Books.

Gaines, Donna. 2003. *A Misfit's Manifesto: The Sociological Memoir of a Rock and Roll Heart*. New York: Random House.

Gamson, Joshua. 1998. *Freaks Talk Back: Tabloid Talk Shows and Sexual Nonconformity*. Chicago: University of Chicago Press.

Ganahl, Dennis J., and Mark Arbuckle. 2001. "The Exclusion of Persons with Physical Disabilities from Prime Time Television Advertising: A Two Year Quantitative Analysis." *Disability Studies Quarterly* 21. http://dsq-sds.org/article/view /278/305.

Gans, Herbert J. 1999. *Popular Culture and High Culture: An Analysis and Evaluation of Taste*. Rev. and updated ed. New York: Basic Books.

Gardner, Eriq. 2012. "Actress Sues over Controversial Vodka 'Rape' Advertisement." *Hollywood Reporter*, March 30. http://www.hollywoodreporter.com /thr-esq/lawsuit-actress-sues-vodka-belvedere-rape-306435.

Garfinkel, Harold. 1967. *Studies in Ethnomethodology*. Englewood Cliffs, NJ: Prentice Hall.

Gay and Lesbian Alliance Against Defamation. 2011a. "2010–2011 Where We Are on TV." http://www.glaad.org/files/whereweareontv2010-2011.pdf.

———. 2011b. "2011 Network Responsibility Index." http://www.glaad.org/files /glaad_nri_2011_updated.pdf.

Geertz, Clifford. 1973. *The Interpretation of Cultures*. New York: Basic Books.

Gitlin, Todd. 1983. *Inside Prime Time*. Berkeley: University of California Press.

Goff, Patricia M. 2006. "Producing Harry Potter. Why the Medium Is Still the Message." Pp. 27–44 in *Harry Potter and International Relations*, edited by Daniel H. Nexon and Iver B. Neumann. Oxford: Rowman and Littlefield.

Griffith, D. W. 1915. *The Birth of a Nation* [film]. David W. Griffith Corp.

Grindstaff, Laura. 2002. *The Money Shot: Trash, Class, and the Making of TV Talk Shows*. Chicago: University of Chicago Press.

Griswold, Wendy. 1981. "American Character and the American Novel." *American Journal of Sociology* 86:740–765.

———. 1994. *Cultures and Societies in a Changing World*. Thousand Oaks, CA: Sage.

Gunelius, Susan. 2008. *Harry Potter: The Story of a Global Business Phenomenon*. New York: Palgrave Macmillan.

Gupta, Suman. 2009. *Re-Reading Harry Potter*. 2nd ed., updated with new material. New York: Palgrave Macmillan.

Hargittai, Eszter, and Gina Walejko. 2008. "The Participation Divide: Content Creation and Sharing in the Digital Age." *Information, Communication, and Society* 11: 239–256.

Heins, Marjorie. 2003. "The Strange Case of Sarah Jones." Free Expression Policy Project. http://www.fepproject.org/commentaries/sarahjones.html.

Herman, Edward S., and Noam Chomsky. 1988. *Manufacturing Consent: The Political Economy of the Mass Media*. New York: Pantheon Books.

Holtzman, Linda. 2000. *Media Messages: What Film, Television, and Popular Music Teach Us About Race, Class, Gender, and Sexual Orientation*. Armonk, NY: M. E. Sharpe.

Holy Bible. 2011. New International Version. Grand Rapids, MI: Zondervan.

Horkheimer, Max, and Theodor Adorno. 2002. "The Culture Industry: Enlightenment as Mass Deception." Pp. 39–45 in *Cultural Sociology*, edited by Lyn Spilman. Malden, MA: Blackwell.

Hughey, Matthew W. 2010. "The White Savior Film and Reviewers' Reception." *Symbolic Interaction* 33:475–496.

Hunt, Darnell. 2003. "Prime Time in Black and White: Not Much Is New for 2002." Report, Ralph J. Bunche Center for African American Studies at UCLA.

———. 2005. *Channeling Blackness*. New York: Oxford University Press.

Hunter, James Davison. 1991. *Culture Wars: The Struggle to Define America*. New York: Basic Books.

Hurt, Byron, dir. 2006. *Hip-Hop: Beyond Beats and Rhymes* [documentary film]. PBS.

India.Arie. 2006. "I Am Not My Hair." Track 11 on *Testimony: Vol. 1, Life and Relationship*. Motown.

Jackson, Linda A., Yong Zhao, Anthony Kolenic III, Hiram E. Fitzgerald, Rene Harold, and Alexander Von Eye. 2008. "Race, Gender, and Information Technology Use: The New Digital Divide." *CyberPsychology and Behavior* 11:437–442.

Jackson, Patrick Thaddeus, and Peter Mandaville. 2006. "Glocal Hero: Harry Potter Abroad." Pp. 45–59 in *Harry Potter and International Relations*, edited by Daniel H. Nexon and Iver B. Neumann. Oxford: Rowman and Littlefield.

Jhally, Sut. 1990. *Dreamworlds: Gender/Sex/Power in Rock Video*. Amherst, MA: Media Education Foundation.

———. 1995. *Dreamworlds 2: Gender/Sex/Power in Music Video*. Amherst, MA: Media Education Foundation.

———. 2007. *Dreamworlds 3: Gender/Sex/Power in Music Video*. Amherst, MA: Media Education Foundation.

Jimi Hendrix Experience. 1967. "If 6 Was 9." Track 7 on *Axis: Bold as Love*. MCA.

Jones, Sarah. 2000. "Your Revolution." Mixed by DJ Vadim. Ninja Tune.

Kasbekar, Asha. 2006. *Pop Culture India! Media, Arts, and Lifestyle*. Santa Barbara, CA: ABC-CLIO.

Keh, Hean Tat. 1998. "Evolution of the Book Publishing Industry: Structural Changes and Strategic Implications." *Journal of Management History* 4: 104–123.

Keller, James R. 2002. *Queer (Un)Friendly Film and Television*. Jefferson, NC: McFarland.

Ke$ha. 2010a. "Tik Tok." Track 2 on *Animal*. RCA.

———. "Take It Off." Track 3 on *Animal*. RCA.

Kidd, Dustin. 2007. "Harry Potter and the Functions of Popular Culture." *Journal of Popular Culture* 40:70–90.

———. 2010. *Legislating Creativity: The Intersections of Art and Politics*. New York: Routledge.

———. 2012. "'She'd Have Been Locked in St. Mungo's for Good': Magical Maladies and Medicine." Pp. 91–100 in *The Sociology of Harry Potter: 22 Enchanting Essays on the Wizarding World*, edited by Jenn Simms. Hamden, CT: Zossima.

Kilbourne, Jean. 2010. *Killing Us Softly 4*. Amherst, MA: Media Education Foundation.

Kissel, Laura. 2009. "Disability Is Us: Remembering, Recovering, and Remaking the Image of Disability." Pp. 17–40 in *Filming Difference: Actors, Directors, Producers, and Writers on Gender, Race, and Sexuality in Film*. Austin: University of Texas Press.

Kring, Tim. 2006. "Homecoming." *Heroes* [TV show]. Season 1: Episode 9. NBC.

Lady Antebellum. 2010. "Need You Now." Track 1 on *Need You Now*. Capitol Nashville.

Lady Gaga. 2009. "Bad Romance." Track 1 on *The Fame Monster*. Streamline.

———. 2011a. "Born this Way." Track 2 on *Born this Way*. Interscope Records.

———. 2011b. "Hair." Track 6 on *Born This Way*. Interscope Records.

Lauzen, Martha M. 2008. "Boxed In: Women On Screen and Behind the Scenes in the 2007–08 Prime-Time Season." Center for the Study of Women in Television and Film.

———. 2012. "Boxed In: Employment of Behind-the-Scenes and On-Screen Women in the 2010–11 Prime-Time Television Season." Executive Summary. Center for the Study of Women in Television and Film.

Lauzen, Martha M., and Douglas M. Diess Jr. 2009. "Breaking the Fourth Wall and Sex Role Stereotypes: An Examination of the 2006–2007 Prime-Time Season." *Sex Roles* 60:379–386.

Lauzen, Martha M., and David M. Dozier. 2004. "Evening the Score in Prime Time: The Relationship Between Behind-the-Scenes Women and On-Screen Portrayals in the 2002–2003 Season." *Journal of Broadcasting and Electronic Media* 48:484–500.

———. 2006. "Genre Matters: An Examination of Women Working Behind the Scenes and On-Screen Portrayals in Reality and Scripted Prime-Time Programming." *Sex Roles* 55:445–455.

———. 2008. "Civilizing Prime Time: Gender and Conflict Resolution in the 2004–05 Season." *Mass Communication and Society* 11:300–318.

Lauzen, Martha M., David M. Dozier, and Nora Horan. 2008. "Constructing Gender Stereotypes Through Social Roles in Prime-Time Television." *Journal of Broadcasting and Electronic Media* 52:200–214.

Lear, Norman, with Tom Gliatto and Paul Chi. 2012. "Picks and Pans Main: TV." *People Magazine* 78(8). http://www.people.com/people/archive/article /0,,20622146,00.html.

Leiner, Barry M., Vinton G. Cerf, David D. Clark, Robert E. Kahn, Leonard Kleinrock, Daniel Lynch, Jon Postel, Larry G. Roberts, and Stephen Wolff. 2009. "A Brief History of the Internet." *ACM SIGCOMM Computer Communication Review* 39:22–31.

Levitan, Steven, and Christopher Lloyd. 2009. "Pilot." *Modern Family* [TV show]. Season 1: Episode 1. ABC.

Lincoln, Anne E., and Michael Patrick Allen. 2004. "Double Jeopardy in Hollywood: Age and Gender in the Careers of Film Actors, 1926–1999. *Sociological Forum* 19:611–631.

Linneman, Thomas J. 2008. "How Do You Solve a Problem Like Will Truman? The Feminization of Gay Masculinities on *Will and Grace*." *Men and Masculinities* 10:583–603.

Lorber, Judith. 1994. *Paradoxes of Gender*. New Haven, CT: Yale University Press.

Ludacris. 2000. "Ho." Track 11 on *Back Again for the First Time*. Disturbing the Peace/Def Jam.

Lyman, Stanford M. 1987. "From Matrimony to Malaise: Men and Women in American Film, 1930–1980." *International Journal of Politics, Culture, and Society* 1:263–290.

Martin, Deanna. 2007. "Secret 'Harry Potter' Printer in Indiana? Maybe." *USA Today*, July 18. http://usatoday30.usatoday.com/life/books/news/2007-07-18 -potter-printer_N.htm.

Marx, Karl. 1978 [1867]. "Capital, Volume One." Pp. 294–438 in *The Marx-Engels Reader*, edited by Robert C. Tucker. New York: W. W. Norton.

———. 1978. "The German Ideology." Pp. 146–200 in *The Marx-Engels Reader*, edited by Robert C. Tucker. New York: W. W. Norton.

McCabe, Janice, Emily Fairchild, Liz Grauerholz, Bernice A. Pescosolido, and Daniel Tope. 2011. "Gender in Twentieth-Century Children's Books: Patterns of Disparity in Titles and Central Characters." *Gender and Society* 25:197–226.

McChesney, Robert. 1999. *Rich Media, Poor Democracy: Communication Politics in Dubious Times*. Champaign: University of Illinois Press.

McIntosh, Peggy. 2009 [1988]. "White Privilege and Male Privilege." Pp. 15–27 in *Privilege: A Reader*, edited by Michael S. Kimmel and Abby L. Ferber. Boulder, CO: Westview Press.

Merton, Robert K. 1938. "Social Structure and Anomie." *American Sociological Review* 3:672–682.

Miles, Hugh. 2005. *Al Jazeera: The Inside Story of the Arab News Channel That Is Challenging the West*. New York: Grove Press.

———. 2006. "Al Jazeera." *Foreign Policy* 155:20–24.

Monaco, Paul. 2010. *A History of American Movies: A Film-by-Film Look at the Art, Craft and Business of Cinema*. New York: Scarecrow Press.

Monae, Janelle. 2007. "Many Moons." Track 3 on *Metropolis: Suite 1 (The Chase)*. Bad Boy Records.

Morley, David. 1992. *Television, Audiences, and Cultural Studies*. Abingdon, UK: Routledge.

Mosher, William D., Anjani Chandra, and Jo Jones. 2005. *Sexual Behavior and Selected Health Measures: Men and Women 15–44 Years of Age, United States, 2002*. Advanced Data from Vital and Health Statistics no. 362. Washington, DC: Centers for Disease Control and Prevention.

MPAA. 2012. "Theatrical Market Statistics 2011." http://www.mpaa.org/resources /5bec4ac9-a95e-443b-987b-bff6fb5455a9.pdf.

Neuendorf, Kimberly A. 2002. *The Content Analysis Guidebook*. Thousand Oaks, CA: Sage Publications.

Norden, Martin F. 1994. *The Cinema of Isolation: A History of Physical Disability in the Movies*. New Brunswick, NJ: Rutgers University Press.

Oakenfull, Gillian. 2007. "Effects of Gay Identity, Gender and Explicitness of Advertising on Gay Responses to Advertising." *Journal of Homosexuality* 53(4):49–69.

Omi, Michael, and Howard Winant. 1994. *Racial Formation in the United States*. New York: Routledge.

Perry, Katy. 2010. "California Gurls." Track 3 on *Teenage Dream*. Capitol.

Pescosolido, Bernice A., Elizabeth Grauerholz, and Melissa A. Milkie. 1997. "Culture and Conflict: The Portrayal of Blacks in U.S. Children's Picture Books Through the Mid- and Late-Twentieth Century." *American Sociological Review* 62:443–464.

Peterson, Eugene H. 2002. *The Message: The Bible in Contemporary Language*. Colorado Springs, CO: NavPress.

Peterson, Richard A. 1997. *Creating Country Music: Fabricating Authenticity*. Chicago: University of Chicago Press.

Peterson, Richard A., and David G. Berger. 1975. "Cycles in Symbol Production: The Case of Popular Music." *American Sociological Review* 40:158–173.

P!nk. 2010. "Raise Your Glass." Track 15 on *Greatest Hits . . . So Far!!!* LaFace.

Press, Andrea L. 1991. *Women Watching Television: Gender, Class, and Generation in the American Television Experience*. Philadelphia: University of Pennsylvania Press.

Radway, Janice A. 1984. *Reading the Romance: Women, Patriarchy, and Popular Literature*. Chapel Hill: University of North Carolina Press.

Ramones. 1977. "Pinhead." Track 7 on *Leave Home*. Sire.

Raynor, Olivia, and Katherine Hayward. 2005. *The Employment of Performers with Disabilities in the Entertainment Industry*. Los Angeles: Screen Actors Guild.

Ritzer, George. 1993. *The McDonaldization of Society*. Thousand Oaks, CA: Pine Forge Press.

———. 1999. *Enchanting a Disenchanted World: Revolutionizing the Means of Consumption*. Thousand Oaks, CA: Pine Forge Press.

Ritzer, George, and Elizabeth L. Malone. 2000. "Globalization Theory: Lessons from the Exportation of McDonaldization and the New Means of Consumption." *American Studies* 41:97–118.

Rosenberg, Alyssa. 2012. "*Glee* Is an Immoral Television Show and It's Time to Stop Watching It." Think Progress. http://thinkprogress.org/alyssa/2012/05/02/475188/glee-is-an-immoral-television-show-and-its-time-to-stop-watching-it.

Ross, Steven J. 1998. *Working-Class Hollywood: Silent Film and the Shaping of Class in America*. Princeton, NJ: Princeton University Press.

Rowling, J. K. 1999. *Harry Potter and the Chamber of Secrets*. New York: Scholastic.

———. 2000. *Harry Potter and the Goblet of Fire*. New York: Scholastic.

Russell, Mark James. 2008. *Pop Goes Korea: Behind the Revolution in Movies, Music, and Internet Culture*. Berkeley, CA: Stone Bridge Press.

Russo, Vito. 1987 [1981]. *The Celluloid Closet: Homosexuality in the Movies*. Rev. ed. New York: Harper and Row.

Schippers, Mimi. 2000. "The Social Organization of Sexuality and Gender in Alternative Hard Rock: An Analysis of Intersectionality." *Gender and Society* 14:747–764.

Schmutz, Vaughn, and Alison Faupel. 2010. "Gender and Cultural Consecration in Popular Music." *Social Forces* 89:685–708.

Schudson, Michael. 1989. "How Culture Works: Perspectives from Media Studies on the Efficacy of Symbols." *Theory and Society* 18:153–180.

Scott-Heron, Gil. 1970. "The Revolution Will Not Be Televised." Track 1 on *Small Talk at 125th and Lennox*. Flying Dutchman/RCA.

Sender, Katherine. 2012. *The Makeover: Reality Television and Reflexive Audiences*. New York: New York University Press.

Sherwood, Jessica Holden. 2010. "The Manly Spokesmen Are Winking" [blog posting]. *Ms. Magazine*. http://msmagazine.com/blog/blog/2010/07/16/the-manly-spokesmen-are-winking.

Shively, JoEllen. 1992. "Cowboys and Indians: Perceptions of Western Films Among American Indians and Anglos." *American Sociological Review* 57:725–734.

Shyminsky, Neil. 2011. "'Gay' Sidekicks: Queer Anxiety and the Narrative Straightening of the Superhero." *Men and Masculinities* 14:288–308.

Simmel, Georg. 2010. "The Stranger." Pp. 302–305 of *Sociological Theory in the Classical Era: Texts and Readings, Edition 2*, edited by Laura Desfor Edles and Scott Appelrouth. Los Angeles: Pine Forge Press.

Smith, Stacy L., and Marc Choueiti. 2009. "Black Characters in Popular Film: Is the Key to Diversifying Cinematic Content Held in the Hand of the Black Director?" Report. Annenberg School for Communication and Journalism, University of Southern California.

————. 2010. "Gender Inequality in Popular Films: Examining On Screen Portrayals and Behind-the-Scenes Employment Patterns in Motion Pictures Released Between 2007–2009." Report. Annenberg School for Communication
and Journalism, University of Southern California.

Snyder, Sharon L., and David T. Mitchell. 2010. "Body Genres: An Anatomy of
Disability in Film." Pp. 179–204 in *The Problem Body: Projecting Disability
on Film*, edited by Sally Chivers and Nicole Markotic. Columbus: Ohio State
University Press.

Steadman, Jana. 2005. "TV Audience Special Study: African-American Audience." Nielsen Media Research.

Straus, Joseph N. 2006. "Normalizing the Abnormal: Disability in Music and Music Theory." *Journal of the American Musicological Society* 59:113–184.

Swidler, Ann. 1986. "Culture in Action: Symbols and Strategies." *American Sociological Review* 51:273–286.

Thomas, Carol. 2004. "How Is Disability Understood? An Examination of Sociological Approaches." *Disability and Society* 19:569–583.

Thornton, Bridgett, Britt Walters, and Lori Rouse. 2006. "Corporate Media Is
Corporate America: Big Media Interlocks with Corporate America and
Broadcast News Media Ownership Empires." Pp. 245–262 in *Censored 2006:
The Top 25 Censored Stories*, edited by Peter Phillips and Project Censored.
New York: Seven Stories Press.

Toney, Gregory T., and James B. Weaver III. 1994. "Effects of Gender and Gender Role Self-Perceptions on Affective Reactions to Rock Music Videos." *Sex
Roles* 30:567–583.

Townsend, Robert. 1987. *Hollywood Shuffle* [film]. Conquering Unicorn.

Train. 2009. "Hey, Soul Sister." Track 2 on *Save Me, San Francisco*. Columbia.

Turner, S. Derek, and Mark Cooper. 2006. *Out of the Picture: Minority and Female
TV Station Ownership in the United States: Current Status, Comparative Sta-
tistical Analysis and the Effect of FCC Policy and Media Consolidation*. Free
Press. Available online at freepress.net.

Usher. 2010. "OMG." Track 6 on *Raymond v. Raymond*. LaFace.

Vanable, P. A., D. J. McKirnan, and P. Stokes. 1994. "Identification and Involvement with the Gay Community." In *Handbook of Sexuality-Related Measures*.
Thousand Oaks, CA: Sage.

Various Artists. 1979. *Walls to Roses: Songs of Changing Men*. Folkways.

Various Artists. 1980. *Gay and Straight Together*. Folkways.

Vila, Pablo, and Pablo Seman, with contributions by Eloisa Martin and Maria Julia Carozzi. 2011. *Troubling Gender: Youth and Cumbia in Argentina's Music
Scene*. Philadelphia: Temple University Press.

Wachowski, Andy, and Lana Wachowski. 1999. *The Matrix* [film]. Warner Bros.

Wallis, Cara. 2011. "Performing Gender: A Content Analysis of Gender Display
in Music Videos." *Sex Roles*: 64:160–172.

Webb, Beatrice Potter. 1998 [1913]. "Introduction to 'The Awakening of Women.'" Reprinted in *The Women Founders: Sociology and Social Theory: 1830–1930,* edited by Patricia Madoo Lengermann and Jill Niebrugge-Brantley. Boston: McGraw-Hill.

Weber, Max. 1978. *Economy and Society: An Outline of Interpretive Sociology.* Volumes 1 and 2. Edited by Gunther Roth and Claus Wittich. Berkeley: University of California Press.

West, Candace, and Don H. Zimmerman. 1987. "Doing Gender." *Gender and Society* 1:125–151.

Whittington-Walsh, Fionna. 2002. "From Freaks to Savants: Disability and Hegemony from *The Hunchback of Notre Dame* (1939) to *Sling Blade* (1997)." *Disability and Society* 17:695–707.

Williams, Raymond. 2002 [1958]. "Culture Is Ordinary." Pp. 91–100 in *The Every Day Life Reader,* edited by Ben Highmore. London: Routledge.

Willis, Paul. 1977. *Learning to Labor: How Working Class Kids Get Working Class Jobs.* New York: Columbia University Press.

Wilson, Britanie, and Jeremy Lucyk. 2012. *A Very Brief History of the Book-Publishing Industry.* Toronto: Centennial College Press.

GLOSSARY

Anomie: A state of normlessness in which existing social norms have broken down and have not yet been replaced by new ones.

Bechdel test: A method for testing the status of women in a film, attributed to a comic strip by Alison Bechdel. To pass the Bechdel test, a film must have (1) at least two or more female characters who (2) have names and (3) talk to each other about something other than men.

Commercial culture: Expressive styles and objects that are mass produced and sold for a profit. Often contrasted with folk culture and high culture.

Consumption: The process of buying and making use of goods and services.

Controlling images: Patricia Hill Collins's conception of stereotypes and other images that are meant to remind audiences of social hierarchies, including racial hierarchies, gender hierarchies, and class hierarchies.

Cultural diamond: Wendy Griswold's system for examining the relationship between culture and society. The four points on the cultural diamond are producers, cultural objects, audiences, and the social world.

Culture: A system of shared meanings embodied in social practices, social relationships, and socially meaningful objects.

Culture industry: The web of corporations that produce commercial culture and the meanings that are embedded in commercial culture objects.

Digital divide: A form of inequality related to access to, and understanding of, the Internet and its associated technologies, such as smartphones and tablets. Digital divides have been identified, and debated, along class lines, gender lines, and racial lines, among others.

Folk culture: Expressive styles and objects associated with local cultures and lower income groups. Often contrasted with high culture and commercial culture.

261

Gatekeepers: Cultural professionals who assess and curate cultural objects. Examples include book critics, awards programs, and television reviewers.

Habitus: A structure of dispositions that we acquire from life experiences, especially from our families. Schools also play a major role.

Hegemony: A form of domination that is based on culture and politics, as contrasted with domination based on violence and military control. The messages embedded in popular culture are often associated with the maintenance and legitimation of hegemony.

High culture: Expressive styles and objects associated with privileged elites. Often contrasted with folk culture and commercial culture.

Hypermasculinity: A cultural process of ramping up the standards and representations of masculinity.

Interpretation: The process of determining the meaning of a cultural object such as a book, film, television show, or work of art. See also Reception.

Interpretive sociology: A social science paradigm that focuses on the ordering power of culture.

Interpretive strategies: Ordered systems that guide the process of making meaning out of cultural consumption. Formal aesthetics can serve as an interpretive strategy, but so can other ideological systems such as feminism, Christianity, or libertarianism.

Intersectionality: A sociological theory that examines inequality and privilege, with a focus on the connections among systems of hierarchy, particularly race, class, and gender.

McDonaldization: George Ritzer's theory for explaining the transformation of systems of capitalist production, leading to increased efficiency, predictability, calculability, and mechanization.

Medical model of disability: A paradigm for understanding disability that focuses on bodily impairment and the capacity for the medical system to treat such impairment.

New means of consumption: George Ritzer's theory for explaining the transformation of systems of capitalist consumption, leading to larger and more rapid consumption experiences.

Popular culture: The culture of "the people," which can refer to either folk culture or commercial culture.

Positivist: A scientific paradigm that focuses on observable phenomena. It has the advantage of not being driven by beliefs or ideology, but the disadvantage of not being able to capture the influence of phenomena that are harder to observe but still powerful.

Power: A force that exerts influence over the behavior of individuals and groups. In some conceptions of power it is held by specific actors. In other conceptions it is independent of actors and moving in multiple directions.

Privilege: The benefit of being situated at the top of a social hierarchy. The concept is associated particularly with the work of Peggy McIntosh, who wrote about white privilege and male privilege. Privilege is often taken for granted and not noticed by those who have it.

Production: The process of creating and distributing goods and services.

Reception: The process of consuming a cultural object. See also Interpretation.

Reflection theory: A paradigm for examining the relationship between cultural objects and society that focuses on how objects reflect social reality, sometimes in a distorted way.

Representation: A cultural depiction of some aspect or group in society. Examples include disability representations, gay and lesbian representations, and racial representations.

Social construction: An ordering system that is based on social reality, but often implying a biological or other basis. Social constructions are powerfully real and shape behavior and social relationships.

Social model of disability: A paradigm for understanding disability that focuses on social order and inequality and treats disability as one of many systems that create hierarchies of human bodies.

Symbolic violence: Pierre Bourdieu and Jean-Claude Passeron's concept of the ways that cultural images reinforce social hierarchies.

Thick description: Clifford Geertz's methodological approach to studying culture from an interpretive standpoint. Deep structures and taken-for-granted ideas are observed through a detailed process of observation.

Tool kit: Ann Swidler's theory of how individuals make use of cultural experiences as resources and strategies that they utilize when making decisions about social action.

INDEX

Abercrombie, Nicholas (scholar), 133
Actors
    with disabilities, 182–183
    wages of, 81, 84, 84 (fig.)
ADA (Americans with Disabilities Act),
    168, 188
Adeleye-Fayemi, Bisi (scholar), 212–213
Adorno, Theodor (scholar), 7, 22
Advertisements
    gay identity and response to, 156–157
    men in, 95 (image)
    women in, 96–98, 99 (image)
Africa, popular culture in, 211–213
"Airplanes" (B.o.B), 79–80
Al Jazeera, 213–214
Aladdin (film), 76
All in the Family (TV show),
    63 (image), 64
Allen, Michael Patrick (scholar), 89, 117
Alternate Channels (Capsuto), 141
Altheide, David L. (scholar), 82–83
American Community Survey, 173–174
American dream, 68, 70, 76
American Horror Story: Asylum (TV
    show), 169
Americans with Disabilities Act (ADA),
    168, 188
America's Next Top Model (TV show), 104
Animation
    gender representation in, 105
    queer roles in, 143
Annihilation, gender and, 127

Anomie, 133
The Apprentice (TV show), 104
Arbuckle, Mark (scholar), 177
Argentina, image in, 207–209
Art, popular culture as, 69
The Artist (film), 108
Asians
    median household income, 73 (table)
    representation in film, 39, 40 (fig.)
    representation in music, 43, 44 (fig.)
    representation in television, 41–43,
        42 (fig.)
    television station ownership by, 52
Audience
    disability and, 183, 185–186
    ethnography, 59–60
    experience and class, 88–92
    gender and, 120–127, 121 (table), 123
        (table)
    influence of, 9
    internalization of meanings by, 9–10
    interviews, 159–162
    racial differences in film
        interpretation, 53–56, 55 (table)
    as receivers of cultural good, 7
    sexuality and, 154–162
    surveys, 90–91
Autoethnography, 187–188
The Awakening (Chopin), 122–123

The Bachelorette (TV show), 104
"Bad Romance" (Lady Gaga), 80

Barber, Karin (scholar), 211–212
Barnett, Lisa (scholar), 89
Bechdel, Alison (cartoonist), 107
Bechdel test, 107–108
Belcher, Catherine L. (scholar), 202–203
Bell, George (television personality), 227
Belvedere vodka ad, 96–97
Benjamin, Walter (scholar), 69
Biden, Joe (politician), 133
Bielby, Denise (scholar), 117
Bielby, William (scholar), 117
The Biggest Loser (TV show), 104, 177
The Birdcage (film), 141
The Birth of a Nation (film), 39
Bisexual identity, 138, 139 (fig.)
Bisexuals
    in music, 143, 145
    in television, 141–143, 144 (fig.)
    See also LGBT
Black Feminist Thought (Collins), 24, 113
Blacks
    median household income, 73 (table)
    representation in film, 39, 40 (fig.)
    representation in music, 43–45,
        44 (fig.)
    representation in television, 41–43,
        42 (fig.)
    representations in literature, 45–46
    technology use by, 58
    television station ownership by, 52
    television viewers, 56–58, 57 (fig.)
    women's performances in music
        videos, 113, 114
The Blind Side (film), 56
Blumer, Herbert (scholar), 194
B.o.B (musician), 79–80
The Bold and the Beautiful
    (TV show), 210
Bollywood, 211
Bomer, Matt (actor), 150
Bordo, Susan (scholar), 109
Boucher, Cindy (scholar), 150, 151
Bourdieu, Pierre (scholar), 46, 70–71, 89
Bourgeoisie, 68
Bradley, Christopher (actor), 149–150
"Break Your Heart" (Cruz), 80
Broadcast networks, 17, 20
Brokeback Mountain (film), 140

Browning, Tod (director), 165 (image),
    166, 168, 175, 221
Bullying of LGBT youth, 132, 136
Bureau of Labor Statistics, 53, 182
Butler, Judith (scholar), 225–226

Calculability, 195
Caldecott Medal books, 45–46, 110
"California Gurls" (Perry), 79
Campaign for Full Citizenship (film), 183
Capital (Marx), 69
Capitalism
    culture industry and, 7, 22
    Karl Marx and, 68–70
    popular culture as a form of
        production, 68–69
    women's movement and, 98–99
Capsuto, Steven (scholar), 141
Cash, Johnny (musician), 45
Cash (autobiography), 45
Cazwell (musician), 151
Cell phones, racial demographics
    of use, 58
Celluloid Closet (Russo), 140
Channeling Blackness (Hunt), 51
Children's books
    gender representation in, 110–112,
        111 (fig.)
    racial representations in, 45–46
Chomsky, Noam (scholar), 17
Chopin, Kate (author), 122
Choueiti, Marc (scholar), 39
Church, David (scholar), 180
The Cinema of Isolation (Norden), 174
CJ Entertainment, 205–206
Class, 63–93
    ambiguity of concept, 92
    audience experiences shaped by,
        88–92
    as dimensions of identity, 11, 24
    film and, 75–76, 77 (fig.)
    global perspective, 198
    modes of cultural production and,
        81–88
    music and, 76, 78–80
    qualitative content analysis, 82–83
    in the social world, 71–74
    taste and, 72–74

television content and, 74
television's caste system, 63–67
Closeness, sense created by popular
     culture, 4
Cohen, Michael (musician), 150
Collins, Patricia Hill (scholar), 15, 23,
     113, 192
Comic books
     disability representation in, 176, 179
     superhero/sidekick relationship,
          145–146, 146 (image)
Commercial culture
     goals celebrated by, 13
     production of, 7
Commodities, popular culture as a
     system of, 69
Conformity, 13, 13 (table)
Conglomerates, major media,
     18–19 (fig.), 20–23
Conrad, Peter (scholar), 171
Consumption
     by middle class, 6
     new means of, 196
Content, demographics of, 15
Content analysis
     qualitative, 82–83
     quantitative, 147–148
The Content Analysis Guidebook
     (Neuendorf), 148
Controlling images, 15, 113
Controversy, studying, 125–127
Cooper, Margaret (scholar), 157–158,
     162
Cops (TV show), 74, 116
Corporations
     identity politics and, 151
     major media, 17–23, 18–19 (fig.)
     matrix of, 218–219
     personhood of, 218–219, 221
     ruling ideas, 70
Corse, Sarah M. (scholar), 122
Counterimages, 15
Creators
     in cultural diamond, 7, 8 (fig.), 9, 10
     interviewing, 118–119
     reflection of social world, 9
Crenshaw, Kimberle (scholar), 24
Crime, 133

Crosby, Stills, Nash & Young
     (musicians), 227
Cross-promotion, 20, 22, 199–200
Cruz, Taio (musician), 43, 78, 80
Cultural adaptation, types of, 13,
     13 (table)
Cultural capital model, 89
Cultural diamond, 7, 8 (fig.), 9, 10, 14,
     222 (fig.)
Cultural efficacy, 47–50, 48 (fig.)
Cultural goals, 12–14, 13 (table)
Cultural objects
     in cultural diamond, 7, 8 (fig.), 9, 10
     efficacy of, 47
     Glee (TV show), 9–10
     glocalization, 200–201
     meaning of, 95–96
Cultural oligopoly, 68, 70
Cultural potency, 47–45, 48 (fig.)
Cultural studies, 112
Culture
     commercial, 7
     meanings of, 6
     shared meaning, 6
     taste, 72–74
     tool kit of resources provided by, 10
Culture industry
     capitalism and, 7, 22
     controlling corporations, 17,
          18–19 (fig.)
     mass media as, 7
     as a matrix, 23
Culture Wars (Hunter), 125
Cumbia villera, 207–209
Curtis, Ian (musician), 180
Cyber bullying, 132
Cyborgs, 179

Dangerous Minds (film), 56
Demographics of content, 15
The Departed (film), 201
The Descendants (film), 108
Description, thick, 180–182
Descriptive analysis, 113–114
The Dialectic of Enlightenment (Adorno
     and Horkheimer), 22
Digital culture, professional associations
     for, 185 (table)

Digital divide, 124
Directors
    gender of, 117
    wages of, 81, 84–85, 84 (fig.)
Disability, 165–189
    audience reception, 183, 185–186
    categories of, 173 (table)
    definitions of, 172–174
    as dimension of identity, 11
    film representation of, 174–176
    global perspective, 198
    meaning of, 170–172
    production and, 182–183
    social model of, 169–172
    in the social world, 172–174
    television representation of, 177,
        178 (fig.)
    visibility of, 174–180
Discrimination, 37
Dobransky, Kerry (scholar), 186
The Dominant Ideology Thesis
    (Abercrombie, Hill, and
    Turner), 133
Domination, 25
Double consciousness, 35–36
Dozier, David (scholar), 115–117
Dramas, TV
    disabled persons on, 177, 178 (fig.)
    gender representation in, 103 (fig.), 104
Dreamworlds (film), 112
Du Bois, W. E. B. (scholar), 35–36
Dubin, Steven (scholar), 46
Durkheim, Emile (scholar), 132–133,
    135
Dykes to Watch Out For (Bechdel), 107
"Dynamite" (Cruz), 80
Dzara, Kristina (scholar), 157–158, 162

Economy and Society (Weber), 170
Efficacy, cultural, 47–50, 48 (fig.)
Efficiency, 195
Egle, Jill (disability advocate), 186
Ellen (TV show), 141
Elliot, Missy Misdemeanor (rapper),
    31–32
Emerson, Rana A. (scholar), 112–113, 114
Eminem (musician), 80
Ethnographic content analysis, 82

Ethnography
    audience, 59–60
    autoethnography, 187–188
    content analysis, 82
    production, 86–88
    of romance novel readers, 123–124
Ethnomethodology, 125
Extremely Loud and Incredibly Close
    (film), 108

Facebook, 157–158, 162
Fame Monster (album), 131
Fashion, 134
Faupel, Alison (scholar), 118
Fear Factor (TV show), 116
Fecteau, Lydia (scholar), 179
Federal Communications Commission
    (FCC), 21 (table)
The Feminine Mystique (Friedan), 101
Feminism
    historical waves of, 101
    as interpretive strategy, 123
Fey, Tina (actress), 105
Film
    class impact on audience, 89–90, 92
    class representations/themes in,
        75–76, 77 (fig.)
    disability representation in, 174–176
    gender of audience, 120–121,
        121 (table)
    gender representations in, 105,
        106 (fig.), 107–109
    gendered production, 117, 117 (table)
    in India, 211
    professional associations for,
        184 (table)
    racial demographics of production
        labor force, 50–51
    racial differences in film
        interpretation, 53–56, 55 (table)
    racial representation in, 39, 40 (fig.)
    sexual demographics in, 138,
        140–141
    sexuality and production, 149–150
    in South Korea, 204–206
    wages for occupation associated with,
        81, 84–85, 84 (fig.)
Finding Forrester (film), 56

Fine, Gary Alan (scholar), 180
Finger, Anne (author), 187
Fire, Kathy (musician), 150
Fiske, John (scholar), 59
Folk culture, 5
Folkways, 125–126
Folkways Records, 150–151
Foucault, Michel (scholar), 135–136, 138
Fourteenth Amendment to the
    US Constitution, 218
Freak, 225–228
    embracing status of, 5
    as slur, 4
    susceptibility to being called, 4
    word as mechanism for undermining
        social power, 4
Freaks (film), 166–169, 167 (image),
    174–175, 221–225
Freaks Talk Back (Gamson), 86
Freakshow (TV show), 227
Freedom Writers (film), 54, 56
The Fresh Prince of Bel-Air (TV show), 64
Friedan, Betty (author), 101
Friends (TV show), 74
Funny Girl (film), 76

Gaines, Donna (scholar), 169
Gamson, Joshua (scholar), 86–87
Ganahl, Dennis (scholar), 177
Gans, Herbert (scholar), 5, 72–74
Garfinkel, Harold (scholar), 125
Gatekeepers, 46
Gay actors, 149–150
Gay and Lesbian Alliance Against
    Defamation (GLAAD), 142
Gay Liberation Front, 150
Gays
    advertising images and, 109–110
    audience interviews with, 159–162
    demographics in US, 138, 139 (fig.)
    in film, 140–141
    in music, 143, 145, 150–151
    Parents and Friends of Lesbians and
        Gays (PFLAG), 151
    production surveys, 152–154
    in television, 141–143, 144 (fig.), 149
    See also LGBT; Sexuality
Geertz, Clifford (scholar), 180–182

Gender
    in advertisements, 95 (image), 96–98,
        99 (image)
    annihilation, 127
    audience and, 120–127, 121 (table),
        123 (table)
    culture and the awakening of,
        98–101
    as dimension of identity, 11, 24
    doing gender, 24
    global perspective, 197
    participation divide, 124–125, 127
    as performance, 225
    production and, 115–119, 115 (table),
        117 (table)
    as social construct, 100–101
    in the social world, 101
    stereotypes, 24–25
Gender confirmation surgery, 102
Gender demographics in the mass media
    in advertisements, 109–110, 111(fig.)
    in children's books, 110–112, 111 (fig.)
    in film, 105, 106 (fig.), 107–109
    in music videos, 112–113
    in television, 102, 103 (fig.), 104–105,
Gender perspectives, 95–128
General Social Survey (GSS), 90–91
Gilligan's Island (TV show), 89
Gini score, 198
Gitlin, Todd (scholar), 119
GLADD (Gay and Lesbian Alliance
    Against Defamation), 142
Glee (TV show)
    cross-promotion in, 20, 22
    identity marker use, 25–26
    review/criticism of, 16
    sociology of, 1–4, 7, 9, 12
    women represented in, 14
Global identities, 197–199
Global perspectives, 191–215
    disability, 198
    gender, 197
    on Harry Potter, 199–204
    inequality, 198
    McDonaldization, 195–196
    racial categories, 197
    sexual identity, 198
Glocalization, 200–201

Goals, cultural, 12–14, 13 (table)
Goff, Patricia M. (scholar), 200
Gone with the Wind (film), 76
Good Times (TV show), 64
Google, 151, 154
Grauerholz, Elizabeth (scholar), 45
Gray, John (author), 100
Griffith, Bill (cartoonist), 166
Grindstaff, Laura (scholar), 86, 87–88
Griswold, Wendy (scholar), 7
Grossman, Naomi (actress), 169
Gruwell, Erin (teacher), 54, 56
GSS (General Social Survey), 90–91
Gupta, Suman (scholar), 203–204

Habitus, 70–71
Hargittai, Eszter (scholar), 124, 186
Harry Potter, global perspectives on,
     199–204
*Harry Potter: The Story of a Global
     Business Phenomenon*
     (Gunelius), 195
Harry Potter and the Chamber of Secrets
     (Rowling), 192
Harry Potter and the Goblet of Fire
     (Rowling), 191–193, 191 (image),
     203–204
Harry Potter and the Philosopher's Stone
     (Rowling), 202
Harry Potter and the Sorcerer's Stone
     (Rowling), 202, 204
Hegemony, 37
Hell's Kitchen (TV show), 104
The Help (film), 108
Herman, Edward S. (scholar), 17
Heroes (TV show), 226–227
"Hey Soul Sister" (Train), 79
High culture, 5, 73
High Culture and Popular Culture
     (Gans), 5
Hill, Stephen (scholar), 133
Hip-Hop: Beyond Beats and Rhymes
     (film), 32
Hip-hop music, 33
Hispanics
     median household income, 73 (table)
     representation in film, 39, 40 (fig.)
     representation in music, 43, 44 (fig.)

representation in television, 41–43,
     42 (fig.)
television station ownership by, 52
Hollywood Shuffle (film), 51
Holtzman, Linda (scholar), 75–76
Homosexuality
     demographics in US, 138, 139 (fig.)
     in film, 140–141
     See also Gays; Lesbians
Horizontal integration, 20, 21 (table)
Horkheimer, Max (scholar), 7, 22
Household income, 71–72, 73 (table)
How I Meet Your Mother (TV show),
     104–105
Hughey, Matthew (scholar), 54, 56
Hugo (film), 108
Hulu, 22
The Hunchback of Notre Dame (film), 175
Hunt, Darnell (scholar), 39, 51
Hunter, Davison James (scholar), 125
Hurt, Byron (filmmaker), 32
Hypermasculinity, 109

I Love Lucy (TV show), 89
Identity
     described, 4
     dimensions of, 11
     intersectionality and, 24
     matrix of, 23–26
     relationship with popular culture,
          10–16
     as stratification mechanism, 15
     as structural, economic, and cultural
          principle, 23
     ubiquity of, 23
IMDb (Internet Movie Database), 14, 52
Income, class and, 71–72, 73 (table)
India, popular culture in, 209–211,
     210 (table)
Inequality, privilege as a mechanism
     of, 25
Infernal Affairs (film), 201
Innovation
     generated by popular culture, 135
     in Merton's five types of cultural
          adaptation, 13, 13 (table)
Institutional retention, cultural potency
     and, 48 (fig.), 49–50

Integration, of individuals into society, 133
Interlock, 21 (table), 22
Internet
  disability and, 186
  gender and content creation, 124–125
  pornography and, 135
  racial demographics of use, 58
Internet Movie Database (IMDb), 14, 52
Interpretation, of meaning of cultural good, 7
The Interpretation of Cultures (Geertz), 180
Interpretive sociology, 170
Interpretive strategies, gender and, 122–123
Intersectionality, 24
Interviews
  audience, 159–162
  creators, 118–119
Isolation, disability and, 174, 183
It Gets Better Project, 129 (image), 130–131, 135, 162
It's Always Sunny in Philadelphia (TV show), 102

Jackson, Patrick Thaddeus (scholar), 201
Jamey's Law, 137 (fig.), 138
The Jeffersons (TV show), 63–64, 68, 70
Jhally, Sut (filmmaker), 112
Jimi Hendrix Experience (musicians), 227
Jones, Sarah (artist), 126–127
Journals, scholarly, 81
JSA: Joint Security Area (film), 206
The Jungle (Sinclair), 135

Kasbekar, Asha (scholar), 209–211
Ke\$ha (musician), 78, 227–228
Keller, James R. (scholar), 154
Kidd, Dustin (scholar), 125
The Kids Are All Right (film), 141
Kilbourne, Jean (filmmaker), 97–98
Killing Us Softly 4 (film), 97–98
Kissel, Laura (filmmaker), 183

Labor force
  class identity and, 70

deskilling of, 195–196
in production of popular culture, 50–53
Lady Antebellum (musicians), 78–79
Lady Gaga (musician), 32, 80, 131–132, 134, 138, 188–189
Lang, Fritz (director), 34
Lang, K. D. (musician), 151
Latinos. *See* Hispanics
Lauzen, Martha (scholar), 115–117
Lear, Norman (television writer), 64–65
Learning to Labor (Willis), 134
Leave Home (album), 168
Lee, Ang (director), 140
Lee, Jay-hyun (media mogul), 205
Lee, Miky (media mogul), 205
Legislating Creativity (Kidd), 125
Leisure, 69
Lesbians
  demographics in US, 138, 139 (fig.)
  in film, 140–141
  in music, 143, 145, 150–151
  Parents and Friends of Lesbians and Gays (PFLAG), 151
  in television, 141–143, 144 (fig.), 149
  See also LGBT; Sexuality
Levitan, Steven (television writer), 65
LGBT (lesbian, gay, bisexual, and transgender)
  Facebook users, 157–158, 162
  representation in television, 142
  suicides, 130, 131, 132, 135
Lincoln, Anne E. (scholar), 117
Linneman, Thomas (scholar), 156
Literature
  gender representations in children's books, 110–112, 111 (fig.)
  in India, 210
  racial representations in, 45–46
  romance novels, 123–124, 123 (table)
  sexuality in, 145–146, 146 (image)
Lloyd, Christopher (television writer), 65
Lorber, Judith (scholar), 100–101
Loser
  in *Glee* (TV show), 1–3, 10, 12
  hand signal for, 1
Love Story (film), 76
"Love the Way You Lie" (Eminem), 80

Low culture, 73
Lower-middle-class, film viewing by,
    89–90
Lower-middle culture, 73
Ludacris (musician), 207
Lyman, L. (scholar), 108–109

The Makeover (Sender), 91
The Male Body (Bordo), 109
Male privilege
    in music industry, 118
    production of, 127
    variation in character of, 101
Mandaville, Peter (scholar), 201
Marlboro Man, 95 (image), 109
Married . . . with Children (TV show), 59
Marx, Karl (scholar), 68–70
Mass media, as culture industry, 7
Mass media matrix, 12, 16–23
    corporations and, 218–219
    The Matrix as metaphor for,
        218–221
    plugging into, 219–220
Matrix
    of identity, 23–26
    of privilege and oppression, 223–224
The Matrix (film), 34, 217–221, 217
    (image), 225
McCabe, Janice (scholar), 110
McChesney, Robert (scholar), 17
McDonaldization, 195–196, 211
McIntosh, Peggy (scholar), 25
McMillan, Terry (author), 47
Mead, George Herbert (scholar),
    193–194
Meaning
    of cultural objects, 95–96
    in global context, 200, 204
    shared, 194
    systems of, 170
Media consolidation, 21 (table)
Media Messages (Holtzman), 75
Media oligopoly, 20, 21 (table)
Medical model of disability, 170
Medicalization, 171
Men
    in advertisements, 95 (image),
        109–110, 110 (image)

film representation of, 109
    film viewing by, 120–121, 121 (table)
    hypermasculinity, 109
    television viewing by, 120
    See also Gender
Merton, Robert (scholar), 13, 13 (table),
    172
The Message (Peterson), 201
Methodological approaches, discussed in
    book, 28–29 (table)
Methodology moment
    audience ethnography, 59–60
    audience interviews, 159–162
    audience surveys, 90–91
    autoethnography, 187–188
    descriptive analysis, 113–114
    interviewing creators, 118–119
    labor force analysis, 52–53
    organizational reports, 184–185
    production ethnography, 86–88
    production surveys, 152–154
    qualitative content analysis, 82–83
    quantitative content analysis, 147–148
    studying controversy, 125–127
    studying cultural efficacy, 47–50,
        48 (fig.)
    thick description, 180–182
Metropolis (film), 34–35
Microcephaly, 166, 169
Middle class
    audience experience with television
        and film, 88–90
    consumption by, 6
    defined, 5–6
    film and, 75
    growth of, 6
    household income, 71–72, 73 (table)
    taste of, 73
    television and, 74
Midnight in Paris (film), 108
Midnight's Children (Rushdie), 210
Miles, Hugh (journalist), 213–214
Milkie, Melissa A. (scholar), 45
Miller, Terry, 130
A Misfits Manifesto (Gaines), 169
Mitchell, David (scholar), 176
Modern Family (TV show), 50, 64–68,
    70–71

Monae, Janelle (musician), 31 (image), 33–34, 49
Money Ball (film), 108
The Money Shot (Grindstaff), 86
Moral authority, provided by society, 133
Morley, David (scholar), 120
Murphy, Ryan (creator of *Glee*), 7, 9
Music
  in Argentina, 207–209
  audience ethnography, 59–60
  class and, 76, 78–80
  disability and, 179–180
  ethnography of alternative rock, 157
  gender in production of, 118
  gender of audience of, 122
  in India, 209–210, 210 (table)
  professional associations for, 185 (table)
  racial demographics of artists, 43–45, 44 (fig.)
  racial perspectives in, 31–35
  sexist lyrics, 207–209
  sexual demographics in, 143, 145
  sexuality and production, 150–151
Music videos
  gender of audience of, 122
  gender representation in, 112–113, 114
My Fair Lady (film), 76
My Summer of Love (film), 141
MySpace, 22

Nationality, 35
Native Americans
  absence from television, 41
  racial differences in film interpretation, 53–54, 55 (table)
  television station ownership by, 52
"Need You Now" (Lady Antebellum), 78–79
"Network Responsibility Index" (NRI), 142
Neuendorf, Kimberly A. (scholar), 148
The New Statesman (magazine), 98
Nigeria, popular culture in, 211–213
Night of the Living Dead (film), 179
Norden, Martin (scholar), 174

Oakenfull, Gillian (scholar), 156–157
Obama, Barack (president), 138
Objects, cultural. *See* Cultural objects
Occupation Employment Statistics (OES), 53
Ocean, Frank (musician), 151
OES (Occupation Employment Statistics), 53
Off the Straight and Narrow (film), 155
The Office (TV show), 104
Oligopoly, 20, 21 (table), 68, 70
Omega Man (film), 179
"OMG" (Usher), 79
Omi, Michael (scholar), 36
Open-ended questions, 91
Oppression, matrix of, 223–224
Organizational reports, 184–185
Out & Equal Workplace Survey, 153–154

Packard, Alicyn (actress), 97
Paradoxes of Gender (Lorber), 100
Parents and Friends of Lesbians and Gays (PFLAG), 151
Parsons, Jim (actor), 150
Participation divide, 124–125, 127
Passeron, Jean-Claude (scholar), 46
Peer review, 81
Perry, Katy (musician), 79
Perry, Tyler (director), 50
Personal Best (film), 141
Pescosolido, Bernice A. (scholar), 45
Peterson, Eugene H. (author), 201
PFLAG (Parents and Friends of Lesbians and Gays), 151
The Philadelphia Negro (Du Bois), 35
Phillips, Sam (record producer), 45
Physiognomy, 174
"Pinhead" (song), 168–169
P!nk (musician), 227
Pistorius, Oscar (athlete), 179
Politics
  identity, 23
  racial, 33, 34
Pop Culture India! (Kasbekar), 209
Pop Goes Korea (Russell), 204
Popular, origin of term, 5

Popular culture
  defining, 5–10
  described, 4
  racial demographics in, 39–50
  racial theory and, 35–37
  relationship with identity, 10–16
  research questions and arguments,
    10–16
  ubiquity of, 16–17
Popular Culture and High Culture
  (Gans), 5, 72–73
Pornography, 135
Positivist social science, 59
Potency, cultural, 47–45, 48 (fig.)
Power
  Chain of Power Relations, 137 (fig.),
    138
  sexuality and, 135–138
  social, 101
Predictability, 195
Press, Andrea (scholar), 88–89
Pretty Woman (film), 76
Prince-Bythewood, Gina (director), 50
Privilege
  concept described, 25
  male, 101, 118, 127
  matrix of, 223–224
  as mechanism of inequality, 25
  white, 25, 37–39
Producers, income of, 84–85
Production
  characteristics of process, 195–196
  class and, 81–88
  of cultural good, 7
  gender and, 115–119, 115 (table),
    117 (table)
  by people with disabilities, 182
  popular culture as form of capitalist,
    68–69
  racial demographics of, 50–53
  sexuality and, 146–154
  surveys, 152–154
  wages associated with occupations,
    84–85 (fig.)
Proletariat, 68
Propaganda, 36
Publishing, professional associations for,
  185 (table)

Qualitative content analysis, 82–83
Qualitative Media Analysis (Altheide and
  Schneider), 82
Quantitative content analysis, 147–148
Quasi-fold low culture, 73
Queer (Un)Friendly Film and Television
  (Keller), 154
Questions, open-ended, 91

Race, 31–61
  audience experience shaped by, 53–58,
    55 (table)
  categories, 37, 38 (fig.), 197
  as dimension of identity, 11, 24
  double-consciousness, 35–36
  labels, 31–32
  misrepresentations in media, 58–61
  popular culture and racial theory,
    35–37
  in production, 50–53
  racial breakdown of the United States,
    37, 38 (fig.)
  representations, 36
  in social world, 37–39
  symbolic slavery, 46–47
Racial demographics, 39–50
  in film, 39, 40 (fig.)
  in literature, 45–46
  in music, 43–45, 44 (fig.)
  of production labor force, 50–53
  of technology use, 58
  in television, 39, 41–43, 42 (fig.)
  of television station ownership, 51–52
  in television viewership, 56–58,
    57 (fig.)
Racial formation, 36
Racial Formation in the United States
  (Omi and Winant), 36
Racial hegemony, 37
Racial labels, 31–32
Radway, Janice (scholar), 123
Rain Man (film), 175
Ramones (musicians), 168–169
Rap music, 33
Ray, Todd (television personality), 227
Re-Reading Harry Potter (Gupta),
  203–204
Reading, ethnography of, 60

Reality TV
  disabled persons on, 177, 178 (fig.)
  gender representation in, 102,
    103 (fig.), 104
Rebellion, 13 (table), 14
Receivers, in cultural diamond, 7,
    8 (fig.), 9, 10
Reception, of cultural good, 7
Reflection theory, 9
Remoteness, sense created by popular
    culture, 4
Representations, 36
Resolution, cultural potency and,
    48 (fig.), 50
Resonance, cultural potency and,
    48 (fig.), 49
Resources, trust in, 80–81
Retreatism, 13–14, 13 (table)
Retrievability, cultural potency and, 47,
    48 (fig.)
"The Revolution Will Not Be Televised"
    (Scott-Heron), 33
Rhetorical force, cultural potency and,
    47, 48 (fig.), 49
Riley, Amber (actress), 1 (image)
Ritualist, 13, 13 (table)
Rituals of popular culture, 134
Ritzer, George (scholar), 195–196, 211
Rocky (film), 76
Rocky Horror Picture Show , 59
Rodemeyer, Jamey (suicide victim),
    129–130, 131–132, 136, 137 (fig.),
    138, 162
Rolling Stone (magazine), 118
Romance novels, 123–124, 123 (table)
Romijn, Rebecca (actress), 102
Rosenberg, Alyssa (critic), 16
Ross, Steven (historian), 75
Rules of Sociological Method
    (Durkheim), 133
Rushdie, Salmon (author), 210
Russell, Mark James (journalist),
    204–206
Russo, Vito (film historian), 138, 140–141

SAG (Screen Actors Guild), 85, 182–183
Sarkeesian, Anita (media critic), 107–108
Saturday Night Live (TV show), 145

Savage, Dan (columnist), 130–131, 135
Savant, 175
Schippers, Mimi (scholar), 157
Schmutz, Vaughn (scholar), 118
Schneider, Christopher J. (scholar),
    82–83
Scholarly journals, 81
Schudson, Michael (scholar), 47
Science fiction, disability representation
    in, 176, 179
Scorsese, Martin (director), 201
Scott-Heron, Gil (musician), 33, 49
Screen Actors Guild (SAG), 85, 182–183
Scrubs (TV show), 22
The Searchers (film), 53–54, 55 (table)
The Secret Life of Bees (film), 50
Seman, Pablo (scholar), 207–209
Sender, Katherine (scholar), 91
Sesame Street (TV show), 49
Sex in the City (TV show), 59
Sex ratio, 197
Sexist music lyrics, 207–209
Sexual Behavior and Selected Health
    Measures (CDC report), 138
Sexual demographics of US, 138,
    139 (fig.)
Sexuality, 129–163
  audience shaped by, 154–162
  as dimension of identity, 11
  in disabled representation, 176
  global perspective, 198
  power and, 135–138
  production of cultural objects and,
    146–154
  production surveys, 152–154
  in the social world, 138
Shared meaning, 6
Shiri (film), 206
Shively, JoEllen (scholar), 53–54
Shyminsky, Neil (writer), 145
Significant symbols, 194
Simmel, Georg (scholar), 2–3, 225
The Simpsons (TV show), 105
Sinclair, Upton (author), 135
Situation comedies
  gender representation in, 103 (fig.),
    104–105
  queer roles in, 143

Skarsgård, Alexander (actor), 188
Sling Blade (film), 175
Slushy, 3
Smith, Stacy (scholar), 39, 105, 117
Snyder, Sharon (scholar), 176
So You Think You Can Dance
    (TV show), 104
Social boundaries
    maintained by freaks, 223, 225
    produced by popular culture, 133–134
Social construction, disability concept
    as, 170–171
Social media
    ethnography and, 60
    gender and content creation,
        124–125
    sexual identity and, 157–158, 162
Social model of disability, 170
Social movements, identity and, 24
Social norms
    generated by popular culture, 133
    males favored by, 197
Social progress, generated by popular
    culture, 135
Social solidarity
    importance of, 135
    rituals that generate, 134
Social world
    class in, 71–74
    in cultural diamond, 7, 8 (fig.), 10
    disability in, 172–174
    gender in, 101
    race in, 37–39
    reflection theory and, 9
    sexuality in, 138
The Souls of Black Folks (Du Bois), 35–36
South Korea, popular culture in,
    204–207
*Spring, Summer, Fall, Winter . . . and
    Spring* (film), 206
Star Trek: The Next Generation
    (TV show), 179
Stephenson, Becky Herr (scholar), 203
Stereotypes, as controlling images, 15
Stiller, Ben (actor), 186
Stonewall Riots of 1969, 140, 150
Stowe, Harriet Beecher (author), 135
"The Stranger" (Simmel), 2–3

Stratification
    identity as mechanism for, 15
    intersectionality, 24
Straus, Joseph N. (scholar), 179
Studies in Ethnomethodology (Garfinkel),
    125
Studying controversy, 125–127
Suicide (Durkheim), 132
Suicides
    LGBT, 130, 131, 132, 135
    sociological perspective on,
        132–133
Superhero/sidekick relationship, in
    comic books, 145–146, 146 (image)
Surtees, Schlitze (circus performer),
    166–167, 167 (image), 169
SurveyMonkey (Web site), 90–91
Surveys
    audience, 90–91
    General Social Survey (GSS), 90–91
    Out & Equal Workplace Survey,
        153–154
    production, 152–154
Survivor (TV show), 116
Swidler, Ann (scholar), 10
Symbolic interactionism, 193–194
*Symbolic Interactionism: Perspectives and
    Methods* (Blumer), 194
Symbolic violence, 46

Taste, class and, 72–74
Teaching Harry Potter (Belcher and
    Stephenson), 203
Technology use, racial demographics
    of, 58
Television
    in Africa, 212
    Al Jazeera, 213–214
    audience ethnography, 59
    audience experiences shaped by
        class, 88–92
    class perspectives, 63–71
    class representations, 74
    disability representation on, 177,
        178 (fig.)
    gender of audience, 120
    gender representation in, 102,
        103 (fig.), 104–105

gendered production, 115–117,
    115 (table)
in India, 210–211
interviewing creators of content, 119
ownership of local stations, 51–52
professional associations for,
    184 (table)
qualitative content analysis, 82–83
racial demographics of production
    labor force, 51
racial representation in, 39, 41–43,
    42 (fig.)
reality, 74
sexual demographics in, 141–143,
    144 (fig.)
sexuality and production, 146, 149
viewership by race, 56–58, 57 (fig.)
wages for occupation associated with,
    81, 84–85, 84 (fig.)
Theater, in Africa, 213
Theoretical approaches, used in book,
    27 (table)
Thick description, 180–182
30 Rock (TV show), 104–105
Thomas, Carol (scholar), 171
"Tik Tok" (Ke$ha), 78
A Time to Kill (film), 56
Titanic (film), 76
To Wong Foo, Thanks for Everything,
    Julie Newmar (film), 141
Toney, Gregory, T. (scholar), 122
Tool kit, 10
Townsend, Robert (director), 51
Trade unions and professional
    associations in the culture
    industries, 184–185 (table)
Train (musicians), 79
Transgender, 102
Translation, 201–202
The Tree of Life (film), 108
Tropic Thunder (film), 186
Troubling Gender (Vila and
    Seman), 207
Turner, Bryan (scholar), 133
28 Days Later (film), 179

Ugly Betty (TV show), 102
Uncle Tom's Cabin (Stowe), 135

Upper-middle-class, film viewing by,
    89–90
Upper-middle culture, 73
Use-value, 69
Usher (musician), 79

Valorization, 123
Value, 69
Vertical integration, 20, 21 (table)
Vila, Pablo (scholar), 207–209
Violence
    in disabled representations, 176
    symbolic, 46

Walejko, Gina (scholar), 124
Wallis, Cara (scholar), 112
War Horse (film), 108
Wayne, John (actor), 53–54
Weaver, James B. III (scholar), 122
Webb, Beatrice Potter (scholar),
    98–100
Weber, Max (scholar), 170, 180
West Side Story (film), 76
Westervelt, Saundra Davis (scholar), 122
White privilege, 25, 37–39
"White Savior Films," 56
Whites
    median household income,
        73 (table)
    racial differences in film
        interpretation, 53–56, 55 (table)
    representation in film, 39, 40 (fig.)
    representation in music, 43–45,
        44 (fig.)
    representation in television, 39, 41–43,
        42 (fig.)
    representations in literature, 45–46
    technology use by, 58
    television station ownership by, 52
Whittington-Walsh, Fiona (scholar),
    174–176
Wikipedia, as resource, 80–81
Will and Grace (TV show), 133, 141,
    155–156, 155 (image)
Williams, Raymond (scholar), 6
Willis, Paul (scholar), 134
Winant, Howard (scholar), 36
Winter's Bone (film), 75

Women
  branding as social inferior, 99–100
  in film production, 117, 117 (table)
  film viewing by, 120–121, 121 (table)
  portrayal in advertisements, 96–98,
    99 (image)
  representation in advertisements,
    109–110
  representation in children's books,
    110–112, 111 (fig.)
  representation in film, 105, 106 (fig.),
    107–109
  representation in music videos,
    112–113
  representation in television, 102,
    103 (fig.), 104–105
  representations of lives of, 14–15
  sexist music lyrics, 207–209

  in television production, 115–117,
    115 (table)
  television viewing by, 120
  See also Gender
Women Watching Television (Press), 88
Women's movement, development of, 98
Women's suffrage movement, 101
Work class, and audience experience
    with television, 88–89
Wright, Chely (musician), 151

X-Men (comic book series), 179

"Your Revolution" (song-poem),
    126–127

Zippy (comic strip), 165–166,
    166 (image)

CPSIA information can be obtained
at www.ICGtesting.com
Printed in the USA
BVOW03s1710100717
488866BV00002BA/4/P